HEART OF THE SAVIOUR

HEART
OF THE SAVIOUR

A Symposium on Devotion to the Sacred Heart

———

EDITED BY JOSEF STIERLI

WITH CONTRIBUTIONS BY
RICHARD GUTZWILLER
HUGO RAHNER
AND KARL RAHNER

ENGLISH TRANSLATION BY
PAUL ANDREWS SJ

HERDER AND HERDER
NEW YORK
THOMAS NELSON AND SONS LTD
EDINBURGH AND LONDON

THE TRANSLATIONS LISTED BELOW ARE BASED ON THE
ORIGINAL GERMAN VERSION OF "COR SALVATORIS", SECOND
EDITION, PUBLISHED BY HERDER, FREIBURG, 1956

HEART OF THE SAVIOUR

SECOND IMPRESSION, PUBLISHED 1958 BY HERDER AND HERDER,
INC., 7 WEST 46th STREET, NEW YORK 36, N. Y.

COR SALVATORIS

EDITORIAL HERDER, AVENIDA JOSÉ ANTONIO, 591
BARCELONA, SPAIN

TRANSLATIONS INTO FRENCH, DUTCH AND ITALIAN
HAVE BEEN PUBLISHED

DE LICENTIA SUPERIORUM ORDINIS

NIHIL OBSTAT: PAULUS O'DEA, S. J.
CENSOR THEOL. DEPUT.
IMPRIMI POTEST: + JOANNES CAROLUS
ARCHIEPISCOPUS DUBLINENSIS
HIBERNIAE PRIMAS
DUBLINI, DIE 20 OCTOBRIS, 1957

LIBRARY OF CONGRESS CATALOG CARD NUMBER: 58—5868
© 1957 BY HERDER & CO GMBH
MADE AND PRINTED BY HERDER DRUCK,
FREIBURG, WEST GERMANY

CONTENTS

TRANSLATOR'S NOTE

Cor Salvatoris, the German original of this book, was published in 1954, two years before Pope Pius XII's encyclical on devotion to the Sacred Heart. In this volume the book and the encyclical are published side by side, with an index to the main themes recurring in both. Readers can judge the extent to which the Pope's words endorsed the doctrine of the book. It is evident at least that the German symposium anticipated the main directive of the encyclical by explaining the devotion's basis in Sacred Scripture, Christian tradition, and the Liturgy.

Two of the authors, Fathers Stierli and Gutzwiller, are Swiss Jesuits; the brothers Rahner are German Jesuits at present professing theology in the University of Innsbruck.

Cor Salvatoris has already been translated into French, Spanish, Dutch, and Italian.

PREFACE

IN his encyclical *Caritate Christi Compulsi* of 3 May, 1932, POPE PIUS XI called devotion to the Sacred Heart "the extraordinary remedy for the extraordinary needs of our time". The words were an invitation to a crusade of prayer and penance, and rang like an echo of the message to St. Margaret Mary Alacoque nearly three hundred years earlier. The Heart of our Lord was shown as the sign of salvation for our unregenerate age, in which the love of men has grown cold and the multitudes have turned away from God.

In the twenty years since this second encyclical on the Sacred Heart (the first was *Miserentissimus Redemptor* of 28 May, 1928), the needs of our time have assumed apocalyptic dimensions. Can we claim that all the sincere Christians to whom the Pope was then making his appeal have responded with a progressive transformation of their lives in the spirit of devotion to the Sacred Heart? We need only ask this question to know the answer.

It is true that the liturgical cycle draws us into the various exercises of the devotion: the First Fridays, with the Communion of Reparation and the Holy Hour, the feast of the Sacred Heart with the solemn act of atonement, and the renewal of consecration to the Sacred Heart on the feast of Christ the King. But nobody will maintain that these pious exercises exert a revitalising influence commensurate with the needs of our age. At the same time they may well be the source of richer blessings than we with our hasty judgements could suspect. There are surely many lives of hidden expiation which accomplish far more for the salvation of the world than our superficial gaze observes.

The fact remains that devotion to the Sacred Heart no longer has that power to attract and influence men that it should have, according to the intentions and the teaching of the Church. There are many explanations why this is so. The first chapter of this book will list several of the obstacles to the devotion. These difficulties are enhanced by our own spiritual pride, which makes us unwilling to stoop to this humble token of God's love, and by our emotional bankruptcy, which is incapable of enthusiasm for the radiant mystery of the royal Heart of our Lord.

Numerous books have been written on the devotion, varying considerably in size and quality: popular pamphlets, pious books of devotion, and mystical writings which emphasize ecstatic experiences and extraordinary apparitions. What is still wanted is a comprehensive exposition of the devotion which is solidly and deeply based in theology, and at the same time speaks the language of those among our contemporaries who still have an ear for spiritual things. Some years ago FRIEDRICH SCHWENDIMANN wrote his *Herz-Jesu-Verehrung und Seelsorge* (published by Josef Stocker, Lucern 1942), which was a complete treatment of the various ways in which the devotion can be presented in pastoral work. But he set himself a purely practical task and limited his message to those who have the care of souls. RUDOLF GRABER'S *Das Herz des Erloesers* (Marianischer Verlag, Innsbruck 1949), contains a theological and historical introduction to the devotion together with an explanation of the Litany of the Sacred Heart, which relates the individual invocations to their basis in divine revelation.

A number of other books on the devotion, old and new (for instance the works of FR. NOLDIN and FR. VERMEERSCH), have voiced the need for a deeper and more stable theological basis for the devotion.

The present work is intended as a contribution, however fragmentary, towards filling this lacuna. It cannot claim for its contents that they are all original nor that they have been rounded into a compact unity. The several chapters originated in conferences given at Easter 1951 to a students' congress in Bad Schönbrunn near Zug (Switzerland). They follow two main lines of investigation: First, they seek to widen the horizon of the devotion by a historical essay, which reaches back beyond St. Margaret Mary not merely to the Middle Ages, but through the theology of the Fathers to where the devotion links up with the revelation of the Old and New Testaments. On this basis the second part attempts to deepen our understanding of the devotion by examining its dogmatic principles and its connections with the Bible and the Liturgy.

A preliminary chapter deals with the obstacles to the devotion, not in order to obstruct the reader's encounter with the mystery of the Sacred Heart, but to show that the adversaries must be taken seriously, and that the real problems are not to be brushed aside lightly. More important still, this critical questioning should open the reader's heart and mind to a personal consideration of the problems. A number of the questions will be answered directly; others will be resolved by the deepening of our concept of the devotion; others again are practical problems which pose tasks for our accomplishment. Rather than overstep the framework of a theological work we have abstained from any treatment of psychological questions, interesting and necessary though such an enquiry is for the doctrine and practice of the spiritual life.

The need for a comprehensive theological exposition of the mystery of the Sacred Heart is still unsatisfied. The contributors nevertheless hope that their work may stimulate progress in that direction, pave the way for a fuller solution, and most of all, that it may intensify men's devotion to the Heart of our Lord.

Feast of Blessed Claude de la Colombière, 15 February, 1954

THE EDITOR

RICHARD GUTZWILLER

THE OPPOSITION

DEVOTION to the Sacred Heart has had a peculiar history. For some time many of the highest authorities in the Church adopted an attitude of reserve and even disapproval towards it. Success, when it came, brought not merely the establishment of the devotion, but, in the words of the second nocturn for the office of the Sacred Heart, a positively triumphal progress. The breviary sketches briefly the lines of this development, from the Fathers of the Church through the medieval mystics to John Eudes and Margaret Mary Alacoque, and on to Pope Pius IX, who extended the feast of the Sacred Heart to the universal Church. With this official recognition the last barriers fell away and the devotion spread through the whole Catholic world. Leo XIII, in consecrating the world to the Sacred Heart, underlined the world-wide importance of the devotion. Finally Pope Pius XI endorsed this papal approval by two important acts: the writing of the encyclical *Miserentissimus Redemptor,* and the raising of the feast to a double of the first class with an octave.[1]

The words of the breviary are no exaggeration. There are churches of the Sacred Heart in every country in the world, statues and pictures of the Sacred Heart in chapels and religious houses, in monastic cells and refectories. The First Friday of every month draws astonishing crowds to the churches. The

[1] Since the original publication of this book, the octave of the Sacred Heart has been suppressed, in the general simplification of the rubrics (decree of the Sacred Congregation of Rites, 23 March, 1955). However the action of Pius XI, and the liturgical prayers for the octave, which will be discussed on the pages 211 ff. are still of interest for the light which they throw on the Church's devotion to the Sacred Heart. |Tr.|

1

month of June is dedicated to the Sacred Heart. The "Messenger of the Sacred Heart" is published in innumerable languages and countries. Scarcely any other devotion can show so remarkable a growth.

However the zenith of this development seems to have been passed. It is as though a certain weariness has crept in, as though the cult of the Sacred Heart, after rising swiftly to a high level of enthusiasm, can be maintained at that level only with effort. Moreover one can detect a passive, and even, in many clerical and lay circles, an active resistance to the devotion.[2]

The reasons for this opposition will be enumerated and discussed with all frankness and clarity in the remainder of this chapter. If they are formulated in rather too pointed a fashion, it is in order that the opponents of the devotion may not feel that their difficulties and objections have been robbed of their sting. Many of the objections reveal a rationalist spirit, which can never really grasp the religious and deeply interior character of the devotion. Others arise because here and there too little account has been taken of the work of theology in establishing, justifying and deepening the devotion. Since this symposium looks primarily to the concerns of theology, it must allow ample room for the exposition of these difficulties. The solutions and answers will be found in the positive expositions later in the book.

The first group of objections is based on externals. But we may not on that account ignore them. Twentieth-century man lives and learns through his eyes; he is more dependent than ever on external impressions and forms, and has a fine feeling for what is genuine and what is counterfeit in image and speech. Now it cannot be denied that the pictorial representation of the Heart of our Lord is in many cases unattractive, if not actually insipid and repellent.

---

[2] This resistance, whether passive or active, hardly exists to the same extent in English-speaking countries as in those of which Fr. Gutzwiller is writing; but the reasons adduced by the author are pertinent wherever devotion to the Sacred Heart is preached. |Tr.|

The Christ of the Sacred Heart pictures is generally sugary and sentimental, often mournful and self-pitying, even effeminate. For a generation that has lived through two world wars, a generation torn by doubts, and engaged in vital social, economic, and political struggles, such a picture has little appeal. It awakens no response in men who are disillusioned and have eyes only for what is true to life.

It is no solution to represent the heart by itself, separated from the human figure of Jesus. Critics can validly object to that as a type of picture forbidden by the Church, at least for use on altars, and so obviously not in harmony with her mind and her wishes. In any case the separation of the Heart from the Person of our Lord offends our modern feeling for completeness. Critics stress, too, that the heart is not in reality the seat of the emotions, and that it fulfils a purely organic function in the body. In fact, a Sacred Heart picture that is artistically satisfying and agreeable to contemporary taste has yet to be created, unless we give the title to the likeness of the crucified Christ transfixed by a lance.

The type of language favoured for prayers and devotions to the Sacred Heart is generally not much better. This is partly due to literal translations which are innocent of any feeling for our idiom and for the impact of certain words on modern ears. Such epithets as "sweetest", such phrases as "prostrate before thy altar", which occur constantly in prayers to the Sacred Heart, do not appeal to the ordinary man: they sound forced. Moreover the complete equating of the Sacred Heart with the Person of Christ results occasionally in turns of speech that sound strange, if not offensive, to our ears. Think of the phrase in the act of consecration for families, composed by Benedict XV: "Vouchsafe, Divine Heart, to preside at our gatherings"; or of the exclamation with which this same prayer closes: "Long live the Heart of Jesus, our King and our Saviour!" It is not easy to see how a heart can preside, or how one can wish long life to a heart.

3

Prayer-books contain many words and phrases which might be justified as the "lights" of a private meditation, but have an extravagant ring when proposed for public prayer. Some lay too exclusive an emphasis on the feelings. Others barely escape the censure of being dogmatically unsound. An instance of the latter is the image of the lonely prisoner in the tabernacle, waiting for souls to visit and console him.

Hymns to the Sacred Heart are frequently trashy and sentimental. Often it is hard to understand why, in place of the expression "Sacred Heart", we do not say simply "Jesus Christ". Not a few thoughtful men ask what authority there is for this usage.

So it has come about that for many people pictures and language are not an aid but an obstacle to a deeper understanding and love of this devotion.

There are others who view the modern devotion as a typical product of the seventeenth century. It is no accident that John Eudes and Margaret Alacoque were contemporaries. In contrast to the coolness and reserve of Jansenism, devotion to the Sacred Heart is all intimacy and ardour. But it is precisely this contrast that dates the devotion. Does not our age demand other forms of piety, a stressing of different themes?

The attitude of many, especially of plain, simple people, to the devotion is clouded by a sense of disappointment in their expectations and hopes. They have been promised in the Sacred Heart a help and an answer to prayer, and they have not found it. They have sung the hymn:

> In need and in danger we never shall falter
> For thou, Lord, art guarding the throne and the altar.

But neither the thrones nor the altars have been protected. The consecration of families and of entire nations has not saved them from the catastrophes of war, defeat and bolshevist oppression. Is it then surprising if their confidence is shaken?

None of these factors, it is true, touches the essence of the devotion, but taken together they have a crippling effect.

More important is the second group of difficulties, which go to the inner core of the devotion. Objections which can claim the support of theology must be taken seriously. It is true that the devotions of the Church are not the fruit of theoretical speculations and theoretical knowledge, but have their origin in the life of the Mystical Body of Christ, and are perennially fresh signs of its vitality. But they must have a theological basis, and theology is therefore justified in passing judgement on them.

Let us start with dogma, and face the fact that theologians do not agree upon what is the object of this devotion. Some hold it is the earthly, bodily Heart of our Lord; and they can justify their position. For this earthly Heart is, through the Hypostatic Union, part of the human nature of the Logos, and therefore worthy of worship. But if it is the object, the question remains why it is precisely the Heart of our Lord that merits this veneration, and not, for instance, his hands, which after all worked miracles, were joined in prayer, bore the wounds, and were raised in blessing.

Accordingly others maintain that the proper object of the cult is the love of Christ. But then you have lost the connection with the Body of Christ. Moreover this view will not be easy to reconcile with the documents of the Church.

The third school of opinion makes the physical human heart of our Lord the object of the cult, but sees this heart as the symbol of love. According to them the heart is the material, Christ's love the formal object of the cult.

This position is almost reversed by the fourth school, which maintains that love is the material object, and its symbolization in the heart the formal object.

Finally a fifth school would find the material object in the "Cor Ethicum", and the formal object in the relation of this "Cor Ethicum" to the plan of Redemption. The Latin phrase is used to embrace the Divinity of Christ, his human soul with all its natural and supernatural gifts, and also his physical heart. The objection has been made to this view, that by overstressing the ethical aspect it does less than justice to the underlying mystical reality, for instance to the genesis of the Church from the blood and water of the transfixed Heart. In any case the Fathers of the Church seem to emphasize the underlying reality rather than the dispositions of our Lord.

This disagreement over the object of the cult is perhaps rather an isolated difficulty. A more central one presents itself when we try to fit the devotion into the general scheme of theology. For theology is necessarily theocentric; and since there are three Persons in God, the doctrine of the Blessed Trinity is the central mystery of all theology, and it is essential to see every other mystery in its connection with this centre. Now Christ in his Divinity is the Logos, the spoken Word of the Father, he is Wisdom in person. The sending, the *missio*, of the Logos into the world is, theologically speaking, a continuation of the inner *Processio* of the Blessed Trinity. Therefore in the Incarnation of the Second Person of the Blessed Trinity it is primarily the Wisdom of God, not his Love, that is made visible. The bestowal of love in the world is the function of the Third Person, the Holy Ghost, who is the *osculum caritatis* in the inner life of the Trinity. *Caritas diffusa est per Spiritum Sanctum* (Rom. 5, 5). To call the cult of the Sacred Heart a manifestation of love seems then to be placing it in a false theological perspective.

Suppose we begin, not with the Logos, but with the Humanity of Christ. Now he is essentially a mediator. He is not the centre of his own life, but points beyond himself, to the Father. Therefore every devotion must be *per Christum ad Patrem*. But devotion to the Sacred Heart, in the shape it has in practice assumed, is concentrated on Jesus; he is in practice not a pointer but the central point.

Theology is something complete and integrated; it cannot

allow that a part should be detached from its totality. But in many respects devotion to the Sacred Heart lacks any clearly defined place in this ordered structure. It seems to be a part arbitrarily detached and taken by itself.

Finally there is one detail of the practice of this devotion for which it is not easy to find a theological explanation: it is the injunction to console the sorrowing Heart of our Lord. Christ is at this moment in glory, and therefore incapable of suffering in body or soul. If in spite of this we speak of the sorrowing Heart of our Lord, our words permit of one of two explanations. They may be construed to refer, not to anything present, but to the suffering of Christ in Gethsemini, when he foresaw the consolation which the future would bring. The theology of this interpretation, as the encyclical *Miserentissimus Redemptor* has shown, is sound; Christ as Logos foresaw not only all future sins, but also all future consolations, and a share in this vision could be imparted to the human knowledge of Christ. But for people who wish here and now to assuage the pain of our Lord, it is certainly no simple matter to refer themselves back to a time two thousand years passed.

Alternatively we could aim to console not the physical but the mystical body of Christ. But in that case the Sacred Heart would mean the heart of the Mystical Body, and this is definitely not the view of the Church in her pronouncements.

We are faced then with dogmatic difficulties which, while not insoluble, are certainly not to be ignored. Their existence throws light on the strange history of the devotion, on the fact that in spite of all petitions and in face of weighty theological opinions, three Popes, Innocent XII, Clement XI, and Benedict XIII, formally discountenanced the cult of the Sacred Heart. It was not until 1765, nearly one hundred years after the revelations to St. Margaret Mary, that the feast of the Sacred Heart was approved for some churches in Poland and in Rome.

Other theological difficulties arise from the exegesis of Holy

Scripture. Scholars point out with some justice that biblical texts are used in the devotion in a way that can hardly be sanctioned. In Matthew XI, for instance, where Christ calls himself "meek and humble of heart", the "Learn of me" which he utters does not mean in the context that men should study and model themselves on his meekness and humility of heart. Rather it has the general sense that they should be his disciples because he does not talk down at them haughtily, like the Jewish doctors of law, but speaks in a plain, simple, and humble way. His meekness is not what they should learn, but why. The sense in which the text is used in many prayers and writings of the devotion is notably different from this.

From the exegetical point of view there are similar difficulties in the text about the transfixed heart of our Lord (John 19, 34). It is a quotation from Zacharias 12, 10, but the original speaks only of transfixing, and does not mention the heart. Even St. John's account does not contain the word "heart". As the Fathers of the Church emphasized, the Evangelist carefully chose the word "side" *(latus, pleura)*. The allusion is to the opening of Adam's side at the creation of Eve rather than to the human heart. Finally when the Apocalypse calls Christ "the Lamb that was slain", *agnus occisus,* the reference is primarily to a lamb slaughtered in preparation for sacrifice by the cutting of its throat, and not to a transfixed heart.

Taken singly these texts do not seem applicable to the cult of the Sacred Heart of Jesus. Neither can the biblical references to the "heart of God" be applied without further ado to the human heart of the Messias, or at least not if we appeal to their inspired character. A biblical basis for the devotion is to be found only by joining together and correlating many different texts, which illumine and explain one another. This task of correlation is generally neglected in books about the Sacred Heart. Instead they cite the individual texts, which by themselves are all too unconvincing.

For many people, the Christ of the Bible seems a larger, more powerful and glorious figure than the Christ of the Sacred Heart prayers. The Old Testament does, it is true, depict the Servant of Yahweh, who bears the burden of his people and wins them redemption by his suffering. But look at the full picture of the Messias. He is before all else the Anointed of Yahweh, who raises up the fallen tents of David, who brings glory and greatness to the Kingdom, and fame, might and domination to the people of God. He it is who brings the Kingdom of God in power.

In the New Testament the Synoptics do indeed portray the poor and humble Christ, who will not extinguish the smoking flax nor break the bruised reed, who treads the road of his Passion and is crucified. But he is also the mighty worker of miracles, the glorious conqueror of sin and of death, whose life ends in the triumph of the Resurrection. The Christ of St. John's Gospel is the Logos in human form. Again and again his humanity is irradiated with the divine glory. Even in the Passion he shows his mysterious power by calling the dead Lazarus to life. Then, living himself and dispensing life, he overcomes death and returns to the glory of his Father.

The Christ of St. Paul is the first-born of all creatures, in whom, through whom, and for whom all else is created (Col. 1). He is the apex of creation's pyramid, the Head of his Body, which is the Church. He is the powerful and mighty Christ, who appears even on the Cross not so much as the humbled One, but as the Victor, who has overcome all thrones, powers, principalities, and dominations. His life is a triumph in which he puts his enemies to shame and, as the "spotless and innocent One", leads all men before his Father and hands over the Kingdom to him. (Col. 2,15).

The Apocalypse shows Christ as the King of kings and Lord of lords. He is victorious over the false prophets, over the Beast and over Satan. He is the Judge of the living and the dead.

This biblical portrayal of Christ lays emphasis not on his Heart, but on the might of his Kingdom and on the victorious power of his life, death and glory. The Christ of the popular devotion to the Sacred Heart appears by comparison as a mere fragment, a part of the whole, and not even the most important part. It is true that the official texts in the Mass, Office, and Litany of the Sacred Heart have a consistently biblical character; but the Christ depicted by many books of devotion is unquestionably different from the Christ of the Bible.

The moralists, too, have their doubts about the devotion. Christian morality is not simply concerned with actions, nor with determining, by means of an elaborate casuistry, whether certain actions are permitted or not. Christian morality, in the spirit of the Gospel, looks primarily to man's disposition. It must therefore attach considerable importance to the attitude of mind, the disposition of soul, that is awakened in the faithful. Now genuine devotion to the Sacred Heart does engender a loving, self-sacrificing disposition which is of great value; but as it is practised here and there, the devotion undoubtedly carries with it the danger of a one-sided development.

It can produce in some men a melancholy, pessimistic, escapist attitude. This can go so far that they abandon the world to its wickedness and, withdrawing into themselves, cultivate an unbalanced mysticism of the Cross, to the neglect of those natural factors which have their place in the building of the Kingdom of God. It is true that ultimately suffering and self-sacrifice are more important than activity. It was through his Cross that Christ redeemed the world. But that is no reason for neglecting action. Even Christ prefaced his Passion with words and deeds.

Moreover the devotion seems to foster an individualist, egocentric frame of mind. To be personally united with Christ, to be alone with him in silent, loving adoration, is important. But for the present age, with its passion for objectivity and its developed sense of community, the thought, sentiments and aims of the devotion to the Sacred Heart must often seem one-sided.

Finally, by harping on the promises of the Divine Heart, we

risk inducing a false sense of security, a sort of spiritual life insurance. There are those who, after making the nine First Fridays, are confident that their salvation is assured. If this security is unreal, then the words and meaning of the promises seem to be weakened. If it is real and justified, it seems impossible to take seriously the injunction to work out our salvation "in fear and trembling".

These are the traits which render the devotion to the Sacred Heart (not indeed as it is revealed in Church documents, but as it frequently appears in practice) unpalatable to many men. They are alienated from it by their very instinct for the strength, sincerity and largeness of the spirit of Christ.

Disapproval is also voiced by certain defenders of the Liturgy. We do not mean the extremists, for whom only the formations of the first centuries are valid Liturgy, and every later development is automatically a perversion. Nor do we mean the unbalanced proponents of a merely objective piety, who have time only for the *opus operatum,* and in their zeal for ontological holiness neglect the ethical. The encyclical *Mediator Dei* has corrected these views where they were to be found. We are referring rather to the strong and justifiable concerns of the liturgical revival. The Liturgy has its own laws of growth; the better they are known and observed, the more assured we may be that both the public cult of the Church's services and the genuine private piety of the individual faithful will develop along the classic lines.

Now it cannot be denied that from a purely external point of view the cult of the Sacred Heart has not yet been properly and definitively incorporated into the Liturgy. One evidence of this is the practice of saying Mass before the Blessed Sacrament exposed during the octave of the Sacred Heart.[3] During such a Mass Christ is present in three ways: on the paten, in the tabernacle and in the monstrance. There is a difficulty too in the placing of the

[3] See above note 1.

feast of the Sacred Heart on the Friday after the octave of Corpus Christi. It does indeed underline the close connection between the devotion to the Sacred Heart and the Eucharist; but on the other hand it makes the veneration of the God-Man's Heart seem a sort of pendant to the Eucharistic mystery. Even the existence of a special cult of the Eucharistic Heart of Jesus shows that the connection between the Blessed Eucharist and the Sacred Heart has not yet been clearly worked out.

There is another vital concern of the Liturgy which reaches even deeper. The Christ of the liturgical cult is the glorified Lord, *Rex aeternae gloriae*. In the Sacrifice of the Mass indeed we have also to "announce the death of the Lord until he comes". But this memento reminds us not so much of the bodily and spiritual suffering of Jesus as of the redemptive and sanctifying power of his sacrifice. It is a memory "both of his blessed passion, and also of his resurrection from the dead, as well as his glorious ascension into heaven". The very celebration of the sacrifice is a glance upwards at the glorified Lord. For the Christ who is present through the Consecration has the glorified, not the suffering body.

One can still sense a cautious probing and an absence of complete satisfaction at the way in which this devotion has been absorbed into the general spirituality of the Church. This is nowhere clearer than in the fact that the present Mass of the Sacred Heart, approved by Pope Pius XI, is the last of fourteen provisional Mass-forms, all different. Look for instance at the form which immediately preceded the present one, at the Mass *Egredimini,* which is still to be found in many missals. The whole Mass is set in a joyful tone and contains no word about reparation, whereas the present Mass, *Cogitationes cordis eius,* bears a different stamp, is set in a different key. There are also great differences between the various formulae of consecration which we possess. When we remember that at present the act of reparation is prescribed for the feast of the Sacred Heart, and the consecration to the Sacred Heart for the feast of Christ the King, it becomes clear that there are still many elements of the devotion to be integrated and clarified. And must we charge the supporters of the liturgical movement with lack of piety or of *sentire cum Ecclesia,* if they draw our attention to these things?

A final difficulty is raised by the students of Church history. History teaches us that there are undulations even in the religious life of Christianity, sharply rising curves which maintain their momentum for a while and then slowly decline. In harmony with the mentality of an age and the needs of a generation, God's Providence and the operation of the Holy Ghost suggest devotions which will help men. After a while their sound grows softer, without ever ceasing altogether. So it was with the devotions to the Holy Name of Jesus, to the Five Holy Wounds, to the Holy Face of Christ; so it is with the veneration of certain saints. Is not the devotion to the Sacred Heart largely subject to the same historical conditions? Where Jansenism had preached a religious coolness and an exaggerated reserve towards God, the veneration of the Heart of our Lord and the glow of his love introduced into piety a deep religious intimacy, a warmth, a *familiaritas cum Christo.* This had a special part to play in christianizing the individualism and subjectivism of the nineteenth century, in assimilating it, and, to an extent, utilizing it for the Kingdom of God. But surely our objectives have changed, and nowadays our first concern must be with the creation of a new world by realizing in it the Christian ideal of the Kingdom. Our first care must be to foster the awareness of our mission to the world. And if that is so, we must ask with all honesty whether the high tide of devotion to the Sacred Heart is not beginning to ebb.

Within the devotion, too, a historically minded observer can note undulations. In patristic times the veneration of the Sacred Heart consisted in sinking oneself in the mystery of the opened side of the crucified Christ, and so in the birth of the Church as the new Eve from the side of the new Adam. For the medieval mystics the opened Heart of our Lord was the open door through which contemplative souls were initiated into the secrets of the interior life. With John Eudes the ethical dispositions of the soul predominate, with Margaret Mary Alacoque the idea of reparation. Is the present form inevitably the definitive one? Or can we expect new movements, which will give another shape to the devotion? And in that case, is it advisable to commit oneself to the present form? Not everything that is living in the Church must necessarily survive for all time in the same shape and with the same intensity. Fresh life is constantly being awakened in the Church, the Mystical Body of Christ, by the Holy Ghost, who is its soul, its *Spiritus Vivificans*. And precisely for that reason a historical consideration of the Church can lead us to see the devotion to the Sacred Heart as something truly great, as a real treasure, and yet to value it in its temporal limitations for just what it was: a help against certain dangers, for a certain length of time, for a certain generation. The present age with its newly found appreciation of, and emphasis on, the Mystical Body, the objectivity of the *opus operatum,* and the individual's responsibility towards the world, may perhaps seek inspiration and help in other forms of piety.

These difficulties vanish if one sees as the object of the devotion the pierced Heart of the crucified Christ, bearing in mind the position of the Cross in God's plan of Redemption, and the power and greatness of Christ, the Victim-Priest. But then one would have to prove that this idea of the Sacred Heart squares with the pronouncements of the Church; if it does not, all our difficulties revive.

The doubts, objections and questions which have been put forward do not all carry the same weight. But all of them, to a greater or lesser extent, find expression today, some voiced as conscious criticisms, others as whispered doubts and misgivings. It remains for the theologian to give them serious consideration and provide satisfactory answers.

ON THE BIBLICAL BASIS OF THE DEVOTION

THERE is good reason for seeking to trace the historical devotion to the Sacred Heart back to its origins in the Bible. It is not as though we were falling into an anachronism common to many pious books, of trying to produce copious scriptural "references" for all the key-points of a devotion which has unquestionably acquired much of its present character in modern times. That approach does no service either to history or to asceticism; indeed it has already done much harm. Still it is undoubtedly possible, within the limits of sound exegesis, to show how the kernel of the devotion is really contained in the Revelation of Holy Scripture, especially of the New Testament. This would silence immediately at least one reproach, cast with increasing emphasis in our own day in the name of a pruned and purified biblical theology: that the pious veneration of the Heart of our Lord should be rejected as a scandalous excrescence, a perversion of Catholic pietism into a sort of romantic passion for Jesus; that it lacks the true modesty of the Gospel, and exchanges the Christian familiarity with God for the loud sensuousness of palpable symbols. Karl Barth has gone so far as to place the Catholic devotion to the Sacred Heart on the same level as modern Protestantism's biographies of Jesus, which have shed all belief in the true Incarnation of the Word. He would see in both forms "an attempt to find an approach to Jesus which ignores his Divinity, and an approach to Revelation which, through its use of human judgements and human experiences, will be within the powers and understanding of all men". Hence his crushing verdict: "The modern Protestant faith in Jesus as a religious hero, and the

15

Catholic devotion to the Heart of Jesus, are to be rejected as the deification of creatures."[1]

This, by the way, is not new. It is ancient and dusty. The Jansenists said it before Barth, and the Church gave its answer to the Pseudo-Synod of Pistoia.[2] But when we listen with charity, we can pick out the element of truth in these strictures. Many features of devotion to the Sacred Heart which were attractive to the late medievals and still more to the age of Baroque may be meaningless to a Christian who has been penetrated by the awful solemnity of the language of the Bible and the theology of grace. That is why we think it so important to try to root the devotion in the Bible. Our task must be to show which key-ideas in the biblical Revelation suggested the first forms of the devotion; how the classical beauty of this original structure was later overgrown, but never quite destroyed, by various short-lived growths of piety, which today have lost their attraction; and finally, how in our day that form of the devotion which alone enjoys the recognition of the praying and teaching Church is rediscovering the simplicity of its early days. Through this intimate history of men's deep love for Christ, we can find our way back to the word of God, as it is cherished and expounded in the living Church; and there we shall discover the fundamental ideas which are perennially valid and therefore ever burgeoning afresh in the Church.

The present frame-work will scarcely allow of more than a cursory attempt to sketch the fundamental traits of the biblical basis for the devotion.[3] Let us start with what is most essential.

---

[1] K. Barth, *Die Kirchliche Dogmatik* I, 2: Die Lehre vom Wort Gottes, Zollikon ²1939, p. 150 f.

[2] Cf. Denzinger, *Enchiridion Symbolorum,* nos 1561–1563.

[3] The following more detailed works were used here: G. Closen, *Das Herz des Erloesers in den heiligen Schriften des Alten Bundes,* in: *Zeitschrift fuer Aszese und Mystik* (= ZAM) 18 (1943), p. 17–30. — I. M. Bover, *Das heiligste Herz Jesu im Neuen Testament,* in: *ZAM* 13 (1938), p. 285–301. — Id., *Paulus und das heiligste Herz Jesu,* Innsbruck 1933. — H. Rahner, *Flumina de ventre Christi. Die patristische*

In the language of Revelation, the hallowed word "heart" and its almost synonymous equivalents (Hebrew: *leb, lebab, beten, me(j)'im, kereb;* Greek: *kardia, koilia, splanchna;* Latin: *cor, venter, viscera*) have the same primal meaning as in all human language. The strictly theological section of this book will discuss this meaning in detail. But the connotation of "heart" in the Old Testament has been well summarized in a recent work: "Heart" is the principle and organ of the personal life of man, the centre in which the being and the activity of man as a spiritual personality are concentrated, and consequently the source and centre of his religious and ethical life. "Heart" is the focal point of spirit and courage, of interior insight, of man's planning and volition, of the ethical decisions of the whole, undivided man.[4]

The same is true for the language of the New Testament. "Heart" stands for a man's most secret thoughts (Mt. 24, 48; Rom. 10, 6); it is opposed to his outward seeming (I Thess. 2, 17; II Cor, 5, 12), and still more sharply to mere lip-service (Mt. 15, 18; Mk. 7, 6). "Heart" is therefore the key word for expressing the newness and redemptive message of the New Testament. It is in the heart, in the depths of the righteous man who is penetrated by the love of God, that the encounter of Revelation and faith, of grace and response to grace, takes place. The grace of Christ is a circumcision of the heart (Acts 7, 51; Rom. 2, 29). Justification is in faith "from the heart" (Rom. 10, 10; Heb. 10, 22). The Spirit is poured out in our hearts (Gal. 4, 6). Love from the heart constitutes perfection (Mt. 22, 37; I Tim. 1, 5). The Christian is called simply "the hidden self of the heart" (I Pet. 3, 4). "So the New Testament too shows the heart primarily as the central point in man which

Auslegung von Joh. 7, 37–8 in: *Biblica* 22 (1941), p. 269–302 and p. 367–403. — Id., *Stroeme fließen aus seinem Leib. Die aszetische Deutungsgeschichte von Joh. 7, 37,* in: *ZAM* 18 (1943), p. 141–149. — A. Lefèvre, *La blessure du Côté,* in: *Le Coeur (Études Carmélitaines* 1950), p. 109 ff.

[4] G. Kittel, *Theologisches Woerterbuch zum Neuen Testament III,* Stuttgart 1938, col. 613.

God addresses, in which the religious life is rooted, and which determines man's ethical disposition."[5] Victor Warnach has traced the connections between this key word of the Bible and a devotion to the Sacred Heart built on a scriptural basis. "The *pneuma* is that profound element in man, at once godlike and intensely personal, which is repeatedly called 'heart' (*kardia*) in Holy Scripture because it constitutes the real directive centre of the person, from which spring all thoughts and feelings, all cares and decisions (Mk. 7, 21 f.; Rom. 8, 27; 10, 10; I Cor. 14, 25; I Thess. 2, 4; II Thess. 3, 5). The same meaning attaches to the equivalent term *leb* (or later *lebab*), which is frequently used in the Old Testament; and in the Liturgy and spirituality of the Church down the centuries, 'heart' has generally retained this spiritual sense. It is from this source that the veneration of the Sacred Heart, which centres round the idea of charity (*agape*), draws its deepest significance. We should mention too the special meaning of the *coeur qui trouve Dieu* for Pascal, who gave a modern but quite justifiable twist to the New Testament concept."[6]

Warnach's suggestion brings us into the centre of our question. We must look to the language of the Bible for a deeper understanding of the devotion to the Sacred Heart. The sense in which the phrase "Heart of our Lord" has been understood from the earliest times in the prayers of the Church and of her devout children, is precisely that of Holy Scripture. Occasionally in the course of history the genuine biblical understanding of the original force of this phrase was lost, or Christians strayed into one of two dangers, that of sensuousness, seeing only the tangible physical heart, or that of a bloodless rationalism, seeing merely the symbol. Whenever that happened, it was time (as it is time today) to seek a remedy in the Bible, to study the hypostatic mystery of the Sacred Heart itself, and there to relearn the

[5] Ibid. col. 615.

[6] V. Warnach, *Agape. Die Liebe als Grundmotiv der neutestamentlichen Theologie,* Duesseldorf 1951, p. 231 (and note 1).

almost hypostatic union that exists between the divine and human elements of the devotion, whenever it is formed in the spirit of the Church.

You might say then that the less understanding Christians showed for the true nature of the Sacred Heart devotion, the dimmer also was their understanding for the divinely inspired language of Holy Scripture. The sensualism and intellectualism of our time have tended to cloud our vision of those truths and concepts which denote something undivided, compact of body and soul. They can be kept within the range of men's knowledge and perception only by the language of the Bible and by this perennially fresh devotion, as it lives and develops within the tradition of the Church. Every failure to understand the eternal word "heart" is a real tragedy of the spirit. And on the other hand, wherever men learn the secrets of the Heart of our Lord Jesus Christ with a knowledge which is authentic (in other words, founded on Scripture) and interior, there something decisive has taken place in the realm of the spirit: God has been understood in the way in which he offered himself for understanding—from heart to heart.

This brings us to the question: does the Word of God in the Old and New Testaments speak expressly of the Heart of the God-Man? Does there exist any strictly biblical phraseology which would serve as a positive basis for devotion to the Sacred Heart?

There is one easy way of answering this question: by quoting from the sort of devout literature which unthinkingly presses into the service of the devotion every scriptural allusion to the "Heart" of God. But that is a different thing from finding a scriptural basis. The pious at their prayers, and the Church when she is solemnly speaking to God, make use of these allusions—the history of the devotion shows it—simply because they delight in their sound and splendour. And the reason for this delight is that liturgists and the devout faithful have still a profound understanding for the rich connotation of "heart" in the Bible.

Consequently they can think of the human Heart of the Redeemer when they read how Yahweh says his "Heart" will remain for the future in the middle of the temple (III Kings 9, 3; II Par. 7, 16), or when they find it written that the eternal God is "wise of heart" (Job 9, 4), or when they meditate on the mystical words about the Bridegroom, about the joy of his heart (Cant. 3, 11), and about his ravished heart (Cant. 4, 9). True, these are only pious applications, but we should not overlook their importance for the development of the devotion to the Sacred Heart. The text about the "wounded heart" of the Bridegroom was meat and drink to the mysticism of the Middle Ages.

To find a strictly biblical basis for the devotion we must inquire deeper. Are there no words in the written Revelation of God which expressly, and in the immediate intention of the Spirit who inspired them, refer to the human heart of the Messias?

One is tempted to point at once to Matthew 11, 29, where our Lord says of himself that he is "meek and humble of heart". But the passage speaks of the Sacred Heart only in a remote and transferred sense, namely in so far as his meekness and 'sincere' humility are contrasted with the proud and heartless character of pharisaical teaching.[7] There is another text which leads us much deeper into the heart-theology of the New Testament. Paul writes to his beloved community in Philippi: "God knows how I long for you all in the bowels of Jesus Christ" (Phil. 1, 8). The Greek word which he uses, *splanchna,* is a strict equivalent for *kardia,* and therefore means "heart" with precisely the connotation which we have outlined above. The messianic prophecy of Ezechiel (11, 19) shows how exact is this parallel between "heart" and "bowels": *I will give them one heart, and will put a new spirit in their bowels.* We can see the same usage in the messianic prediction of Jeremias (31, 33): *I will give my law in their bowels*

---

[7] Cf. Herder's *Bibelkommentar* XI, 1, Freiburg, p. 166. — M. J. Lagrange, *Évangile selon St. Matthieu,* Paris 1923, p. 230.

and I will write it in their heart, and this is fulfilled by the unique and everlasting sacrifice of the human Messias: *I will give my laws in their hearts, and on their minds will I write them* (Heb. 10, 16). "Entrails" and "bowels" *(splanchna, viscera)* are therefore the same as "heart" for the spiritually minded faithful (Phil. 2, 1; Philem. 7 12; Col. 3, 12; I John 3, 17) and therefore the same also for Jesus Christ, in whose "most tender charity" Paul loves his Philippians. This phrase then shows the apostle speaking expressly of the Heart of our Lord; it has a fundamental place in the story of men's tender love for the human Heart of God. Eric Peterson's note on the passage has caught the meaning admirably: "The 'Heart of Jesus Christ' is the love which is active in the martyrs and in the saints. The Church's veneration of the Heart of Jesus means therefore the glorification of that love which burns in the martyrs and the saints, and which, as love of Jesus Christ, is diametrically opposed to all merely human sentimentality and familiarity."[8]

However, these rather casual allusions to the heartfelt love of our Lord are not enough for us. There does exist also a clearly-defined series of assertions about the Heart of our Lord; and in the light of these, it is not only the right, but even the sacred duty, of anyone who seeks to understand the Scriptures, to sketch the divinely inspired concepts which might constitute a biblical theology of the heart.

This series consists of the Old Testament prophecies whose reference to the future Messias can in every case be guaranteed by the explicit revelation of their fulfilment. They afford glimpses of the "heart" of the Redeemer who was to appear in human form, glimpses which, taken together, merge into a complete picture of the innermost dispositions of the Messias. All these allusions to the Heart of the Messias fit with theological exactitude into the

---

[8] E. Peterson, *Apostel und Zeuge Christi. Auslegung des Philipperbriefes,* Freiburg 1940, p. 4 f.

same basic structure. They explain how the Messias will dispense to the redeemed Israel and to the whole world of heathens the streams of grace and the living heart of spirit and flesh; and they indicate the terms and the pledge demanded by God for this profusion of grace; God requires the surrender, suffering, and death, in which the Heart of the Messias must be immolated. This promise of the Messias is the ultimate content of Old Testament revelation; and we can perhaps capture its force in a phrase: Living *spirit* will be communicated to the redeemed through dead *heart*.

Here we are careful to discuss only those messianic texts of the Old Testament whose reference to Jesus is guaranteed by the witness of the New. This is the only way to avoid the merely devotional "application" of phrases from the Bible (and as a rule only from the Vulgate text) based solely on piety or on the contemplative love of Jesus, and therefore quite inadequate for textual or historical purposes. What we wish to prove, in a sober yet passionate love for the written Word of God, is that God really intended the revelation of the Heart of the Messias, which is to be annihilated, and through that annihilation is to dispense life; and that this revelation belongs to the original message and meaning of the inspired Scripture.

We can begin with the messianic verses of Psalm 40 (39), 7-9:

> Sacrifice and oblation thou didst not desire,
> but thou hast given me an ear ready to listen.
> Burnt offering and sin offering thou didst not require,
> then said I, Behold I come.
> That is what is laid down for me where the book lies unrolled.
> To do thy will, O my God, is all my desire.
> I carry thy law in the midst of my heart.[9]

---

[9] In this and other scriptural quotations the Douai version has been modified with an eye to the Hebrew text, in order to meet more exactly the points of H. Rahner's explanation.

This prayer is spoken in the name of the future Messias, as we know from the testimony of the Epistle to the Hebrews (10, 5–7): it is the prayer of our Lord "as he comes into the world". In whatever sense we understand this entry into the world, whether as the moment of the Incarnation or as his entire sojourn in the days of his flesh (Heb. 5, 7), this messianic prayer epitomises all that passed in the Heart of Jesus of Nazareth: surrender to the will of the Father who sent him, even to the surrender of his dead body in the sacrifice of atonement. For a linguistic understanding of this theology of the heart, it is important to see how the psalm-verse reads in the Greek Septuagint version, which was that used by the author of the Epistle to the Hebrews: "that law of thine which is written in my *koilia*." The Latin Vulgate text renders this simply as *in medio cordis mei*. It is evident already (and this will be important when we come to discuss the theology of our Lord's Heart in the New Testament) that the connotation of *koilia* and *kardia* is the same: both mean "heart". The Heart of the Messias, around which God has formed a human body, is the innermost sanctum of the temple. There stands the altar of the sacrifice which redeemed the world.

The nature of the Messias' self-surrender and sacrifice is revealed still more profoundly by Jeremias (30, 21). He reveals the dispositions of the Messias' Heart in a magnificent crescendo of prophecy, to the point where it submits to death and so ensures the destiny of the messianic work. This Messias is heralded as the new David (cf. Jer. 30,9) who in his humanity will spring from the very stock he is to reedem. And thus runs the word of Yahweh:

> Their prince shall be of themselves,
> and their ruler shall proceed from the midst of them.
> I will bring him near, and he shall approach me,
> for is not this the man
> who gives his heart in pledge, and so draws near to me?

"Approaching" is to be understood here as the movement of a priest towards the altar in answer to God's invitation. Even in the early history of Israel it was ordained: "Whom the Lord shall choose, they shall approach him" (Num. 16,5; Ex. 19, 22). One does not assume the priestly dignity, one is called to it. So also here: the king, the new David, is at the same time a priest by vocation. But his office is "to give his heart in pledge". He alone is called to and empowered for that task, and his "approaching" consists precisely in the pledging of his life.[10] "This priest and king drew near to God for an office of sacrifice which he alone could undertake. The altar was the Cross. In this office of sacrifice he must give his heart in pledge, he must plight his life, in order to buy and ensure the treasures of salvation for all men. And no man was there to redeem the pledge of his life-blood. His life became God's to dispose of, and in this holy office of sacrifice it was destroyed. Jesus in very truth gave his heart in pledge when he drew near to God for the priestly office of sacrifice."[11]

It is then the proper and most profound function of this heart to surrender itself. When the prophet Isaias (53, 12; cf. John 10, 17) rejoices over the completion of the messianic Redemption, his joy is based on the surrender of the "soul" to death: *Numerous foes will he receive for his booty because he has delivered his soul unto death.*

In the same way the prophetic vision of Jeremias reaches beyond this pledged heart to the Day of Judgement. It sees the disregarded love of the Redeemer's heart changed into the majestic anger of God, which breaks forth from the Messias and brings "the plans of his heart" to eternal realization (Jer. 30, 23–4):

> Behold the whirlwind of the Lord, his fury going forth,
> a violent storm: it shall rage over the head of the wicked.
> The Lord will not turn away the wrath of his indignation
> till he have executed
> and performed the thought of his heart:
> In the latter days you shall understand these things.

[10] A. Condamin, *Le Livre de Jérémie*, Paris 1920, p. 219 f.
[11] G. Closen, op. cit., p. 24 f.

It is fitting that this powerful chapter from the messianic prophecy of Jeremias should be read in the present liturgy of the
feast of the Sacred Heart. For it is surely "the richest and
deepest text about the Sacred Heart in Holy Scripture, the
finest of all those that expressly mention the Heart of the
Messias"[12].

So far, our quotations from the Old Testament have focussed
attention on the nature of the messianic work. They have shown
that work taking shape in the depths of the Redeemer's human
heart and issuing in the sacrifice of obedience. Now we shall see
the glance of the inspired prophets penetrate the abysses of that
heart and glimpse something of its interior, personal life in all its
love, its sorrow unto death, and its intoxicated joy. The primal
word "heart" implies both this interior life and the messianic activity which springs from it.

To initiate us into these mysteries, there is the dying prayer of
the Messias, Psalm 22 (21), a prayer of evangelical simplicity,
which was intoned by our Lord in his death-agony (Mt. 27, 46)
and distorted by the scribes into blasphemous and cowardly
mockery (Mt. 27, 43). "That the Scripture might be fulfilled", the
Roman soldiers divided among themselves the clothes of the executed man (Ps. 22, 19 and John 19, 24; Mt. 27, 35 Vulg.). Every word
in this death-hymn is messianic. The Spirit of God speaks here of
the Heart of the dying Redeemer (verse 15): "My heart is become
like wax melting in the midst of my bowels." Again we see the
equivalence of *kardia* and *koilia*. The innermost being of the
Messias finds expression in the cry of his breaking Heart; spiritual
annihilation and the death agony of the physical heart are both
implied in the image of melting wax. This terrifying death-plaint
made a strong impact even on the early Christians. They heard it
as an outcry of the Heart of Jesus, and were moved to a compassion
almost medieval in its depth and tenderness. About 150 A.D. Justin,

---

[12] Ibid. p. 25.

in his Dialogue with the Jew Tryphon, explains the verse as follows:

> The words, "My heart is become like wax, melting in the midst of my bowels", are a prediction of that which Jesus was to undergo in the night when they went out against him in the Garden of Olives in order to arrest him. For it is written in the memoirs of the apostles that his sweat ran down to the earth as drops of blood, and that his Heart quaked and dissolved within him, in order that we may know that the Son, in accordance with his Father's will, really did endure this for our sakes, and that we might not imagine that as Son of God he had no feeling for all that happened and befell him.[13]

This sensitive reading, directed against any Greek "spiritualizing" tendency, is beyond question the finest interpretation of the prophetic verse. It leads us by biblical paths to an essential element of the Sacred Heart devotion, to an intense compassion with the broken human Heart of the Messias.

This death-hymn from the depths of the Heart of our Lord offers us still more: at verse 23 it bursts into a breathtaking song of joy over the results of this anguish of the heart; for it is going to transform the world.

> Your heart shall live for ever! The furthest dwellers on the earth will bethink themselves of this and turn to the Lord.

Here too life comes through death. The living hearts (vv. 27—28) spring from the dead Heart.

The New Testament moreover entitles us to consider Psalm 69 (68), the prophetic death-cry out of the abyss, as referring, at least in certain verses, to the Messias and his work. (John 2, 17; 15, 25; Rom 15, 3; Acts 1, 20). Verse 22, which predicts the offer of gall and vinegar as the Messias' drink, is preceded immediately by the lamentation:

---

[13] Justin, *Dialogus cum Tryphone Judaeo* 103, 7–8.

Reproach has broken my heart and I am cast down:
and I looked for compassion, but there was none;
and for comforters, but I found none.

Time and again this text has enkindled the love of the devout souls who wished to comfort our Lord in his anguish. Let us consider it apart from the reverent emotion which softens the harshness of the outcry, and leave it all its fearful edge. God here inspires the prophecy of a despair to be tasted and endured by a human heart which has been brought to death by suffering. The new translation of the Psalms has sharpened the meaning of the Scripture precisely at this point: *Opprobrium fregit cor meum et defeci,* is the new version, in contrast with the line hitherto so current in pious books: *Improperium expectavit cor meum. My heart has expected reproach.* The Heart of the Messias will break in despairing loneliness: that is the revolutionary truth which the prophet here glimpses. In this light we can understand the cry of joy which emerges from this death-hymn (from verse 31 on): it is the jubilation of the Sacred Heart, which gathers "heaven and earth and the sea" into its song of praise, and in one phrase sums up the effect of the Redemption which will spring from the broken Heart: "You who seek God, your heart shall live again" (verse 33: Hebrew *lebab,* Greek *psyche,* Latin *cor*). The heart which is broken by distress brings comfort and strength to the hearts of men.

Psalm 16 (15), 9 adds one last trait to this Old Testament picture of the Messias' Heart:

Therefore my heart has been glad and my tongue has rejoiced:
my flesh too shall rest in hope.

St. Peter used this verse as a witness to the Messias in his first sermon:

Since David was a prophet, he said of the Christ, foreseeing his resurrection, that he would not be left in the place of death, nor would his body see corruption (Acts 2, 30-31).

Paul attests the same thing (Acts 13, 35). This psalm is the heart's paean of joy at being delivered from all suffering. Overflowing with thanks and firmly rooted in the peace of God, it speaks to him:

> In thee is the fulness of joy; at thy right hand are delights that will endure for ever (Ps. 16, 11).

It is the joy of the redeemed, who know that they can never again be separated from God; it streams from the heart, overflows the tongue, possesses even the body which is no longer subject to death. This is the joy of the Messias' Heart, of this new and eternal David who stands at the head of the redeemed people and says (verse 3):

> These are the faithful souls in the land; my love is all for them!

Now from the rest of the sermon in which St. Peter testifies to the messianic character of this psalm, we know what it is that constitutes this glorious dominion of the King, which draws the redeemed people into its glory:

> This Jesus has God raised again, whereof all we are witnesses. Being exalted therefore at the right hand of God, he has claimed from his Father the promise of the Holy Spirit, and has poured forth that Spirit, as you see and hear (Acts 2, 32–34).

Again the insoluble paradox: the crucified one has become Lord and Messias (Acts 2, 36); the Heart of our Lord, annihilated in death, is now the unfailing fountain from which the Spirit is poured forth. When they heard this message "their hearts were stung" (Acts 2, 37). The heart is the origin and goal of every action in the kingdom of him who surrendered his Heart.

There is a sermon of St. Paul (Acts 13, 34–35) which explains still more clearly the prophetic depths of Psalm 16. Speaking of our Lord's glorious resurrection, the apostle connects verse 10 of the psalm with Isaias' phrase (55, 3): *I will make an everlasting covenant with you: the privileges I have promised to David.* The resurrection of the son of David fulfilled the promise which began with the words (Is. 55, 1): *All you that thirst, come to the waters.* Now that Jesus is glorified, the living water of the Spirit begins to flow from him (John 7, 39; Tit. 3, 6). The messianic Redemption will be complete when the new David comes for ever in his glorified humanity, *the root and stock of David, the bright and morning star. And the spirit and the bride say: Come. And he that thirsts, let him come. And he that will, let him take the water of life, freely* (Apoc. 22, 16-17). *So there is gladness in my heart.*

All these mysterious prophecies fuse into one sublime picture of the inmost dispositions of the future Messias; and the element that fuses them is that fundamental word so beloved of the Holy Ghost: the Heart. The Heart of the Lord's Anointed is submissive to the God who sent him, it is humble and self-sacrificing. It is a Heart full of majestic anger, or sunk in mortal anguish, or leaping with ecstatic joy. All the throbbing human life of this Heart is spent in the accomplishment of the messianic mission, in saving mankind by sacrifice, and dispensing to the souls of the redeemed the living water of the Spirit. Blood and water, heart and spirit, death and life, are indissolubly united in the Christology of the Old Testament. There could be no finer summary of this messianic concept than the prayerful phrase of the Church: *Qui corde fundis gratiam—Thou who pourest forth grace from thy heart.*

It is possible to confirm in detail the biblical accuracy of this prophetic vision of Christ by comparing it with the message of the New Testament. This tells us about the Messias who wins glory by the sacrifice of his life, and dispenses the water of the Spirit. It is a doctrine of fundamental importance for the whole future history of the devotion to the Sacred Heart, and one which we must expound with some precision. It affords an approach, and historically the only correct approach, to an understanding of the patristic doctrines which gave rise to the earliest form of the devotion, and which are being rediscovered by the devotion as at present recognized by the praying Church. Everything depends upon a correct exegesis of the revelation which Jesus made of his own messianic office in John 7, 37–41.

There is one reading of this passage (or rather one way of

punctuating it) which rests on the early Christian tradition of exegesis and on an important family of manuscripts. It runs as follows:

> On the last and great day of the feast,
>
> Jesus stood and cried, saying:
>
> If any man thirst, let him come to me,
>
> And let him drink, who believes in me.
>
> As the Scripture says:
>
> Fountains of living water
>
> Shall flow from his bosom.

In the more usual version, the one popularized by the translations (or rather suggested by the different position of comma and full stop) the text must be read as follows:

> If any man thirst, let him come to me and drink.
>
> He that believes in me, as the Scripture says,
>
> Fountains of living water shall flow
>
> from his bosom.

We can see at once the radical difference of meaning resulting from the different division of sentences. In the first case the streaming of living waters is predicated of the Messias, from whose body they spring. In the second they spring from the body of the believer. Now if it can be shown that the former punctuation, and therefore the former interpretation, is the original one, and that intended by John, then we possess a wonderful witness to the doctrine, foreshadowed even in the Old Testament, of the Messias who pours from his Heart the living waters of the Spirit.[14]

In fact this is the case—we have attempted to prove it elsewhere from the findings of scriptural interpretation and the development of exegesis.[15] Here we are concerned only with the

---

[14] In the second paragraph of *Haurietis Aquas,* Pope Pius XII quotes John 7, 37–9 with the punctuation and sense here defended by H. Rahner. |Tr.|

[15] *Biblica* 22 (1941), p. 269–302 and p. 367–403.

essential outlines of the interpretation, in so far as they influenced the early history of devotion to the Sacred Heart.

"On the great day", the last day of the feast of Tabernacles, the Chosen People recalls the messianic promise of living water (Is. 12, 3; Ez. 47, 1–12; Zach. 13, 1). The Messias is expected as the Bearer of Salvation, "who will be like unto Moses" (Deut. 18, 15; Acts 3, 22; 7, 37). Like Moses, the new Messias will make living water stream from the rock, which he will split with a touch of his wooden staff. The solemn libation of water in the Temple was a symbol and hint of this expectation, and it was into the midst of this solemnity that Jesus directed his compelling cry and announced himself as the fulfilment of this messianic expectation: *If any man thirst, let him come to me. And let him drink of me, who believes in me.* He is the rock from which living water will flow, the Moses who will open this fountain in himself. The Messias was expected as the second and authentic Moses, who would accomplish the two miracles of the multiplication of bread and the striking of water from the rock. When therefore Jesus revealed himself on these two occasions, the people cried out: *This is the prophet, this is the Messias* (John 6, 14; 7, 41).

If we read the text correctly, this water flows from the "body" of the Messias. The Greek original has here the word *koilia*, which we know well by now; its literal meaning is "entrails". The most competent experts on the Aramaic mother-tongue of our Lord assure us that it is simply a synonym for "heart" and "heart's core", with precisely the extension of meaning that we have already seen in the usage of the Old Testament. Consequently the Messias wished to proclaim aloud at this solemn moment: "If any man is thirsty and believes in me, let him come and drink of me. For it is written in Scripture: Streams of living water shall flow from my heart." Jesus is appealing expressly to the Old Testament prophecy.

If we accept the meaning to which tradition has accustomed us, it becomes impossible to find any text which refers to streams of water springing from the believer's heart. But if we take the deeper meaning, that this stream is said to flow from the Messias' heart, then we can support it from the Old Testament with all those texts which were solemnly recalled on the last day of the feast of Tabernacles. Chief among these was Zach. 13, 1: *In that day there shall be a fountain open to the house of David and to the inhabitants of Jerusalem: for the washing away of sin and of uncleanness.* Connect this text with that which immediately precedes it (the revelation of the Messias as the "Pierced One" and of the "pouring out of the spirit of grace on the inhabitants of Jerusalem" (Zach. 12, 10), and you find yourself in those paths of scriptural understanding at which our Lord himself was hinting when he cried: "The Scripture says: Streams of living water shall spring from the Heart of the Messias."

Now the apostle John himself explains (7, 39) that this living water is the Holy Ghost, and includes all the treasures of salvation which are given us together with the Spirit of our Lord, all the blessings proper to a redeemed soul which is pressing forward to a state of glory. But these blessings are given only under a proviso: "When Jesus is glorified". "Glorification" here connotes the messianic passion and death (John 12, 28; 13, 31; 17, 4) together with the bodily transformation which can be attained only in this way. The gift of the Redeemer is therefore the Spirit which he has released to us through the sacrifice of his life. As Moses, the first Saviour, caused the spring to flow, so too the second Saviour, the Messias, will open a "fountain of water"[16]. Jesus by his death brought to fulfilment the Jews' hope of salvation, for his Heart is that cloven rock from which spring the living waters of the Spirit. *The rock was Christ* (I Cor. 10, 4).

All the predictions of this seventh chapter of St. John are fulfilled in the instant that Christ's Heart is pierced on the Cross

---

[16] Strack-Billerbeck, *Kommentar zum Neuen Testament aus Talmud und Midrasch* II, Muenchen 1924, p. 481.

(John 19, 34). The blood and water from his wounded side not only prove the reality of his death, but also bear solemn witness that the scriptural prophecy of these messianic graces is now fulfilled. The living water, working redemption through the blood of the sacrifice, is about to flow. Now we shall have "spirit", but only in blood. Now we shall have grace, but only from a pierced heart. This revelation of the Messias, whose Heart is the source of the Spirit, forms the perfect framework for the two scriptural passages which St. John now adduces as having been fulfilled: Exod. 12, 46 and Zach. 12, 10. The former speaks of the lamb in which no bone will be broken; now it transpires that this referred to the true Lamb of God (Is. 53, 7; Jer. 11, 19; John 1, 29; I Pet. 1, 19), not only because they broke no bone of the dead Jesus, but much more because this symbol suggests the wonderful apocalyptic vision of the "Lamb that was slain" (Apoc. 5, 12). The mysterious duality of Old Testament prophecy, which showed the Messias as suffering, and at the same time glorious through his suffering, is here resolved in luminous clarity. A "lamb" is the "Lord of lords and King of kings" (Apoc. 17, 14), the redeemed people is "bride and spouse of the Lamb" (21, 9), the powers of death and sin wage war against the Lamb (17, 14), and the end is the marriage of the Lamb (19, 7). All that is to be kept in mind when we read in John 19, 36 how the prophecy of the Paschal Lamb was fulfilled in the piercing of Jesus' Heart.

The believer can wash himself white in the blood of this Lamb: a sublime and paradoxical mixture of images, which can be understood only if we think of the water and blood streaming from the Heart of the dead Messias. And there is still another allusion. The fact that a stream of water issues from the wounded Heart of this Lamb points to Apoc. 7, 17 and 22, 1, where the crystal stream of living water issues from the throne of the Lamb, and the Lamb leads the redeemed to the fountain of life. It is as though the Redemption is crowned with a heavenly Feast of Tabernacles, in which the homecomers enjoy for all eternity the fountain that springs from the Redeemer.

In this glittering world of biblical images and ideas we can grasp more profoundly the second text which St. John saw realized in the pierced Heart of Jesus:

I will pour out upon the house of David and upon the inhabitants of Jerusalem the spirit of grace and of prayer:
and they shall look upon me whom they have pierced (Zach. 12, 10).

God is speaking here about himself; he himself as man will be the "first-born", who is mourned and bewailed, and to whom men will look up even though they have pierced him. God himself in his redeeming humanity dispenses the living water of the Spirit; he pours it forth as the great "Pierced One". All this is accomplished, and the reign of the Spirit begins, in the moment that his Heart is opened. The messianic work will be completed when the glorified Jesus comes again: *Behold he comes with the clouds, and every eye shall see him: and they also that pierced him* (Apoc. 1, 7). There we have St. John's picture of the Sacred Heart, a picture of infinite majesty.

Now at last we can claim a deeper understanding of the biblical allusions to the communication of the Spirit, as it was predicted in John 7, 37 and revealed in John 19, 34 in the sign of blood and water. The living water from the wounded side of our glorified Lord has been spreading in the Church, since the day of Pentecost, the graces won for us by the Heart of Jesus, broken in death.

We speak easily of the "pouring out" of grace. The phrase is stale for us from pious custom. But it is in itself a remarkable expression, and a favourite one in the inspired word of God; for it carries the suggestion of the "living water" of grace, and so also of the living source of this water, which is the Heart of the Messias (Is. 44, 3; Ez. 36, 25; Zach. 12, 10; Joel 2, 28; Acts 2, 17; 2, 33; 10, 45). The day of Pentecost marks the fulfilment of Joel's prophecy, the pouring out of the Spirit. It is therefore in a strict sense the inauguration of the Last Day, and the prophecy of Joel unveils the eschatological mystery of the Heart of Jesus:

And it shall come to pass in the last days, says the Lord, that I will pour out my spirit upon all flesh (Joel 2, 28; Acts 2, 17). The Spirit goes forth over all flesh because it issues from the Word made flesh. From his Heart it overflows into all hearts (Gal. 4, 6; Rom. 8, 15). This heart-to-heart contact between God and man is achieved even under the earthly disguise of the sacrament of baptism, 'by the laver of regeneration and renovation of the Holy Ghost, whom God hath poured forth upon us abundantly through Jesus Christ our Saviour' (Tit. 3, 5–8). From this source flow all other graces, even the prophetic and mystical charismata of the Church in this world. They are all a preparation for the breaking of the Last Day. The writings of the mystics do in fact show the images of this biblical theology of the heart recurring with a kind of sublime insistence; when a man is intimately illumined by the light of the approaching day, he begins to drink at the fountain of our Lord's Heart, he experiences the mysterious exchange of hearts of Ezechiel's prophecy (Ez. 36, 26–29), and hides himself in the rock of the Pierced Heart. The genuine mysticism of the Church invariably reverts to the language of the Bible. But the definitive revelation of the Spirit who is bestowed on us from the blood of God's Heart begins only when the Spirit and the Bride say: *Come! and he that thirsts let him come, and he shall drink of the water of life, freely* (Apoc. 22, 17).

Are we correct in our interpretation of the Scripture? The history of these ideas in the early Church, the early history, namely, of devotion to the Sacred Heart, assures us that we are. This is the history we have now to narrate. It will be seen that today more than ever before the Church wishes to return to the theology of the biblical Revelation of the Sacred Heart, and to see it as the source from which flow streams of living water; and that living water brings us all that we understand by grace and the Church, by baptism, mysticism and eternal life.

The criterion of genuine devotion to the Sacred Heart is the degree to which its biblical basis is appreciated.

THE BEGINNINGS OF THE DEVOTION
IN PATRISTIC TIMES

THE history of the devotion to the Sacred Heart, which will be outlined in this and the following two chapters, yields two conclusions: first, that it is only since Pius XI gave the feast of the Sacred Heart its liturgical status that we possess a clear-cut form of the devotion which is recognized as binding for the prayer of the Church; and secondly, that this form of the devotion is a conscious return to the fundamental notions which were drawn from the Bible and elaborated by the theology of the first Christian millenium. It must be admitted that the first real devotion to the loving and wounded heart of the God-Man appeared only in the early Middle Ages, and therefore it is only since 1000 A.D. that it has taken forms articulate enough to give it a coherent history. Nevertheless it is historically incorrect to describe the preparations of the first millenium simply as "the dawn of the devotion"[1], or to write it off with such brief and misleading formulas as "In the first thousand years of Christianity, the concept of the Sacred Heart of Jesus was unknown."[2] The citing of three or four places in patristic writings

---

[1] A. Hamon, *Histoire de la Dévotion au Sacré-Coeur*, II: *L'Aube de la Dévotion*, Paris 1925.

[2] K. Richstaetter, *Lexikon fuer Theologie und Kirche* IV, Freiburg 1932, col. 1013. — Cf. also K. Richstaetter, *Illustrious Friends of the Sacred Heart*, London 1930, p. 15f. — For a more detailed history of the patristic beginnings of the devotion the following works are useful: G. Kanters, *Le Coeur de Jésus dans la littérature chrétienne des douze premiers siècles*, Paris–Avignon 1930. — Fr. X. Franciosi, *Le Sacré-Coeur et la tradition. Extraits des Pères, des Docteurs, des Hagiographes*, Tournai-Paris 1908. — J. Bainvel, *Développement historique de la dévotion au Sacré-Coeur*, Paris 1919. — S. Tromp, *Die Geburt der Kirche aus dem Herzen Jesu am Kreuze*, in: *ZAM* 9 (1934), p. 233–246. — H. Rahner, *Stroeme fließen aus seinem*

where, apparently by accident, the words "Heart of Christ" occur, is no way of documenting or disposing of this early history. The main task of the present chapter is to show how, between the foundations of the devotion in the New Testament and the sudden burgeoning in the early Middle Ages of veneration for the human Heart of Jesus, patristic theology nurtured those elements which were later, in the second millenium and right down to our own day, to be reproduced with perennial freshness yet with an almost sublime monotony by devout Christians, by mystics, and by the liturgical prayers of the Church.

Before beginning this exposition it may be well to indicate in general the point of passage in patristic theology at which the biblical foundations link up with the earliest forms of the devotion proper. It is the point to which the Church has returned when giving the devotion its present form.

The Church's presentation of the devotion is dominated by the image of the Heart that dispenses the waters of grace to redeemed mankind. *Qui corde fundis gratiam—who pourest forth grace from thy Heart*: that is the sum and substance of all the hymns of the feast. It is also the fundamental idea in the biblical Revelation of the Heart of the Messias, which was sacrificed and by its sacrifice communicated the Spirit. So fathers and theologians, from Augustine and Cyril of Alexandria to Canisius, in the lessons of the feast and during its octave[3] speak repeatedly of the fountain of living water taking its rise from the wound in Jesus' side. Through this biblical image they express the loftiest mysteries of Revelation: the living water, streaming from a pierced

Leib. Die aszetische Deutungsgeschichte von Joh. 7, 37–8, in: *ZAM 18* (1943), p. 141–149. — Id., *Grundzuege einer Geschichte der Herz-Jesu-Verehrung,* in: *ZAM* 18 (1943), p. 61–83. — Id., *Die Kirche aus dem Herzen Jesu,* in: *Korrespondenzblatt des Innsbrucker Priestergebetsvereins* 69 (1935), p. 98–103. — In this chapter we have made use also of two unpublished studies: H. Rahner, *Fons Vitae, Eine Untersuchung zur Geschichte der Christusfroemmigkeit in der Urkirche,* Innsbruck 1930; Id., *Ecclesia ex latere Christi,* Innsbruck 1935.

[3] See above p. 1, note 1.

heart, crystallizes the truth that the "Spirit" has again been poured out on the human race, but only because he who possessed the Spirit in all its fullness has immolated his Heart. This Spirit is the fountain-head and the quintessence of that which it effects, of grace; and this grace is the Church, and in the Church the second birth by the sacrament of baptism. Consequently the Church and baptism issue from the Heart of our Lord, and with them all the graces of light, of mystical comfort and of strength. So this sublime image of the living water that springs from the Heart of Jesus is one of the fundamental and formative metaphors, as it were one of the archetypes, from which asceticism and mysticism have been perennially renewing their substance even down to our own day.

The early history of the devotion is ultimately the story of the interpretation of the phrase in John 7, 38: *Streams of living water flow from his body*. This can be shown—if we anticipate the result of all this historical development—by a close juxtaposition of all the prayerful phrases that the Church employs in the present office for the feast of the Sacred Heart. From the Heart of our Lord issues the "Spirit" in the shape of the sevenfold stream of water (hymn for Vespers, last verse). This Spirit causes the genesis of the Church, which springs therefore from the Heart of Jesus: *And from the opened heart there sprang | The Church of Christ, his Bride* (hymn for Vespers, third verse). In this Church mankind is called home from sin and death to the fountains of life, which stream from the Heart of Jesus: *At this fountain the nations draw | The pardon of their sins* (hymn for Matins, fourth verse). All forgiveness for sins is granted through the "flood of mercy and grace" which gushes from the human Heart of God, as we sing in the majestic preface of the feast—a clear reminiscence of Psalm 35, 9-10 and of Is. 66, 12. These are the "torrents of peace and of pleasure" in which the Old Testament saw the realization of the messianic salvation. So the antiphon of the first nocturn turns in supplication to the Heart of Jesus: *In thee is the fountain of life, and with a torrent of joy dost thou overwhelm us, O Lord.* The paean of thanks which Isaias puts into the mouth of the redeemed is now fulfilled: *You shall draw waters with joy from the fountains of the Saviour* (Is. 12, 3, Vulg.), and this text recurs as the versicle all through Lauds and Vespers.

Against the background of this biblical imagery, which sees the Heart of Jesus as a fountain of water, the phrase from John 7, 37 stands out in impressive relief. It is no accident that of all the doctors of the Church, St. Peter Canisius should be chosen, in the homily for the sixth day of the octave, to point out the intimate connection between John 7, 37 and 19, 34; for he is the mystically favoured man who once drank at the spring in Jesus' Heart, as he himself describes. Mysticism and liturgical prayer often draw from the same sources, which rise from ancient unplumbed depths outside this world. So the Church, in the second antiphon at Lauds on the feast of the Sacred Heart, turns in prayer to the text: *Jesus stood and cried aloud: If any man thirst, let him come to me and drink.* This prayer of jubilation recurs as a communion verse at Easter: *If any man thirst, let him come to me and drink, Alleluia, Alleluia.* For the most precious gift of the risen Lord is the fountain of the Spirit issuing from his glorified Heart.

From this final form of the cult of the Sacred Heart, as crystallized for us by the Church in the magnificent new office for the feast, let us look back to where the germ-elements of the devotion first make their appearance. As we indicated in the chapter on the biblical foundations, the starting-point must be the interpretation of John 7, 37 and 19, 34. We saw that this mysterious word of our Lord about the streams of living water that flow from his *koilia,* that is, his Heart, has come down to us in two different textual versions, and consequently in two different interpretations. The more widely known reading, as preserved in the best early Christian manuscripts, especially in those which owe their origin to the theological life of Alexandria, runs as follows: *If any man thirst, let him come to me and drink. He that believes in me, as the Scripture says: Out of his belly shall flow rivers of living water.* It is evident at first glance that this version is not particularly favourable to the interpretation that the "Heart" of the Messias is itself the fountain of this living water. It is rather the "interior" of the believer that overflows with this water—though he must first have drunk of Christ, so that even this reading implies that Jesus is indicating himself as ultimately the real fountain.

Even in this interpretation, the text of John 7, 37 was of capital importance for the early history of the devotion to the Sacred Heart. It is in Alexandria that we meet the most ancient commentary on it, from the pen of Origen, whose asceticism, while of great theological profundity, is permeated by Greek spiritualism.[4] In his often dangerous urge to spiritualize away the body, he tends to ignore the corporeal reality of the man Jesus and of the wound in his side, from which the living water flowed. Instead, he constructs a mystical and spiritualist vocabulary, and at this text of St. John begins to speak of the "Heart" of our Lord as the *Hegemonikon,* the innermost self, the source of thoughts and of wisdom, from which the true gnostic, the mystically favoured man of the spirit, drinks the living water of wisdom. Thanks to the decisive influence of Origen, this tradition, softened and transformed into a more simplified asceticism by Ambrose, affected Augustine and through him the whole asceticism and mysticism of the Middle Ages. But as we can see from this cursory sketch (which is developed at greater length in my history of the patristic interpretation of John 7,37)[5], it sacrificed much of the original meaning of the Messias' self-revelation. In fact Origen himself comes on one occasion to speak of the alternative explanation, when he describes Christ as the rock (recalling I Cor. 10,4), which was pierced on the Cross and yielded the stream of water: "Christ

---

[4] Cf. A. Lieske, *Die Theologie der Logosmystik bei Origenes,* Muenster 1938.
[5] *Biblica* 22 (1941), p. 273–279.

was struck on the Cross, and he caused the streams of the New Testament to spring forth from himself. Had he not been trans-fixed, and had not water and blood streamed from his wounded side, then we would for ever have had to suffer thirst after the word of God."[6] Therefore those who despise this word of God can never drink of the true fountain: "For they do not listen to him who stands in the temple and cries: *If any man thirst, let him come to me and drink.*"[7] So even in the interpretation which owes its general acceptance to Origen, and which sees the waters streaming from the interior of the believer, the interior of our Lord is ultimately the source at which the heart of the believer is sated.

A further significance attaches to this teaching of Origen, this intellectual explanation of John 7, 37, with its shifting of the sense from the man Jesus to the divine Logos, from the sacramental to the mystical, from heartfelt love to gnostic knowledge. With this teaching was associated a figure who was to have a fundamental importance in the history of the devotion. Origen is the first to show us the apostle John as the prototype of the gnostically illu-mined man, who drinks the streams of living water "at the Heart of our Lord". We shall come to speak of this in more detail later; here we shall content ourselves with noting the starting-point, just where we would least expect to find it, in the exegesis and textual criticism of the Alexandrian school, which normally follows other paths.

The Alexandrian explanation of St. John's phrase has sunk deep into tradition and into the biblical text. There is, however, a second interpretation which we can trace back from source to source almost as far as the very group that gathered round the Evangelist; and this we are historically justified in considering as

---

[6] *Homily on Exodus* 11, 2 (C. S. G. VI, p. 254, l. 4–9).

[7] *Homily on Jeremias* 18, 9 (C. S. G. III, p. 162 f.). — Cf. also Origen's *Commentary on the Canticle of Canticles* 2 (C. S. G. VIII, p. 167, l. 20): "Christ is the spring, and streams of living water gush forth from him."

the origin of the early Christian, and so also of the early medieval veneration of the Sacred Heart. We can call it the Ephesian reading. In the last chapter we indicated the punctuation on which it is based. The following glance through the history of this interpretation shows that this form of the text is the original one.[8] The first definite and unambiguous witness for it is provided by Hippolytus of Rome, who explains the phrase in his commentary on Daniel, the oldest extant exegetical writing of the early Church, prior in date to Origen. He speaks of the four streams that once arose in Paradise, and finds their antitype in the salvation brought by Christ to his Church. Christ himself is this Paradise. From his body, which is the Church, spring forth the streams of living water to make the earth, dead in sin, into a Paradise again: " A stream of unceasing waters flows now, and four streams divide off from it, surging over the whole earth. This we can see in the Church. For Christ is the stream, and he is preached in the whole world through the fourfold Gospel. Flowing over the whole earth, he sanctifies all who believe in him. This is what the Prophet heralded with the words: *Streams flow from his body (koilia)*."[9]

According to the ancient tradition that goes back to Ephesus, this prophet is none other than the apostle John. The stream of water—in the image of the four rivers of Paradise—is the fourfold Gospel, seen as the sum and substance of the Redemption flowing from the Body of the Messias. Hippolytus here offers that explanation of the mysterious phrase in John 7,37 which originates in Asia Minor, in the theological circle of the living apostle, John. The teacher of Hippolytus, Irenaeus, who had sat at the feet of Polycarp of Smyrna, also understood it thus; and Polycarp had seen John and heard the words of life from John's own lips.

[8] *Biblica* 22 (1941), p. 367–403.—See above p. 30, note 14.
[9] *Commentary on Daniel* I, 17 (C. S. G. I, 1, p. 29, l. 11–16).

For Irenaeus too the Body of Christ is the Church, from which the waters of the Spirit flow forth over the whole earth and unite us men into the one Body of Christ. "But the Holy Ghost is in all of us, and he is that living water, which the Lord dispenses to all who believe in him in the right way."[10] This water flows only from the true Body of Christ, which is the holy Church. Hence Irenaeus can say simply: "The Church is the fountain of the living water that flows to us from the Heart of Christ. Where the Church is, there is the Spirit of God, and where the Spirit of God, there is the Church and all grace. But the Spirit is truth. He who has no part in this Spirit will receive no nourishment or life at the breast of our mother Church, nor can he drink of the crystal-clear spring which issues from the Body of Christ."[11]

What the presbyter of Lyons preaches here as a theological defence against the gnostic heresies, is at the same time the conviction of the devout Christian community. We have a classical witness to this in the report which a member of the Church of Lyons sent from Vienne to his brethren in the faith in Asia Minor, concerning the martyrdom of the deacon Sanctus. In all the fearful agony of his tortures, this early Christian hero remained steadfast, and replied to all questions always the same word: "I am a Christian." The source of this strength is given by the letter from Lyons in these words, which form one of the great testimonies to the early Christian devotion to the Sacred Heart:

"But he remained unshaken and steadfast, unyielding he persevered in his confession. For like a gentle and strengthening dew from heaven there flowed onto him that living water which goes forth from the Heart of Christ."[12] Before the gaze of the martyr stands the glorified Christ, the living rock, from whose interior

[10] *Adversus haereses* V 18, 2 (Harvey II, p. 374, l. 5–7).

[11] *Ibid*. III 24, 1 (p. 132, l. 2–7).

[12] Text quoted in Eusebius, *Church History* V 1, 22 (C. S. G. II, 1, p. 410, l. 10–13).

the heavenly fountain flows. This phrase *ek tes nedyos Christou* is a direct allusion to John 7,37; such was the text of John as it was read in Lyons. Therefore we have a right to translate it as "from the Heart of Christ".

In the theology of Asia Minor this text was seen in association with the Pauline image of Christ as the water-giving rock (I Cor. 10,4). This is clear from a remark of Justin, who had found the Christian faith in Ephesus and has given us, in his "Dialogue with the Jew Tryphon", the first text-book of a biblical and messianic Christology. "We Christians, he says, are the true Israel which springs from Christ; for we are carved out of his heart *(koilia)* as from a rock."[13] The most perfect way in which a Christian can show his mettle and the stock from which he is sprung, is by surrendering his life in martyrdom. "It is a joy for us to go to death for the name of the glorious rock. He makes living water overflow into the hearts of those who through him love the Father of the universe, and he satiates those who wish to drink the water of life."[14] For Justin there is a close connection between John 7,37 and 19,34; it is significant that he, surely in continuation of an originally Johannine tradition of preaching, and following in this St. John himself (Apoc. 1,7), loves to call Jesus simply the Pierced One: Christ is the great Pierced One, in whom is realized the word of the prophet Zacharias: *He will pour out the spirit . . . and on that day there shall be a fountain opened to the house of David and to the inhabitants of Jerusalem for the washing away of every sin and uncleanness* (Zach. 12,10; 13,1).[15]

Another witness to the Johannine tradition of the Church in Asia Minor, Bishop Apollinaris of Hierapolis, offers the same interpretation. In a fragment from a work on the feast of Easter, he speaks of the mysterious unity of the divine and human in

[13] *Dialogue* 135, 5 (Otto, *Corpus Apologetarum* I, 2, p. 480, l. 4–6).

[14] *Ibid.* 114, 4 (p. 408, l. 8–11).

[15] *Ibid.* 14, 8 (p. 54); 32, 2 (p. 106); 64, 7 (p. 230); 118, 1 (p. 422); Apologia I, 52 (Otto I, 1, p. 142, l. 2).

Christ, of the blood of his redemptive death, and the life of the Holy Ghost which wells up from this blood. Then: "It is Christ who has let his side be pierced, it is he who let flow from this wounded side the two streams which make all things clean again: water and blood, that is *logos* and *pneuma,* word and spirit."[16] He has the same vision as St. John had in the Apocalypse, when he saw the slaughtered Lamb as the source of living water (Apoc. 7,12; 22,1). The mosaics and sculptures portraying the Lamb from whom the waters spring, bear eloquent witness to the formative influence exercised by this image on the early Christian devotion to Christ.

The correct interpretation of John 7,37 was preserved also in the early Latin Church. Many codices of the Old Latin Bible give the sentence with the right punctuation, and at the same time, as we know from the "Testimonies" of Cyprian (which afford extremely old material) point to Christ as the source of life, as the spiritual rock and the Pierced One. We find traces here of the influence of Ephesian theology in the West. It was especially the early African Church (which received the faith immediately from Rome) that lent its voice to this authentic theology of the heart. The stream of the spirit, as Cyprian is constantly emphasizing, flows only inside the Church, "for the Lord cries: Let him who thirsts come and drink of the streams of living water which flow from his body."[17] *De ventre eius,* however, means simply his wounded side, as is evident from the following text: "If men thirst, says Isaias, then God will give them water in the desert. He will make it spring for them from the rock; for the rock will be split and water will flow and my people shall drink. This was fulfilled in the Gospel when Christ, who is the true rock, was split by the thrust of the lance in his painful death. Alluding to the prediction of the prophet, he cried: If any man thirst, let

[16] Fragment 4 from the work *Super Pascha* (Otto, *Corpus Apologetarum* IX, p. 487). [17] *Epistola* 63, 8 (C. S. E. L. 3, 2, p. 706, l. 16 ff.).

him come, and let him drink who believes in me. As the Scripture says: Streams of living water shall issue from his body."[18] The equivalence here of *venter* with *cor* is certain from the Old Latin translation of Psalm 40,9, which has *Lex tua in medio ventris mei* for the *cor* of the Vulgate translation.

Still clearer, especially in its explicit reference to the mystery of the Church issuing from the wounded side of Jesus, is the witness of an unknown author, possibly earlier than Cyprian and from the circle of Tertullian, who composed the book *On Mounts Sinai and Sion*. "The Christians' law is the holy Cross of Christ, the Son of the living God. Now the Prophet says (Ps. 40,9): Thy law in the midst of my body. Christ was therefore pierced in the side of his body, and from his side flowed the mixture of blood and water. From this he built his holy Church, and in the middle of the Church he keeps holy the law of his Passion. He himself foretold: Let him who thirsts come, and let him drink who believes in me. For it is written: Streams of living water shall go forth from his body."[19]

The genesis of the Church from the Heart of Christ, intimated in this passage, is expressed more clearly in the poetic work *Adversus Marcionitas,* which is based on Justin's theology. It compares the Church with the rivers of Paradise. "According to the apostles, the Church issues from the body of Christ *(ex utero Christi,* poetically imitating the *koilia* of Justin) full of the glory of the Father, and it washes away all stains and makes the dead seed live again."[20] Since all this is effected through baptism, the author of the tract *De Rebaptismate* (falsely ascribed to Cyprian) can say simply that baptism flows from the fountain of our Lord:

"Therefore let all who thirst come and drink, for the Scripture says: From his body flow swift and copious streams of living water. These streams were first revealed in the Passion of our Lord,

---

[18] *Epistola* 73, 10 (C. S. E. L. 3, 2, p. 786, l. 3 ff.).
[19] *De Montibus Sina et Sion* 9 (C. S. E. L. 3, 3, p. 115, l. 9–15).
[20] II, 43 f. (PL 2, 1064 C).

from whose side, transfixed by the lance of the soldier, blood and water flowed."[21]

The *Tractatus Origenis,* which are so important for the history of spirituality, yet so little exploited, have the same message to give. Composed probably by the Spanish bishop Gregory of Elvira, they preserve for us the early Roman tradition of Novatian and Hippolytus, ultimately, therefore, the tradition of Ephesus: "When the people was suffering thirst in the desert, Moses struck the rock with his staff, that is with wood, and the streams of water gushed forth. In this the mystery of baptism was prefigured. For the rock is the symbol of Christ, as the Apostle says: They drank of the spiritual rock that followed them. But the rock was Christ. No question of it then: that rock was the symbol of the flesh of our Lord, which was struck with the wood of the Cross and now dispenses living water to all who thirst. So it is written: Streams of living water will go forth from his body."[22]

One could document this theology of the heart with countless texts from the Latin fathers. They confirm our thesis that the sublime picture which the early Christians had of the Sacred Heart, as the fountain which dispenses Spirit from the wounded side, was formed by connecting John 7,37 with John 19,34. Gospel, Church, Grace, Baptism: these are the gifts of the transfixed Heart of the glorified Lord, and the symbol which crystallizes them is the water of the Spirit. Even the early Christians at their simple prayer knew and loved this thought. On the wall of the Baptisterium in the Catacomb of St. Priscilla, some anonymous Roman scratched the words from John 7,37: *Whoever thirsts, let him come.* Another hand wrote: "Redeemed through the wound of Christ."[23] We know from the Church regulations made by Hippolytus at the beginning of the third century, that at the ninth hour of the day Christians meditated with special intensity

---

[21] C. 14 (C. S. E. L. 3, 3, p. 87, l. 14–19).

[22] *Tractatus Origenis* 15 (Edit. Batiffol, Paris 1900, p. 165).

[23] Diehl, *Inscriptiones latinae christianae veteres* I, n. 2477 and 1614.

on the piercing of Christ's side.[24] Jerome, Caesarius of Arles, Rufinus, Marius Victorinus, Isidore of Seville, were all witnesses to this image of Christ. One of the most influential of them, Ambrose, gathered all these ideas into a prayer which has the mystical ardour and beauty of a genuine canticle to the Sacred Heart. He is exhorting the faithful to drink at the fount of living water, which is Christ himself:

> Drink of Christ, for he is the rock, from which the water springs.
> Drink of Christ, for he is the fountain of life.
> Drink of Christ, for he is the stream whose torrent brought joy to the city of God.
> Drink of Christ, for he is Peace.
> Drink of Christ, for streams of living water flow from his body.[25]

It is true that elsewhere Ambrose explained John 7,37 in Origen's way, and ignored the connection with the blood and water that flowed from the pierced Heart of Jesus. This more ascetical explanation of his, which was adopted also by Augustine, had a decisive influence on posterity. Nevertheless there are hints in medieval theology and especially in the Benedictine mysticism of the eleventh and twelfth centuries, that the original sense of the Johannine quotation was never completely forgotten. Ever since the beginnings of theology in Asia Minor, the authentic explanation of John 7,37 has played its part in developing the image of Christ as the dispenser of the Spirit, who makes living water stream from his wounded side. The history of this Ephesian form of interpretation leads us into a conceptual world quite different in character from the Alexandrian. Everything in it is warmer,

---

[24] C. 36, 5 (G. Dix, *The Treatise on the Apostolic Tradition of St. Hippolyt. of Rome* I, London 1937, p. 64); cf. J. Stadlhuber, *Das Stundengebet des Laien im christlichen Altertum,* in: *Zeitschrift f. kath. Theologie* 71 (1949), p. 139–146.

[25] *Explanatio Psalmorum* 1, 33 (C. S. E. L. 64, p. 29, l. 18–22).

more palpable and human and, as it were, more sacramental than in the spiritualism of Origen. For the starting-point of this interpretation is the great battle over the genuineness of the human nature of him who died on the Cross. That human nature had to be defended against the gnostic tendency to spiritualize. John, Irenaeus, Ignatius and Hippolytus were passionate in their affirmation of the reality of God's bloody death on the Cross, which has merited for us the Holy Ghost. Along with them, an ancient and venerable tradition of nearly two thousand years has referred the phrase in John 7,37 to Jesus himself, and the image it suggested of the great Pierced One, who dispenses the water of grace from his inmost Heart, could never again be forgotten.

All this biblical and patristic thought about the fountain of grace from our Lord's side enables us to grasp more clearly two elements which are of vital importance for the shaping of the early medieval devotion. First the special veneration for the apostle John, who rested on the breast of our Lord and was permitted to drink at the source of this living water.[26] We have already encountered this idea in Origen, who was the first to formulate it clearly. He makes the apostle John "drink at the Heart of our Lord the streams of living water", that is the waters of mystical knowledge and of the divine mysteries.[27] Henceforth John becomes more and more the man of grace who drinks the "torrents of the Gospel" at the Heart of Jesus.[28]

In this connection we should mention the two much-quoted

[26] There is no need to show what an essential element this was in the mystics' devotion to the Sacred Heart right down to the time of St. Peter Canisius and St. Margaret Mary. For further details see H. Rahner: *De dominici pectoris fonte potavit,* in: *Zeitschrift f. kath. Theologie* 55 (1931) p. 103–108.

[27] *Commentary on the Canticle* I (C. S. G. VIII, p. 93, l. 14–16); on this point see also K. Rahner, *Coeur de Jésus chez Origène?* in: *Revue d'Ascétique et de Mystique* 15 (1934), p. 171–174.

[28] The witnesses to this tradition are assembled in the article mentioned above (n. 24) and, for the Middle Ages, in H. Preuss' book, *Johannes in den Jahrhunderten,* Guetersloh 1939; also in K. Richstaetter, *Die Herz-Jesu-Verehrung,* p. 263f.

"Sacred Heart texts" which are generally adduced from Augustine and Paulinus of Nola. It was especially thanks to them that this Origenist tradition lived on to influence the Middle Ages. We can almost hear the undertones of Origen when Augustine says: "Among his fellows and collaborators, the other evangelists, John received from our Lord (on whose breast he lay at the Last Supper, in order thereby to signify that he drew loftier mysteries from his inmost Heart) the special and peculiar gift that he should say such things of the Son of God as would stimulate, without satisfying, the spirits of little ones, who are still incapable of comprehension; but for the more mature who have reached the adult state, these same words serve to exercise and nourish their souls."[29] In the same way Paulinus too thinks of the Heart of Jesus as the seat and source of all wisdom, when he writes of John: "John, who rested blissfully on the breast of our Lord, was inebriated with the Holy Ghost; from the Heart of the all-creating Wisdom he quaffed an understanding which transcends that of any creature."[30]

The second element is still more essential, especially for an understanding of the present liturgical form of the devotion: it is the genesis of the Church from the Heart of our crucified Lord.[31] Here it becomes particularly clear how all the spiritual treasures won for us by the messianic salvation can be summed up in the "Church", which is the supreme gift of the transfixed Heart. Both dogmatically and historically, this vision of the Church proceeding from the Heart of our Lord was the fundamental notion of the early Christians on the subject of the Sacred Heart. Here is the vision of holy Church as it appeared to the believing eyes of the first Christians: as the Virgin Mother, the Queen in golden robes, the Mother of the living, the second Eve, who

---

[29] *Tractatus in Joannem* 18, 1 (PL 35, 1536 A).

[30] *Epistola* 21, 4 (C. S. E. L. 29, p. 151, l. 13–15).

[31] Detailed patristic references in S. Tromp, *De nativitate Ecclesiae ex Corde Jesu in cruce: Gregorianum* 13 (1932), p. 489–527.

issues from the wounded side of the Bridegroom as once the first Eve came from the side of man, formed by the divine power of the blood that flowed from the pierced Heart of the Redeemer, filled with the life-giving force of the Holy Ghost, who sprang as living water from the Heart of Jesus.

To discover the origin of this profound theology of the Church as the second Eve coming from the side of the heavenly Adam, we must go back to the writings of the New Testament. Here we see in germ the two notions which were to be brooded on and combined in the theological reflection of the second century until they yielded the idea we have been considering.

The Old Testament typology, which finds expression especially in the letters of St. Paul, asserts that the ancestor of the human race was "a figure of him who was to come" (Rom. 5, 14), that Christ is therefore truly the second, the spiritual Adam (I Cor. 15, 45), because in a far more lofty sense than the first Adam he became the ancestor of a new race, and the author of life (Acts 3, 15; Heb. 2, 10). This theology of Christ as the second Adam moved the early Church to ask whether the mysterious creation of the mother of all the living, of Eve, out of the side of the sleeping Adam, could not also be a significant type of what was to come in the messianic future. Paul once compared the church of Corinth with the virginal Eve before original sin (II Cor. 11, 2–3), and in his teaching on the relation between the individual church and the universal Church he undoubtedly wishes to give to the Church as such the title of Virgin Mother of the living, maidenly Mediatrix of the life dispensed by the heavenly Adam. Indeed the fifth chapter of the letter to the Ephesians seems to refer still more precisely to the origin of the Church as the second Eve. Paul says: *For no man ever hated his own flesh, but nourishes and cherishes it, as also Christ does the Church: because we are members of his body, flesh of his flesh and bone of his bones* (Eph. 5, 29–30). Paul is thinking here of the relation between Adam and Eve as a type of the *magnum mysterium* between Christ and his Church, which is symbolized in every marriage. The extra phrase "flesh of his flesh and bone of his bones", the cry of Adam when God led to him the companion who had been formed from his ribs (Gen. 2, 24), points to the origin of the spiritual Eve, the Church: she went forth from the flesh of the life-giving Adam, she is formed, as Paul has said a little earlier, from the suffering of the God-Man and from the holy bath of baptism: *Christ loved the Church and delivered himself up for it: that he might sanctify it, cleansing it by the laver of water in the word of life* (Eph. 5, 25). In a word, the Church issued *ex sanguine et aqua,* from the blood of the passion and from the fountain of baptism, through the bath of regeneration in the Holy Ghost, who as living water "is poured out in our hearts" (Gal. 4, 6; Tit. 3, 5).

Ex aqua et sanguine: with these words we touch on the second fundamental thought from which devotion to the Sacred Heart was to grow. In the theology of St. Paul it was not yet evident whether the origin of Eve from the side of Adam might not also be a significant type for the future story of salvation. Nowhere in Scripture is the idea clearly expressed. But the teaching of St. John adumbrated a mysterious connection between Christ's redemptive sufferings, the side of the crucified second Adam, and the effusion of the Spirit in which St. Paul saw the birth of the Church. "Blood and water" from the pierced side of the Redeemer are attested by the evangelist with peculiar solemnity as symbolizing all the treasures of salvation.

In any case, this scriptural doctrine about the origin of the Church from the wounded side of Christ is part of the earliest deposit of Christian teaching. Already at the end of the second century Tertullian assumes its familiarity when, in his little book of instructions for catechumens, *De Baptismo,* he initiates the faithful into the mysteries of the wounded side of Christ[32]; and in his *De Anima,* in an almost casual and off-hand way he slips

---

[32] *De Baptismo* c. 9 (C. S. E. L. 20, p. 208).

this sentence into the middle of learned considerations on sleep: "If Adam was a type of Christ, then the sleep of Adam was a type of the sleep of Christ, who slept in death, in order that through a similar cleaving of the side the true mother of the living might be formed, namely the Church."[33] Therefore according to Tertullian, Christ is the source of all new life. From the Cross gushes forth the water of baptism[34] which carries with it the Spirit that builds the Church.[35]

Such then is the beautiful form of early Christian devotion to the Sacred Heart; in the first Christian millenium a wonderful chorus of voices arises from all centuries and all countries to praise the wounded side from which the virgin mother Church came forth. It is the doctrine of Cyril of Jerusalem in his simple catechesis, it is the message of Ambrose in his talks to the newly-baptized, and of John Chrysostom when he preaches in the splendid basilica at Antioch: "The lance of the soldier opened the side of Christ, and behold . . . from his wounded side Christ built the Church, as once the first mother, Eve, was formed from Adam. Hence Paul says: Of his flesh we are and of his bone. By that he means the wounded side of Jesus. As God took the rib out of Adam's side and from it formed the woman, so Christ gives us water and blood from his wounded side and forms from it the Church . . . there the slumber of Adam, here the death-sleep of Jesus."[36] The sermons of Augustine to his simple flock in Hippo Regis harmonize perfectly with this universal teaching, and his words on the Heart of Jesus will be echoed by the mysticism of the Middle Ages: "Adam sleeps that Eve may be born, Christ dies that the Church may be born. While Adam sleeps,

---

[33] *De anima* 43 (C. S. E. L. 20, p. 372, l. 2–5).

[34] *Adversus Judaeos* c. 13 (C. S. E. L. 70, p. 318f.).

[35] *Adversus Marcionem* III, 23 (C. S. E. L. 47, p. 417, l. 5–7).

[36] S. Haidacher, *Eine unbeachtete Rede des hl. Chrysostomus an Neugetaufte*, in: *Zeitschrift f. kath. Theologie* 28 (1904), p. 183f. Cf. also H. Rahner, *Mater Ecclesia*, Einsiedeln 1944, p. 17f.

Eve is formed from his side. When Christ is dead, his side is smitten with a spear, that thence may flow sacraments to form the Church."[37] And he returns to the theme in the famous Tract 120 on St. John: "The first woman was called *Life* and *Mother of the living*. The second Adam with bowed head slept upon the Cross, in order that a spouse might be formed for him from that which flowed from his side as he slept. O death, by which the dead come to life again! What could be cleaner than this blood! What than this wound more healing!"[38]

This Augustinian doctrine on the origin of the Church found an echo in the popular catechesis. We can catch it in an instruction of the bishop Quodvultdeus of Carthage: "Now let our Bridegroom mount onto the Cross and sleep there in death, and let his side be opened and the virgin bride come forth. As once Eve was formed from the side of Adam, so let the Church be formed now from the side of the dying Christ, as he hangs there on the Cross. O wonderful mystery! the bride is born from the bridegroom!"[39] We hear another echo in the thoughtful inscription with which, about the year 430, the deacon Leo, later Pope Leo the Great, adorned the pillars of the Church of St. John Lateran. The baptismal poem sings of the Church as the virginal mother giving birth to new life in the baptismal font, the waters of which take their rise from the Heart of Jesus:

Virgineo faetu Genitrix Ecclesia natos
quos spirante Deo concipit, amne parit . . .
Fons hic est vitae qui totum diluit orbem
sumens de Christi vulnere principium.

From her virginal womb Mother Church delivers in the stream (of baptism) the children whom she has conceived under the breath of God. This is the fountain of life, which

---

[37] *Tractatus in Joannem* IX, 10 (PL 35, 1463 D).
[38] *Ibid.,* CXX, 2 (PL 35, 1935 B).
[39] *De symbolo ad Catechumenos* II 6, 15 (PL 40, 645 A).

takes its rise from the wound of Christ and washes over the whole earth.[40]

Time was not to wither this primitive doctrine. In Carolingian sermons, on Roman miniatures, in the theology of the great scholastics, in mystical prayers of the burgeoning devotion in the eleventh century, the mystery finds everywhere utterance and expression. The love for Mother Church has here its deepest roots. The royal Church, princess of peoples, gathering up in a golden chalice the blood of the Bridegroom's Heart, radiant with a mother's joy and dignity, which has become hers through this blood, such is the beloved image which was repeatedly fashioned by the artists of the early Middle Ages. It is perhaps in their inscriptions, painted on manuscripts or engraved in stone, that we catch the most delicate expression of their love for the Church: "Behold the Church as she gathers up the bloodstream of the Lamb, in humility indeed, yet worthy of such dignity", is written on a ninth-century book-cover.[41] The Gothic art of the so-called *bibles moralisées* — for instance in the magnificent *codices* of the Vienna National Library — illustrated the birth of the virginal Church from the Heart of our Lord beside a picture of Baptism, in which this birth of the Church is being perennially reenacted. Later still, at the end of the Middle Ages, a woodcut shows the Church carrying the chalice of divine blood under the proud inscription:

Sein Gewalt ist dir geben,
Du bist das ewig Leben.[42]
(His power is given to thee;
thou art eternal life.)

---

[40] Cf. F. J. Doelger, *Die Inschrift im Baptisterium S. Giovanni in Fonte,* in: *Antike und Christentum* 2 (1930), p. 253–257. Text in Diehl, *Inscriptiones latinae christianae veteres* I, n. 1513.

[41] On the cover of the Aschaffenburg Gospel-Book in Munich.

[42] On a woodcut from South Germany in the Museo Civico of Pavia; cf. W. L. Schreiber, *Handbuch der Holz- und Metallschnitte des XV. Jahrhunderts* VIII, Leipzig 1930, p. 112, n. 1871 p.

The whole history of patristic teaching on the wound in Christ's side can be summed up in the single formula: *Fons vitae*. From St. John, who drank at the breast of our Lord, and from Justin and Irenaeus, who show us the fountain springing from the pierced Heart of Christ, a tradition of thought and writing stretches unbroken down the centuries. It is to the deep foundation laid by this early Christian notion that the present devotion to the Sacred Heart, as expressed in the liturgy, is returning. From that beginning the development of the devotion has come full circle back to the point from which it started: the "streams from the Heart of Christ" of which the prophets spoke, which Jesus promised as living water, and poured from his pierced side onto his Church, are today, as the prayer of the one, holy Church, flowing over the whole earth.

JOSEF STIERLI

DEVOTION TO THE SACRED HEART FROM THE END OF PATRISTIC TIMES DOWN TO ST.MARGARET MARY

THE nature of a thing reveals itself more clearly in its living history than in any abstract definitions, classifications and distinctions. That is why instruction in history, if properly understood, is one of the surest and most indispensable guides of mankind.

The difficulties listed above in chapter one will have suggested some of the reasons which make the historical approach particularly appropriate in a consideration of the devotion to the Sacred Heart. Consequently this condensed and rather simplified account of the devotion's main lines of development has a purpose beyond the merely historical; it is intended as an essential means of clarifying the nature and meaning of devotion to the Sacred Heart. "The history of this devotion", writes Hugo Rahner, "is today more than ever the best explanation of its present form."[1]

The two previous chapters have sketched the first steps in the development of the doctrine of the Heart of our Lord. This history begins in fact in the books of the Old and New Testament. Even though many of the interpretations of Sacred Heart texts from Holy Scripture may call for a critical question-mark, there does nevertheless exist a doctrine of the Sacred Heart which can be solidly based on the Bible. These biblical affirmations about the mystery of the Sacred Heart[2] fall into two groups: in the first, the Heart of Jesus has a subjective, personal connotation; it means the whole interior life of Jesus Christ, rooted in and unified

---

[1] Hugo Rahner, *Grundzüge einer Geschichte der Herz-Jesu-Verehrung,* in: *ZAM* 1943, p. 61 ff.

[2] As Pius XII insists in *Haurietis Aquas* (Paragraph 13), the Bible contains no clear mention of any veneration or love for the physical heart of the Word

by love and really symbolized by the pierced physical Heart of our crucified Lord. In the second group, this same pierced Heart of our Lord, pouring out blood and water on Golgotha, is seen objectively in its redemptive role, as the source of all the messianic treasures of salvation. These are epitomized in "Spirit", and are unfolded gradually in the birth of the Church from the Heart of the Pierced One and in the unceasing flow of the seven holy sacraments and of all the abundant graces of salvation which lead us to eternal life.

In the first Christian millenium, patristic theology developed the second aspect of the mystery of the Sacred Heart, the notion of the inexhaustible fountain of grace in the Heart of the Pierced One. This theology of the Sacred Heart did not consist simply of a small selection of suitable texts of Scripture; rather it formed an essential element in the whole complex of patristic thought. To this day the Church has never ceased to cherish these treasures of patristic thought; they have enriched all subsequent devotion to the Sacred Heart even down to the present Liturgy.

Was there also in patristic times any spirituality of the Sacred Heart, in which the theology of the Fathers was translated into personal devotion? There is very little direct evidence for it, but we have positive reason for leaving the question open. Surely this rich theology about the fountain of grace from the pierced Heart of the Redeemer would naturally and almost of necessity be translated by the believing soul into prayer?

The theological heritage of patristic times persisted as an organic growth into the Middle Ages. But partly for extrinsic reasons such as the stimulus of the crusades, and much more in consequence of the medieval temperament, this age rediscovered the other aspect of the mystery, the personal disposition of our

---

Incarnate, considered precisely as the symbol of his ardent charity. However it is evident from the rest of the encyclical, and from chapter two above, p. 15, that there is ample justification in the Old and New Testaments for Fr. Stierli's reference to "biblical affirmations about the mystery of the Sacred Heart". |Tr.|

Lord's Heart. What resulted was a fruitful synthesis of objective and subjective aspects; the treasures of salvation from the pierced Heart of the Crucified were seen as gifts of the personal love of the Redeemer's Heart. It was a vision that spontaneously and inevitably spurred men on to a true devotion, which meant a personal return of love for this gift of Christ's Heart.

The fourth and latest phase of the cult is dominated by the name of St. Margaret Mary Alacoque. The Church now accepts the veneration of the Heart of Jesus into its own official prayer. That which has hitherto been almost exclusively private in practice receives from the Church an official character; from being the prayer of many individuals it becomes a concern of the whole Church. To this exterior development there corresponds in the interior life a special emphasis on reparation, as it is demanded by the visions of Paray-le-Monial. In his encyclical *Miserentissimus Redemptor* Pius XI laid the theological foundations of reparation and proposed the means of putting it into practice.

We shall show in this chapter how the patristic theology of the Sacred Heart was further developed in the Middle Ages, and how the private devotion to the Heart of Jesus took shape from it. The story of how the teaching and praying Church assimilated the medieval heritage into its Liturgy, and moulded the main lines of the modern devotion, remains for the next chapter.

Though history resembles in a way the uninterrupted flow of a stream, yet we can note certain characteristic traits in its course, and so define the periods which are dominated by these traits. On this principle we can distinguish three periods in the medieval devotion to the Sacred Heart:

1. The *early period with the transition from the patristic to the Middle Ages*: the initiative still rests with the theologians, who are deepening and developing the patristic ideas;

2. Then the *period of the great mystics*, the golden age of medieval devotion to the Sacred Heart, at least the peer of the first period in theological depth, and far surpassing it in religious vitality;

3. Finally the *period of the renewal and expansion* of the devotion among the ordinary laity.

Our division departs in one point from that generally accepted by historians: we extend the medieval period of the devotion to the year 1700, that is, to the beginning of an essentially new development. Geographically, the witnesses and champions of the cult are scattered through the whole of the West, but with an unmistakable concentration in the countries of German language and culture, which seem to have shown a peculiar aptitude for these religious values; perhaps one should recognize here a special vocation from God.

One of the most interesting questions, to which nevertheless hardly any historical research has been devoted, is that of the transition from patristic theology, which saw the wound in Jesus' side as the source of grace, to the medieval preaching of the Heart of Jesus as the express object of a particular devotion. One thing seems to be clear: there was no sudden discovery of the Sacred Heart in the Middle Ages, as many accounts seem to imply. We are faced rather with a gradual and unconscious process of development and transformation. On the one hand we have patristic texts with a medieval ring. On the other, the medieval teaching on the Sacred Heart, especially in its first period, retains the patristic habits of thought.

The organic transition is accomplished first of all on the lines of the exegesis of the Canticle of Canticles. Then came the special contribution of Anglo-Saxon and Carolingian theology, which showed the Church emerging as a bride from the wounded side, and catching in her chalice the fountain of blood and water from the interior of Christ. There are recollections in this image of the theological idea that wisdom, mysticism, and the interior life are drawn from the Heart of Jesus as from a fountain; moreover the veneration of St. John, and the notion of God being born in the heart of every believing Christian, live on to perpetuate the legacy of Origen.

The transition from patristic to medieval ways of thought began in late antiquity. Hugo Rahner has established this[3], and in doing so has corrected all previous historical accounts, such as Richstätter's[4] and Hamon's.[5] The beginnings of the change can be seen already in the spirituality of the Spanish church, with its anti-Arian bent, and in the medieval undertones of the Gallican liturgies, with their glowing love for the blood and wounded side of our Lord. It is evident too in Irish piety. Both Gallican and Celtic spirituality show Syrian influences at work. But the Syrian Church, ever since the days of St. Ephraem, had cultivated a warm-hearted and intimate devotion to the Passion, Cross, and wounded side of our Lord, and it communicated this to the West. One channel of this influence was Rome, where in the eighth century Syrian popes left their mark on the Roman liturgy, for instance in the *Improperia* of Good Friday.

Strictly speaking, the early period of the medieval devotion is confined to the years 1100—1250. The devotion was still the preserve of theologians, in direct continuation of the patristic tradition.

The first name to deserve mention is St. ANSELM OF CANTERBURY, not as the father of Scholasticism, but as the mystic who summed up the twofold biblical significance of the Sacred Heart: "The opening of the side of Christ reveals the riches of his love, the love of his Heart for us." It is then the intimate vision of the mystery of Christ that leads him to the mystery of the Sacred Heart. But another way opens to him from the mystery of the Passion through the opened side into Christ's Heart; and St. Anselm prays that his own heart too be pierced by the word of God.

Beside him stands St. BERNARD OF CLAIRVAUX, who is likewise

---

[3] In the article quoted above note 1 and in his contributions to this book.

[4] K. Richstaetter, *Illustrious Friends of the Sacred Heart,* London, 1930.

[5] A. Hamon, *Histoire de la dévotion au Sacré-Coeur,* 4 volumes (Paris 1923), p. 31.

led to the mystery of the Sacred Heart by his mystical love for Christ, especially in the mysteries of his birth and his Passion.

"The secret of his Heart lies visible through the clefts of his Body; visible too the great mystery of his love, and the bowels of his mercy."[6]

This mysticism of the heart reaches its maturest development in his unfinished commentary on the Canticle of Canticles. Bernard had written on the first three chapters of the Canticle when he fell seriously ill, so he called his friend WILLIAM OF ST. THIERRY to his sick-bed in order to discuss with him the plan of the whole commentary. William made notes of Bernard's ideas and they flowed quite spontaneously into his own writings. They speak of the ardent longing to know the whole Christ, and so to penetrate even to his Heart: *usque ad ipsum cor Iesu!*

Bernard's Commentary was continued by GILBERT OF HOY-LAND, Abbot of Swenshed on the Scottish border, who brought it down to the fifth chapter. In doing so he found particular occasion for deeper explanation at the verse which was to become a classic one in the mysticism of the Sacred Heart: *Vulnerasti cor meum, soror mea sponsa—Thou hast wounded my heart, my sister, my spouse* (Cant. 4, 9).

The influence of Bernard spread to his numerous disciples, among whom we must mention Abbot GUARRICUS OF IGNY. The VICTORINES too were stimulated by him. RICHARD OF ST. VICTOR, influenced no doubt by William of St. Thierry, confesses: "Nothing is kinder, nothing more gracious, than the Heart of Jesus." And alluding to Ez. 36, where God promises us a heart of flesh and blood in place of our stony hearts, he says: "Our Emmanuel has more than all others a heart of flesh."

Among German-speakers, the first to deserve mention is the Benedictine ABBOT WILLIRAM OF EBERSBERG (1048—1085), for his work on the Canticle of Canticles. At the height of the In-

[6] *Sermo* LXI, 4 (PL 183, 1072).

vestiture quarrel he makes Christ say to the Church: "Come from Lebanon, my bride! Hasten to me in the purity of your baptism. If you preserve yourself as lovely as you were made in baptism, see what graces I will grant you even in this world. I shall make the kings and emperors, who are now rising against you with cunning and fury like panthers and lions, I shall make them reverence the prints of your feet, and be converted to Christian piety. You have wounded my heart, my sister, for whom I became man, my spouse, whom I wedded to me through the dowry of my blood. For your sake I suffered on the Cross the wounds of the nails and of the lance."[7]

ABBOT RUPERT OF DEUTZ († 1135) collected, from the patristic and medieval theology available to him, everything that he could find about the opening of our Lord's side and its meaning.

Another commentary on the Canticle based on patristic sources is that of the Benedictine ABBOT WOLBERO OF ST. PANTALEON in Cologne († 1167). Yet his explanation of the text is completely medieval: in the piercing of the side he sees the love of the transfixed heart of the Bridegroom.

The earliest Middle High German collection of sermons, composed by the PRIEST CONRAD about 1180, drew abundantly from patristic sources, and prolonged in a way the Ephesian tradition.

CAESARIUS OF HEISTERBACH (about 1189) appears in contrast rather as one of Origen's school, for he speaks of the spiritual Heart of our Lord, of his loving and self-sacrificing will.

The Johannine theme of Origen reappears in ABBOT GOTTFRIED OF ADMONT († 1165): "John rested on the breast of our Lord. In the breast is the heart of man, in the heart is wisdom." Therefore this Heart of our Lord is the seat of wisdom and of divine sweetness and love.[8]

The Trudberter Canticle, which originated probably in

---

[7] Williram's German paraphrase of the Canticle of Canticles, edited by Seemüller (1878), p. 27f.   [8] PL 174, 671.

the Alsatian monastery of Hohenburg, connects the bridal role with Mary and her intimacy with Christ, "whose most kind and gracious Heart has predestined us to eternal life." — "To the wound in my side you should turn your mouth and heart at all times, and in so doing think of all those whom I have redeemed with my blood, both the living and the dead."[9]

The first prayer to the Sacred Heart in Middle High German shows how a deep theological knowledge of the Sacred Heart could blend with its fervent veneration:

"Lord Christ, Son of God, for the dread with which your Sacred Heart was seized when you, Lord Christ, surrendered your holy limbs to suffering, and for your love and loyalty towards men, I beg you to comfort the pain of my heart, as you comforted the pain of your disciples in the days of your resurrection."[10]

Among the early medieval devotees of the Sacred Heart must also be counted the disciple of the Victorines, ECKBERT OF SCHOEN-AU, Abbot of a Benedictine monastery situated near St. Goars-hausen. The prayer-book which he put together for his sister, the abbess Elizabeth of Schoenau, is full of patristic ideas about the grace-dispensing side of our Lord.

Two more examples will indicate how largely the theology of the Sacred Heart enriched personal piety even in this early period:

The first is the truly classical hymn to the Sacred Heart, *Summi Regis Cor, aveto*. It is almost certain now that it was written by BLESSED HERMANN JOSEPH in the Premonstratensian monastery of Steinfeld in the Eifel. The hymn unites intimately the liturgical image of Christ as the *Rex Gloriae* on the Cross with the picture

---

[9] *Das Hohelied,* erklaert von Rilindis und Herrat, edited by J. Haupt (1864), p. 140.

[10] From a twelfth century prayer-book which belonged in the fourteenth century to Queen Agnes of Hungary, passed into the possession of the monastery of Muri (Switzerland), and was burnt in the sack of the monastery in 1841.

of the man of sorrows, whose Heart, pierced by the lance, is overcome by suffering and love, and demands a return of love and sympathy. In the same way the image of the bodily, pierced Heart is combined with that of the spiritual Heart, wounded by suffering and by love. Finally it shows us the twofold existence of this Heart: the Heart of bleeding wounds and the Heart glorified in splendour, into whose sanctuary the elect long to enter.

The counterpart to this classiscal hymn is formed by the first recorded vision of the Sacred Heart in the Middle Ages, that granted to Saint LUITGARD OF ST. TROND.

Luitgard at the age of seventeen had determined to consecrate herself entirely to our Lord, but she was harassed by the advances of a young man. Then Christ appeared to her in human form. Opening his garments, he showed her the wound in his side, red as though with fresh blood, and said: "From now on seek not the flatteries of a foolish man. This must be the constant object of your contemplation and love!" She became a Benedictine and later a Cistercian. As a special grace she received an understanding of the Latin psalms. But the help in prayer for which she hoped from them was still denied to her. So she complained to our Lord:

"What use to me, an uneducated peasant girl, is the knowledge of the mysteries of Holy Scripture?"

"What then do you want?" asked our Lord.

"I want your Heart!"

"And still more do I want yours!"

"Yes, Lord, but in such a way that you temper the love of your Heart to that of mine, and that I may possess my heart under the sure protection of yours!"

And our Lord exchanged the two hearts.[11]

In the second, most abundantly blessed period of the medieval devotion to the Sacred Heart, the patristic heritage merged completely into the language and piety of the Middle Ages.

---

[11] Richstaetter, *op. cit.,* p. 44.

Three forces in particular promoted this development. First of all the strong emphasis on the mystery of the Passion had its effects on mysticism and on every sphere of spirituality. The external stimulus to this came from the Crusades and their contact with the Holy Land. But devotion to the Passion was influenced in a more vital way by deep emotional meditation on the life and suffering of Christ. The mysticism of the Passion looked directly to our Lord's suffering Heart, which in its suffering was pouring itself out in love. Hence the strongest characteristic of this medieval devotion to the Sacred Heart: the object of it was, above all, the suffering, wounded Heart, which calls for a return of love.

Besides the mystery of the Passion, other formative factors were a special love for St. John the apostle and an abundance of commentaries on the Canticle of Canticles. The introduction of the feast of Corpus Christi served to underline the close connection between the Eucharist and the Heart of Jesus, and gave the devotion a Eucharistic note, while on the other hand the Eucharist was seen as a gift and an abiding presence of this loving Heart of our Lord.

At the height of the Middle Ages, the devotion no longer looked to theology as its mainstay. The latter was developing more and more towards its scholastic form, and was beginning at the same time to lose contact with life. Into its place stepped mysticism, which was however formed completely by theology. The most prominent place was taken now by German piety, which at this period was unparalleled in any other country of Europe. This contrast is not based simply on the fact that German sources have been more thoroughly explored, but on the actual state of the devotion in these regions. The leading roles in this development were taken by the Franciscans, by the religious women of Helfta, and above all by the Dominicans. Through the apostolic activity of the two mendicant orders, the traditional doctrine about the love-pierced Heart of our Lord as the source of grace, further transformed and refashioned, was accepted more and more by simple, unlearned religious. This influence showed itself especially in the convents of nuns which were served by the two mendicant orders. But even in this period the cult of the Sacred Heart was still not really a popular devotion.

In her vision of 4 October, 1673, ST. MARGARET MARY ALACOQUE recognized in ST. FRANCIS OF ASSISI, whose feast it was, one of the really great friends of the Sacred Heart. The 'legend of St. Francis' lends strength to this testimony. It tells how Brother Francis received from the crucifix of St. Damian the commission to restore the house of God, and continues: *Ab illa hora vulneratum et liquefactum est cor eius ad memoriam dominicae passionis.*[12] What touched his heart so deeply was not simply the external suffering of Christ, but the Passion of his Heart; and the spirit of St. Francis has never ceased to direct his sons to the suffering Heart of Jesus.

This is immediately clear in St. BONAVENTURE, who in his deep devotion to the Passion has become even for our days a herald of the mystery of the Sacred Heart. The *Itinerarium Mentis in Deum,* truly a 'Pilgrim's Route-Map of the heart on the Way to God', shows how the only way to the Father is a burning love for the crucified Christ *(via autem non est nisi per ardentissimum amorem Crucifixi)* and this love is perfected in a true communion of hearts.[13] Many isolated passages in his theology, but above all his little book *Lignum Vitae,* preach the mystery of our Lord's Heart. In his letters too the warm love of his own heart finds utterance.

For a long time the *Vitis Mystica,* a small intimate Sacred Heart book which was used even in the liturgy, was ascribed to Bonaventure. Probably it is of German origin, either from Franciscan or from Cistercian circles. But the fact that it was attributed to Bonaventure proves how well known he was as a venerator of the Redeemer's Heart. We read there: "The Heart of our Lord

[12] *Legenda S. Francisci, Acta Sanct. Oct.* II, 732–42.
[13] *Opera Omnia,* ed. Quarachi, tome V, 293.

was pierced with a lance, that by the visible wound we might recognize the invisible love. The outward wound of the Heart shows the soul's wound of love." From the external Passion the author penetrates to the interior suffering of the Heart, and quotes that phrase of Psalm 68 which still stands in the present liturgy of the Sacred Heart, an echo of countless repetitions in the course of seven centuries: "My heart hath expected reproach and misery. And I looked for one that would grieve together with me, but there was none: and for one that would comfort me, and I found none." Then he exhorts us to a practical veneration of the Sacred Heart: to praise the divine Heart, to pray to it with unswerving trust, to show it the deepest compassion, to seek there the cleansing from our sins, and there also to set up our abode.[14]

We can catch the early Franciscan spirit again in the piety of St. ANGELA OF FOLIGNO and in the yearning of St. MARGARET OF CORTONA to dwell deep in the Heart of our Lord. The spirit of these women is diffused among the Italian groups of Franciscans which gather round them.

It is among the South German Franciscans that the development from the seraphic mysticism of the Passion to devotion to the Sacred Heart is most marked. We can take as a forerunner DAVID OF AUGSBURG, the novice-master and later companion of Berthold of Regensburg. He is completely imbued with the spirit of St. Francis, and of his disciple Bonaventure. The pierced Heart of our Lord is for him a symbol of love: "From the burning Heart of Jesus flows his blood, hot with love." — "Jesus showed us from the Cross his faithful Heart, glowing with love, since the death of our souls touched him more nearly than the death of his Body." — "Ah, dearest Lord Jesus Christ, what great love and faithfulness wilt thou show to the soul when thou displayest thy riches and openest thy Heart to thy beloved friends!"[15]

---

[14] *Op. Bonaventurae,* tome VIII; cf. Richstaetter, *op. cit.,* p. 76–77.
[15] Richstaetter, *op. cit.,* p. 59.

David has left us also some Sacred Heart prayers, combining forceful theology with mystical ardour:

"Beloved Lord Jesus Christ, warm, burn through my heart, which longs for thee, with the love-warm blood which flowed from thy burning Heart on the holy Cross. That it flowed from a hot Heart, it was itself a living witness. Thy Body was dead and cold, and thy blood of itself could not have flowed, nor even have been moved. It should naturally have ceased to circulate, as we see in dead bodies. But not so with thee! By this it is given us to understand that it was still so hot with the glow of thy Heart's love that it ran down like a sweet fountain from thy wounded side."[16]

BERTHOLD OF REGENSBURG, the most powerful preacher of medieval Germany, was an enthusiastic pupil of David of Augsburg. Although his penitential sermons to the masses of the people did not give him much occasion to speak of the mystery of our Lord's Heart, still we do find references to it in his extant sermons. On one occasion he preached from the town-walls of Zurich to unnumbered thousands on how, during Holy Mass, a man could meditate on the whole life, passion and death of Christ. When the priest breaks the host after the Pater Noster, we should recall that on the holy Cross "our dear Lord's sweet pure Heart was broken" and that "Longinus thrust the lance through our Lord's holy side into his sweet Heart."[17]

From the ranks of South German Franciscans there originated in the second half of the fifteenth century a collection of sermons and religious tracts, "The Preachers of St. George", called after the Abbey of St. George where the manuscript was found. More than twenty moving passages witness to the growing knowledge of the mystery of Christ's Heart:

"Our Lord let his pure Heart be opened with a sharp spear, the Heart which is full of all wisdom, all mercy and all purity. He

[16] Richstaetter, *op. cit.,* p. 60. [17] Richstaetter, *op. cit.,* p. 64.

suffered his Heart to be opened, that we might find it open if we came to it, and also that we might open our hearts to him. Thus he poured forth that stream from his Heart, that we might see that his love was perfect and pure without any deceit."[18]

Under the direction of the Abbess Gertrude of Hackeborn, a sister of Blessed Mechthild, the monastery of Cistercian nuns at Helfta, near Eisleben[19], reached the highest level of feminine culture known to the Middle Ages. At the same time it became a centre of noble striving for holiness and of extraordinary graces of prayer. The nuns had learnt from St. Bernard a mystical love for Jesus, from St. Benedict the solemn splendour of the liturgy, and from the Dominicans of Halle, their neighbours and spiritual directors, a special devotion to the Passion; but the decisive influence that made Helfta a vigorous centre of devotion to the Sacred Heart was the supernatural one, the sublime mystical graces of which it was the focus. Among the many great women of this convent, three deserve special mention.

MECHTHILD OF MAGDEBURG, who combined in her nature a masculine boldness and strength with high poetic gifts, was blessed by God with rich graces of prayer. She entered Helfta late in life, after she had lived as a Beguine in Magdeburg, engaged in works of charity.

At the bidding of her confessor she described her visions in a book entitled *The Flowing Light,* which tells of her intimacy with our Lord in the mystery of his Heart: "In my great sufferings God revealed himself to my soul, showed me the wound of his Heart and said: See how they have made me suffer. Then my soul said: Ah, Lord, why didst thou suffer such great misery, why is thy holy blood shed so lavishly? By thy prayer alone all the world might surely have been easily saved and justice satisfied? No, he

[18] Richstaetter, *op. cit.,* p. 67.

[19] We can disregard here the dispute over the religious allegiance of Helfta, whether it should be considered a Cistercian or a Benedictine Abbey. It is certain that the nuns of Helfta had been won over to the reforms of St. Bernard.

answered, that would not have been sufficient for my Father. For all this poverty and toil, all this torment and shame, all this was but a knocking at heaven's gate until the hour when my Heart's blood ran down to earth — only then was heaven opened."[20]

Mechthild sees in the Sacred Heart above all the interior life of our Lord, burning with love, to which men answer with abuse. This inner life is incarnate in the wounded, glowing Heart. Her mysticism of the Sacred Heart is dominated by the mystery of the Passion. She wishes to share the pain and disgrace of the Heart of Jesus and so to find her rest in him.

> Do you truly wish to be converted?
> Behold your Spouse, the whole world's Lord,
> See how he hangs there, high on the Cross,
> Before the whole world, all covered with blood,
> His eyes dimmed and full of tears,
> His sweetest Heart overflowing with love:
> Remember then the sharp spear's wound
> Which pierced even to the depths of the Heart —
> And weep over that which you have done.[21]

At her entry into Helfta in 1270, Mechthild found there two young nuns who were to play important roles in the history of the devotion: St. Gertrude the Great and Blessed Mechthild of Hackeborn.

MECHTHILD OF HACKEBORN, noble by birth and artistic by temperament, had received a careful education, and while still a young nun was entrusted with the direction of the convent school. Our Lord favoured her with great graces, but for many years she kept them hidden. Her only confidantes were St. Gertrude and another nun to whom Mechthild entrusted her secrets after the death of her sister, the abbess Gertrude. At the command of the new

---

[20] *Fließendes Licht* 6, 26; Richstaetter, *op. cit.,* p. 91.
[21] *Fließendes Licht* 7, 27; Richstaetter, *op. cit.,* p. 92–3.

abbess, these two religious wrote an account of Mechthild's spiritual favours, and so, without the latter's knowledge, there came into being the *Liber Specialis Gratiae,* the book of special graces. When Mechthild heard of it she was inconsolable. Then our Lord appeared to her, laid the book on his Heart, and said: "Everything in this book flowed forth from my Heart and will flow back to it again."

When she asked our Lord whether she should refrain from revealing the graces of God to others, she received the answer: "Impart them to others according to the rich generosity of my overflowing Heart: give me to others according to my bounty, not according to your own."[22]

To Mechthild's eyes, Christ is not so much the Man of Sorrows as the glorified Lord, enthroned in the glory of heaven, in other words the liturgical Christ. Her own life was indeed a series of pains and crosses but she found rest and consolation, refuge and peace in the Heart of the glorified Christ.

Besides the *Liber Specialis Gratiae* Mechthild left a valuable legacy of prayers to the Sacred Heart. They were lifelong favourites of St. Peter Canisius, who copied some of them into a little book and carried them always with him. Even on his death-bed he had this book, black from constant thumbing, in his hands.

A few short quotations suffice to show the astonishing familiarity of this soul with our Lord:

"She saw how the Lord opened the wound of his sweet Heart, and said: Behold the greatness of my love. Wilt thou learn to know it, thou wilt find it nowhere so clearly as in the words of the Gospel: *As the Father has loved me, so have I loved you.* The Lord united his sweet Heart with the soul's heart, bestowed on her all the graces of contemplation, devotion and love, and made her rich in all good things."

"He made her rest tenderly on his heart and said: Take thou

---

[22] Mecht. II 43; Richstaetter, *op. cit.,* p. 96.

wholly my divine Heart. And the soul felt how the Godhead poured itself into her with mighty force like a stream."

"In consequence of all these great favours, she was impressed with a wonderful devotion to the divine Heart, and as often as the Lord appeared to her, she received a special gift from his Heart, as is recorded in many parts of the Book of special graces." — " She herself used often to say: 'If all the good things were written down that have been granted to me by the gracious Heart of God, they would fill a bigger book than the book of Matins.'"[23]

St. Gertrude the Great, who went to Helfta at the age of five and grew up there, first as a student and then as a nun, was not prevented by almost continuous suffering from becoming the greatest of the great women of this convent. Her interior life was characterized by an abundance of the most sublime graces of prayer, which gave her spirituality a strong apostolic bent.

The treatises which she wrote in German have been lost, but we still possess her two best-known Latin works, the *Legatus Divinae Pietatis* (The Ambassador of Divine Love) and *Exercitia Pietatis* (Spiritual Exercises). These seven-day exercises contain a large number of prayers to the Sacred Heart which are remarkable for their great intimacy. The whole fifth day is given over to meditation on the Heart of Jesus and on love for it; but on other days too we frequently meet the mystery of the Sacred Heart.

"Dear Jesus, hide me in the wound of thy most loving Heart, away from all that is not thee. Bless me, gentlest Jesus, bless me and have mercy on me according to the bounty of thy most gentle Heart. — O sweetest Jesus! To thee, sole love of my heart, I offer myself as a sacrifice, to live henceforth for thee alone. Do thou then so form my heart after thine, that I may be worthy to walk according to thy good pleasure."[24]

The influence exercised by St. Gertrude's *Legatus Divinae Pietatis*

---

[23] Mecht. I 21; I 1; II 19; Richstaetter, *op. cit.,* p. 96.
[24] Gertrude, *Legatus div. piet. et Exercitia* 667; Richstaetter, *op. cit.,* p. 104.

has been widespread, and still continues today. In sublime images, often drawn from her own mystical experiences, the Heart of Jesus presses ever more into the foreground.

"The Sacred Heart represents itself to her now as a treasure-house which contains all good things; now it appears as a lute touched by the Holy Spirit. Now it is a fountain from which refreshing streams flow into the fires of purgatory; another time it becomes an altar on which Christ offers himself in Holy Mass."[25]

In St. Gertrude's works the Heart of our Lord is associated chiefly with the mystery of the Passion: "Someone who had great experience in the spiritual life counselled her to honour perpetually the Heart of the Crucified, burning with love." This is her own account, and we can safely assume that the advice came from her spiritual director, a Dominican. This emphasis on the Passion is at once an echo and a fruit of the great personal grace which she received in 1288:

"Through thy wounded Heart, dearest Lord, pierce my Heart so deeply with the dart of thy love, that it may no longer be able to contain earthly things, but may be governed by the action of thy Divinity alone." So she had prayed and persuaded others also to pray. God's answer came in the mystical experience in which her heart was pierced.[26]

The key-note of her devotion to the Sacred Heart is love, confidence and holy joy, all penetrated with the spirit of the liturgy. The Heart of Jesus remained for her always a fruitful school of virtue and a source of the richest graces. "Because thou hast entirely resigned thine own will, I pour out the peace and joy of my Heart into thine. The oftener thou dost communicate, so much the greater shall thy bliss be."[27]

"I have presented my Heart to thee so often as a sign of our most constant love. When, therefore, because of this, thou wilt ask me

[25] Fr. Hamm, *Vom Schrifttum der hl. Gertrud d. Gr.,* in Pastor Bonus 1920, p. 468.

[26] Gertrude, *Legatus* II 5; Richstaetter, *op. cit.,* p. 105.

[27] Gertrude III 53; Richstaetter, *op. cit.,* p. 109.

for anything, point to my Heart, which I took for love of men in the Incarnation, that I may bestow on thee from it the grace thou askest me for."[28]

The demonstrations of grace with which her life had been blessed reached their climax at the hour of her death:

"Turning to the most loving Heart of God, she beheld how the divine Heart, in which every kind of good is hidden, opened itself to her as a paradise of joy and bliss. There all the sighs of the most holy Humanity of Christ, and all the thoughts of his most Sacred Heart, grew like roses, lilies and violets, and shed their perfumes."[29] So from the fountains in the Redeemer's Heart she drew a special grace for her death-bed.

Her real apostolate in the service of the Sacred Heart is that which only began with her death, and which has been exercised through her writings, especially since the sixteenth century, on a worldwide scale.

At the height of the Middle Ages it was the Dominicans who did most to promote the cult of the Sacred Heart. Here again Germany was prominent, with its forty-six monasteries of the order and more than seventy convents of Dominican nuns. As preachers, writers and directors of souls the Dominicans carried the spirituality of their order to the large public which came under their apostolic influence. Their action was felt especially in convents of nuns and among religiously minded laymen.

They thought and spoke of the Sacred Heart in terms of their mystical devotion to the Passion: in meditation on the sufferings and death of Christ the soul is led through his five wounds, tokens of love, to his Heart, filled with pain and wounded by love. From this mysticism of the Passion, combined with a deep devotion to the Blessed Eucharist, the Dominicans shaped a complete asceticism centering round the mystery of the Sacred Heart.

---

[28] Gertrude IV 25; Richstaetter, *op. cit.,* p. 110.
[29] Gertrude V 30; Richstaetter, *op. cit.,* p. 113.

We might start with St. ALBERT THE GREAT, whose theology of the Sacred Heart, as expressed in sermons and theological tracts, has been the subject of a monograph by Raimund Erni.[30] Albert's doctrine illustrates clearly how the medieval devotion to the Sacred Heart depends at every step on patristic theology.

"The water from his side and that which he poured from his Heart are witnesses of his boundless love."[31]

On the eighth day after the Resurrection our Lord appeared to his disciples behind closed doors and showed them "his side, in which rest all the riches of God's knowledge and wisdom; he showed his Heart, which had already been wounded by his love for us before it was struck by the point of the lance."[32]

"By the blood of his side and of his Heart our Lord watered the garden of his Church, for with this blood he made the sacraments flow from his Heart."[33]

"Why was he wounded on the side near his Heart? In order that we may never tire of contemplating his Heart."[34]

By the Heart of Jesus Albert understands primarily the bodily heart, especially when he speaks of the precious blood which flows from the wounded side. But he speaks also of the heart in the spiritual sense, as the source and centre of the soul's faculties and operations. He alludes for instance to the joy of the Sacred Heart at the institution of the Blessed Eucharist: "His Heart overflowed with love and joy at being completely one with us and filling our hearts with joy and jubilation."[35] In the same way he thinks of the sorrows of our Lord's Heart, which was buffeted and pierced already at the tomb of Lazarus.[36] On the Mount of Olives this anguish is accentuated. "A sword wounded his soul here before ever the lance pierced his physical Heart." [37]

---

[30] Raimund Erni, *Die Herz-Jesu-Lehre Alberts d. Großen,* Lucerne 1941.
[31] *Sermo 27 de Eucharistia* (B 13, 777). [32] *In Joannem* 20, 20 (B 24, 684). [85].
[33] *De Eucharistia* d. 2 tr. 2 c. 5 (B 38, 302) and *De Sacrificio Missae* III 4 (B 38,
[34] *In Joannem* 20, 20 (B 64, 683). [35] *De Eucharistia* d. 2 tr. 1 c. 2 (B 38, 217–18).
[36] *In Joannem* 11, 38 (B 24, 451–452). [37] *In Matthaeum* 26, 37 (B 21, 172–173).

The Heart of our Lord is full of compassion, and therefore invites us to share in his sufferings (cf. Albert's explanation of the text of Mark 7,34 and 10, 47). The Heart is in a special way the seat of the virtues. Above all it is the seat and the symbol of love, which moves Jesus to institute the Blessed Eucharist and suffer the piercing of his side.

As a living witness of the tradition which began with Origen and was later to be enriched by Meister Eckhart, Albert saw in the Heart of our Lord the seat of wisdom. In his writings we meet the apostle John, who had drunk the treasures of divine wisdom at the Heart of Jesus. At the Last Supper Jesus revealed to him the mysteries of the divinity. John was to have not only a more intense love than the other apostles, but also a more perfect knowledge. So at the breast of our Lord he received sublime revelations about the divinity of Christ.[38]

Albert often treats of the connection between the Precious Blood and the Heart of Jesus. It was because he wished to give the last drop of blood for us that he let his Heart be opened after death. Albert's theology here recalls the purest patristic traditions. The Heart of Jesus is intimately linked with the work of Redemption, and therefore also with the Church and the sacraments. He returns constantly to the familiar ideas of the birth of the Church from the opened Heart, of the marriage on the Cross and the sanctification of the Church through his blood.

"In three ways did he espouse himself to the Church on the Cross: through his blood; through the stretching out of his arms to embrace his bride in intimate love; and after his death through the opening of his side, from which the Church proceeded with the principal mysteries, the blood of redemption and the water of atonement."[39]

Next to Albert stands MEISTER ECKHART, one of the great preachers of the mystery of the Sacred Heart. He too approaches

---

[38] *In Marcum 3,* 7 (B 21, 404).   [39] *In IV Sententiarum* d. 1 a. 2 (B 29, 9).

this mystery through the Passion: "On the Cross his Heart burnt like a fire and a furnace from which the flame bursts forth on all sides. So was he inflamed on the Cross by his fire of love for the whole world."[40]

TAULER, from whom the young Canisius in Cologne was to draw rich inspiration, was a man of lasting influence. He ranks second only to Berthold of Regensburg among the preachers of medieval Germany, and was one of the greatest mystics of all time. His attachment to the apostle John rests on a deep spiritual affinity: "If thou wilt rest with St. John on the lovely Heart of our Lord Jesus Christ, thou must devote thyself to the lovely example of our Lord Jesus Christ. Upon that thou must diligently meditate. In him thou must see his gentleness and humility, and the deep burning love which he bore towards his friends and his enemies, his obedience, and the submission which he showed on every occasion when his Father called him. Add to this the profound pity which embraced all mankind, and his blessed poverty."[41]

We must "knock at the tenderly disclosed Heart and the opened side of our Lord. Therein should we hide ourselves with great devotion and the acknowledgement of our utter poverty and nothingness, like poor Lazarus before the rich man's gate, when he begged for a crumb of his pity."[42]

It must be admitted that Tauler is not responsible for all the writings and sermons which have been attributed to him, nor for all the references to the Sacred Heart to be found there. But these texts are certainly a contemporary witness to Dominican piety; this is true for instance of Tauler's *Exercises*, a book of devout and intimate meditations on the Passion, which speaks some fifty times of the Heart of Jesus. Here, for example, are some reflections on the opening of Jesus' side:

"What more could he still do for us, that he had not done? He

[40] Quoted in Richstaetter, *op. cit.*, p. 123.
[41] Richstaetter, *op. cit.*, p. 127.   [42] Richstaetter, *op. cit.*, p. 127.

has opened his very Heart to us, as the most secret chamber wherein to lead our soul, his chosen spouse. For it is his joy to be with us in silent stillness, and in peaceful silence to rest there with us."

"He gave us his Heart, all wounded, that we may abide therein until we are wholly cleansed and without spot; until we are made like unto his Heart, and rendered fit and worthy to be led with him into the divine Heart of the Father."

"He gives us his Heart wholly and entirely, that it may be our home. Therefore he desires our heart in return that it may be his dwelling-place. He gives us his Heart as a resting-place, dyed with the purple of his blood, adorned with red roses. In return he asks for our hearts, decked with the white lilies of good works."[43]

BLESSED HENRY SUSO, born in 1295 near the lake of Constance, was a disciple of Meister Eckhart. The development of the devotion to the Sacred Heart owes a great deal to him; not that he elaborated the concept of the Sacred Heart any further, but from his own spiritual life, enriched by deep familiarity with the traditional doctrines, he was able to stimulate the practical exercise of the devotion. The channels of this influence were mainly his writings, his booklet on Holy Wisdom, his autobiography and also the hundred meditations on the Passion, where his love for the Sacred Heart breaks through on every page:

"O Eternal Wisdom, my heart reminds thee how, after the Last Supper, on the Mount of Olives, thou wast bathed in thy bloody sweat because of the anguish of thy loving Heart."

"O Lord, thy Heart bore all in tender love. O Lord, thy Heart, burning with love, must enkindle mine with love."[44]

In the Little Book of Spiritual Wisdom we read:

"O Lord, thou didst not only suffer death for me, but thou didst also seek out the most intimate and secret depths of love in

[43] Richstaetter, *op. cit.,* p. 131–2.
[44] Richstaetter, *op. cit.,* p. 134.

which suffering can or may be experienced. Thou didst really act as if thou hadst said: Behold, all you hearts, was ever a heart so full of love? Look on all my members; the noblest member I have is my Heart; my Heart I have allowed to be pierced through, to be slain and consumed, and crushed into small pieces, that nothing in me or upon me might remain unbestowed, so that you might know my love!"[45]

How richly endowed Suso was, we know from his own account:

"It seemed to him one day, as if the divine Heart, in spiritual wise I know not how, directly inclined itself towards his heart, and that in inmost longing his heart was wholly enclosed in it; and it seemed to him as if the divine Heart, the Eternal Wisdom, spoke to his heart most lovingly and without words. He arose, and full of joy he cried in exultation of spirit: Now, O Love most beloved, I loose my heart from all, and in complete detachment from things created I embrace thine invisible Godhead."[46]

Suso's life was crossed by countless sufferings of soul and body. The most cruel trial of all was a grievous slander on his priestly honour, which seemed to compromise his apostolic work beyond hope of remedy. But he sought help and consolation in the Heart of our Lord: "Here is my complaint to the sorrowful Heart of Jesus Christ!" [47]

With such a wealth of mystical devotion among the Dominicans, it is the more remarkable that the mystery of the Sacred Heart never appears in either the theology or the piety of St. Thomas Aquinas. We can do no more than record the fact of this absence, which is the more puzzling for the commentators of St. Thomas when they see the importance of the idea of the Sacred Heart for his master, Albert the Great.

In consequence of the spiritual links between the two branches

---

[45] Richstaetter, *op. cit.,* p. 134.   [46] Richstaetter, *op. cit.,* p. 136.
[47] *Autobiography,* quoted in Richstaetter, *op. cit.,* p. 135.

of the order, the Dominican Nuns of the fourteenth century also showed a deep devotion to the Sacred Heart. It is stamped on innumerable prayers and manuscripts which their monasteries have handed down to us, and on many accounts of the extraordinary graces which were granted to souls through the veneration of the divine Heart.

Among these nuns we should mention especially MARGARETA EBNER of Maria-Moedinger near Dillingen. On one occasion she saw in a dream a glorious picture, a sign of her intimate union with the Sacred Heart: she seemed to be standing before the great crucifix in the choir. "Then our Lord Jesus Christ bent down from the Cross and allowed me to kiss his opened Heart and from it to drink his blood."[48]

For her too the apostle John was the guide to the Heart of Jesus: "When I remembered how St. John rested on the sweet Heart of my Lord Jesus Christ, I was moved by such a sweet grace that I could not express it in words. And when I thought on the sweet drink which he drank from the breast of Jesus Christ—I cannot put it into words—I sat still for a while in such joy and longing that I would gladly have died of love."[49]

So she prayed: "I beg thee, O my Lord, that thou wouldst wound us wholly with the pain of thy Heart. May thy Heart, as a true love-token of thy goodness, be as deeply impressed on us as thou hast ever granted this favour to the loving desire of an upright heart."[50]

To CHRISTINA EBNER was granted the grace of tasting in mystical ecstasy the truth, still remembered from early Christian times, that the Heart of Jesus is the source of all graces. During Holy Mass she had a vision of our Lord on the Cross, and he allowed her to drink from the wound of his Heart like a bee from a blossom.[51]

---

[48] Richstaetter, *op. cit.*, p. 137.   [49] *Ibid.*, p. 137.
[50] *Ibid.*, p. 138.   [51] *Ibid.*, p. 139.

The diary of ADELHEID LANGMANN gives us an insight into the vigour of devotion to the Sacred Heart at this time. She too had St. John for a guide.

"Bethink thyself, O Lord, that because of her tears of repentance thou didst forgive Mary Magdalen all her sins, and didst raise her to a life of contemplation. I pray thee, O Lord, through all the love which thy tender loving Heart had for her, and which thou still bearest to all who love thee, that thou wouldst forgive me all my sins and lead me to a contemplative life. Be thou always in my soul and in my heart, that nought may turn my heart away from thee, that I may renounce all that is contrary to thee and fulfil all thy most loving Will." [52]

Our Lord came to her very graciously and said: "My divine Heart stands open before thee. Take what thou wilt for thyself. However much thou mayest ask me for, I will grant thee a thousand times more. Bow thyself down on my Heart and rest there with St. John." [53]

The thriving convents of the Swiss Dominicans at Oetenbach, Toess, and Katharinental, were centres of a lively devotion to the Sacred Heart, especially under the inspiration of Blessed Henry Suso.

It strikes one as strange that the first flowering of the cult of the Sacred Heart in the CISTERCIANS, under the influence of St. Bernard himself, was soon followed by a period of decline. Only in the fourteenth century did the revival start, stimulated powerfully by Dominican mysticism. Here also, as among the Dominicans, the memory of the bitter Passion of our Lord and of the Blessed Eucharist are the sources and symbols of devotion to the Sacred Heart.

ST. CATHERINE OF SIENA, surely one of the most remarkable women in the history of the Church, is also linked spiritually and personally to the Dominicans. *La mia natura è fuoco!* (Fire is my

[52] *Ibid.,* p. 140.   [53] *Ibid.,* p. 140.

being) was her own characterization of herself. She is the saint of the great burning heart, which could find a worthy object of its love only in the Heart of Christ.

During the long years of loneliness, when she was praying and doing penance shut up in a little alcove in her father's house, she was maturing and being prepared by the guidance of the Holy Spirit for her role in the history of the Church. She herself knew nothing of this role, and she strove at first with all the strength of her longing to remain in her cloistered intimacy with God. Her union with Christ was growing ever more intimate, as Caraffi, one of her first biographers, records:

"The name of Jesus was always on her lips, and Jesus alone possessed her heart. Jesus accompanied her in the streets. Her glances were turned towards him alone, and rested only on objects that could lead her to Jesus."[54] Raymond of Capua, her confessor, confirms this testimony: "From this moment on, Catherine's holy Bridegroom began to live in such intimacy with her that anyone ignorant of what had happened previously will find our account incredible or absurd. Our Lord appeared to her very often, he remained longer than usual with her; sometimes he brought his glorious mother or some other saint with him, but more often he came alone and conversed with Catherine as with an intimate friend."[55]

One day during the Carnival, when the town was loud with merrymaking, Jesus appeared to her in a solemn vision: "Behold, I, thy Creator and Redeemer, espouse myself to thee in the faith which thou must preserve intact until the day when thou wilt celebrate eternal nuptials with me in heaven." As a sign of this marriage of love, he put a ring on her finger. The year 1370 crowned this grace with the vision of the exchange of hearts: Catherine's heart entered into Jesus' Heart, and Jesus' Heart

---

[54] *Acta Sanctorum,* April III 853–959. Supplement to the *Legend* of Raymond of Capua.   [55] *Legend* I 2.

gave itself to that of his bride. "Think of me, and I will unceasingly think of thee!" our Lord begged of her.

Possessed by this love, Catherine could not bear to be better
off than her Lord and Bridegroom, and she came to share more
and more completely in the sufferings and sacrifice of Christ.
When our Lord in a vision offered her the choice between a crown
of pure gold and the crown of wild thorns, she grasped eagerly
for the symbol of the Passion. In Florence our Lord imprinted
the marks of his wounds on her, though at her request they remained invisible. In this way she was co-crucified with Christ
and bore in her heart a wound which would heal only in heaven.

Catherine drew all her intoxicated love for Christ from the
blood of his Heart. This blood is of great significance in her
thought and her piety. "O holy blood, you burn and sear my soul
in the furnace of the divine love. You enclose it in the flames of
the divine love. For the soul cannot taste you without being
seized and compassed by your flames. You yourself were poured
out in the fiery flames of love." So she prayed; and we hear the
same tones of love in her letters: "Bury yourself in the wounds
of the crucified Jesus. Bathe yourself in the blood of the crucified
Jesus. Intoxicate yourself in the crucified Jesus and clothe yourself
with him. Sate yourself with contempt, with shame and abuse,
and bear them for love of the crucified Jesus. Fasten your love to
the Cross of Jesus."[56]

In her intoxication with the precious blood from Jesus' Heart,
Catherine offers herself to be immolated with Christ for the salvation of the Church and of the world. Her apostolate shows itself
first in her love and solicitude for the poor. She is seized too with
a great love for sinners, which moves her to struggle and make
sacrifices for their conversion. Then comes her mission of peace
in an Italy blood-stained and divided. Finally she is ready for her
great task on behalf of the Church and the Papacy. Her burning

[56] Käppeli, *Briefe der hl. Katharina von Siena,* Oldenburg 1931.

love for Christ is directed to the *dolce Cristo in terra* (the sweet Christ on earth), the Sovereign Pontiff. She cares for the Church with a mother's tenderness, because beneath the turbid waters of its sins she perceives a deep current, the stream of blood flowing from the Heart of Jesus. So she offers her own heart for the salvation of the Church: "Eternal God, accept the sacrifice of my life for thy Mystical Body, the holy Church! I can give no more than what thou hast given me. Take my heart and impress it on the face of thy Bride."

The account of her vision continues: "Then the eternal God turned graciously towards me; he tore out my heart and pressed out its blood over the Holy Church. And for this I say thanks, and a thousand times thanks, to the most high and eternal God, who placed us on the battlefield, to fight like a knight for his Bride with the shield of his holy faith."[57]

The halcyon days of devotion to the Sacred Heart, in the golden age of medieval mysticism, were soon followed by a decline. A sort of paralysis, organically connected with the widespread weakening of religious life, seemed to strike the great Franciscan and Dominican Orders.

The fifteenth century, however, brought a surge of new life into the Church. It was not yet the full and comprehensive reform of head and members which had long been called for, and for which the best men of the time were working. In Italy, for instance, there were Catherine and Bernardine of Siena, and in Germany the reform movement of Cardinal Nicolaus of Cues. Parallel to these incipient reforms, devotion to the Sacred Heart assumed a new intensity; it became a characteristic expression of the religious revival, and maintained its vigour through all the tumults of the division of creeds right on into the century of the Enlightenment. We have good reason therefore to extend this third period to the time of St. Margaret Mary Alacoque.

[57] Orazioni XXVI 373 and *Legend* of Raymond of Capua.

Instead of the Franciscans and Dominicans, the Carthusians were now the most active preachers of the mystery of the Sacred Heart. They found strong support in the *Devotio Moderna* of Ruysbroek and his school; and in the Benedictines and the two great mendicant orders, the general religious revival brought a fresh lease of life to the traditional devotion to the Sacred Heart.

This last period is distinguished by the following characteristics: the devotion to the Sacred Heart, which in the early period was cultivated almost exclusively by the theologians, and in the time of the mystics had extended its influence to the monasteries, was now shared more and more by the ordinary laity. Hundreds of manuscripts from this period disclose to us a great variety of prayers to the Sacred Heart. Artistic representations of the Sacred Heart become more and more numerous. At the same time we find the beginnings of a liturgical expression of the mystery.

It is not a time for new ideas; rather the traditional notions are rediscovered and worked into a living piety. Meditation on the Passion is still the way that leads men to the wounded Heart of our Lord, and with it is always linked the cult of the Blessed Eucharist. Moreover, the idea of reparation begins to show itself, infrequently but unmistakably, in relation to the Blessed Eucharist. Reparation is thought of primarily as an atonement for the irreverences shown to our Lord in the sacrament of his special love.

It is not surprising that the Carthusians, with their ideal of the interior life and of vicarious reparation, should be active in spreading devotion to the Sacred Heart. They too came under the influence of the Dominicans in the great age of the mystics. It was LUDOLF OF SAXONY who formed the link between the two orders; for nearly thirty years he had been a fellow-member of the Order of Preachers with Eckhart, Tauler and Suso, and had become familiar with the traditional devotion to the Sacred Heart. The marks of this long familiarity are evident in his *Life of Jesus,* which was to be one of the two books responsible for the conversion of St. Ignatius on his sick-bed at Loyola. Here is Ludolf's explanation of the piercing of the side: "The Heart of Christ was wounded for us with the wound of love, that through the opening of his side we may in return enter his Heart by means of love, and there be able to unite all our love with his divine love into one love, as the glowing iron is one with the fire. Therefore, for the sake of this wound which Christ received for him on the Cross, when the dart of unconquerable love pierced his Heart, man should bring all his will into conformity with the will of God. But to fashion himself into conformity with Christ's sufferings, he should consider what surpassingly noble love our Lord has shown us in the opening of his side, since through it he has given us the wide open entrance into his Heart. Therefore, let man make haste to enter into the Heart of Christ: let him gather up all his love and unite it with the divine love."[58]

One of the great apostles of devotion to the Sacred Heart in the Carthusians was HEINRICH EGHER OF CALCAR, who died in 1408 at Cologne. He was one of the pioneers of the Order, as founder and organizer of new houses, as prior of several monasteries, and as visitor of the Rhenish province for many long years. He used these positions to ensure a firm footing for the devotion in his own monasteries and to extend it further through a quiet apostolate.

Of the many witnesses and apostles of the devotion among the Carthusians of the fifteenth century, we must mention at least three more eminent names. First of all, DOMINIC OF TRIER, many of whose ideas were to be adopted by Landsberger a century later. The Heart of our Lord is for Dominic the principle of his whole asceticism, the focal point of his striving for holiness. We find that he already has the idea of the Apostleship of Prayer and of recommending the picture of the Sacred Heart for veneration. He still speaks with the accents of the old German mysticism, but he has shifted the emphasis to the sphere of asceticism.

"If you wish to be easily and thoroughly cleansed from sin,

---

[58] Ludolphus de Saxonia, *Vita Jesu Christi* II 615; Richstaetter, p. 177.

freed from all your imperfections, and enriched with many graces, you must cut off all unnecessary occupations, and surrender yourself to the eternal charity which is taught by the Holy Ghost, in order to become its disciple. Yield yourself entirely to the divine will in the Heart of our Lord Jesus Christ . . . To this most merciful Heart of our Lord and God raise your heart in spirit, after you have first recollected yourself interiorly. Do this in all places and at all times, but especially at the Divine Office and in all your prayers and work, as the Lord himself commands: 'Come unto me all you that labour and are heavy laden and I will refresh you.' 'My son, give me thy heart and let thine eyes keep my ways.' 'Put me as a seal upon thy heart', to which you will answer earnestly: 'My heart is ready, O Lord, my heart is ready.'" [59]

DENIS RYCKEL, called "the Carthusian", who died at Roermond in 1471, was originally a disciple of Ruysbroek and combined high mystical graces with solid learning and a literary activity. He is second only to Albert the Great among medieval German theologians. As master of novices he was constantly showing his disciples the way to the Heart of our Lord: "Our Saviour was led into the Praetorium to be scourged. He suffered the torture voluntarily and without resistance, with a Heart full of love, which longed to endure this shameful punishment for our sins. On the Mount of Calvary the torturers cruelly tore the clothes from his holy Body. Oh, how must the divine Heart of Jesus have suffered again, this Heart so innocent, so modest, so pure." [60]

"O Lord Jesus Christ, in union with the praises thou hast offered to God from all eternity, I desire now to offer up these praises and prayers, beseeching thee through thine infinite mercy to give me a contrite and devout heart, a very humble and pure heart, a very fervent and faithful heart, a heart like unto thine; a heart that thou wilt keep holy, that thou wilt bind to thine own

---

[59] Appendix to Tauler's *Exercises* 165–167 a; Richstaetter, p. 179.
[60] *Exhortationes novitiorum* Art. VI; Richstaetter, p. 183.

Heart in order that I may be attached to thee alone, may see and seek only thee, may ever bless, praise and love thee in all things and above all things."[61]

NICOLAUS KEMPF, who was a professor in the University of Vienna before he entered the Carthusians, wrote three ascetical tracts in which he alludes repeatedly to the mystery of the Sacred Heart.

One of the most active centres of the devotion in the tumultuous period of the Reformation was the Charterhouse at Cologne. Many valuable works were composed there, but its monks served the Church still more by the industry with which they preserved the spiritual heritage of the dying Middle Ages, and made the texts of the German mystics accessible to the rest of the world in Latin translations. It was here that Nicolaus of Esch, Canisius' teacher, and also Ludwig Blosius, found the inspiration for their own devotion to the Sacred Heart, no less than for the Sacred Heart apostolate that grew out of it.

PETER BLOMEVENNA was an initiator of this spiritual reform. He undertook the printing of the works of his fellow-Carthusian Denis, and as prior of the monastery encouraged in his community an intimate devotion to the Sacred Heart. He died at Cologne in 1536, the year of Canisius' arrival in the city.

Beside him stands JUSTUS LANDSBERGER. who as novice-master, superior, preacher, and writer worked mightily for the spread of the devotion. In his own books he offers few new ideas, but tradition finds ample utterance through him; he frequently transcribes entire paragraphs of older works. It is in the *Pharetra Divini Amoris* that he treats at greatest length of devotion to the Sacred Heart.

His greatest services, however, were as a collector and translator of old German texts on the devotion. For example, to mention only the most valuable of his contributions, he put St. Ger-

---

[61] Innocent le Masson, *Semaine du Sacré-Coeur,* p. 232; Richstaetter, p. 184.

trude's *Messenger of Divine Love* within the reach of everyone by having the original Latin text printed. It was his work that introduced St. Gertrude for the first time to a very wide circle of readers.

The most painstaking translator of the German mystics was LAURENCE SURIUS, the loyal friend of St. Peter Canisius. This prolific author was responsible for a four-volume collection of the Councils, a large book of sermons, and six volumes of lives of the saints. He edited a large number of medieval writings on the Sacred Heart, among them Tauler's *Exercises* together with three short works which are full of the ideas and prayers of the devotion: the *Ascetical Instructions* of Dominic of Trier, the *Exercises* of Nicolaus of Esch, and some poems of Landsberger. At the request of the Benedictine Abbot Ludwig Blosius, he translated the German writings of Suso into Latin and published them in 1555; he also translated Ruysbroek into Latin.

The mystical devotion to the Sacred Heart, awakened to new life in the Charterhouse of Cologne, can be traced down to LUDWIG BLOSIUS. His *Monile Spirituale,* which was translated into most of the languages of the West, was drawn to a great extent from the writings of St. Gertrude and Blessed Mechthild; from them he borrows all his texts on the Sacred Heart; but he quotes also from Tauler, Ruysbroek, Landsberger and Harphius.

From Blosius the tradition passes to St. FRANCIS DE SALES, whose piety, under the inspiration of St. Ignatius' *Spiritual Exercises,* is completely penetrated with the mystery of the Sacred Heart. St. Frances' influence affected in turn St. Jane Frances de Chantal and the Order of the Visitation, where it fused with another tradition coming from the Society of Jesus. Even before St. Margaret Mary, the mystery of the Sacred Heart was known to the Order of the Visitation. But this knowledge was more limited than is sometimes assumed; otherwise it would be hard to understand the opposition met by the visionary of Paray-le-Monial within her own community.

In this period of transition a very lively devotion to the Sacred Heart was to be found also in Ruysbroek and the *Devotio Moderna*. RUYSBROEK's first ministry was as a secular priest among the people of Brussels. Then he felt himself drawn to solitude, and in his isolation composed a number of mystical works. In them he shows himself preoccupied with the Passion of Christ and the mystery of the Sacred Heart, which was for him closely connected with the Eucharist. Through the grace of the Sacred Heart the soul should free itself from all created things in order to arrive at union with the most Holy Trinity:

"Arise, flee, and avoid this deceitful world! Thou seest thy Lord with arms outstretched to receive and embrace thee. Abide in the hollow place of his wounds, like the dove 'in the clefts of the rock'. Place thy mouth to the open wound of his side, and taste and inhale the heavenly sweetness which proceeds from his Heart. Thou must carry thy Lord's love and sufferings in thy heart, that he may live in thee and thou in him. Then will it come to pass that the whole world will be to thee a cross and a disgust, and thou wilt long to die, to follow thy Beloved into his kingdom." [62]

He who has entirely renounced the world finds in the Saviour's Heart the fullness of the Holy Spirit and eternal love: "Christ is our brother, he spreads his arms out wide. Into them you must flee, and he will defend you against all foes. You shall dwell in the wound of his side, whence all streams of grace proceed. Lastly you must live in his most loving Heart, for in it is the fullness of the Holy Spirit and Eternal Love." [63] There is a peculiarly medieval emphasis in this resumption of patristic theology: Ruysbroek sees the fountain of grace from Christ's side as an expression of personal love.

A fine little work on asceticism, *De Spiritualibus Ascensionibus* —

---

[62] *Werken van Jan Ruusbroec* III Deel 116; Richstaetter, p. 187.
[63] *Rusbrochii Opera a L. Surio conversa* 732; Richstaetter, p. 187.

On Spiritual Climbing, was to make GERHARD OF ZUETPHEN for two hundred years the favourite spiritual author of the clergy and educated laity. The matter for meditation is taken principally from the scenes of the Passion, with the main stress on the interior suffering of our Lord's Heart.

THOMAS A KEMPIS, canon of the Windesheim Congregation, gives his most fervent and profound teaching on the mystery of the Sacred Heart in his *Prayers and Meditations on the Life of Christ:* "Enter then, enter thou, my soul, into the right side of thy crucified Lord, pass through the holy wound into the most loving Heart of Jesus, which out of love was pierced by the lance, that thou mayest rest in the clefts of the Rock (Cant. 2, 14) from the trouble of the world. Enter then, o man, to the worshipful Heart, to the hidden Heart, to the silent Heart, to the Heart of God which opens to thee its portals. Enter, thou blessed of God; why standest thou without? Opened to thee is the well of life, the way of salvation, the ark of heaven, whence issue many perfumes. There is the source of the divine stream to still the thirst of thy craving soul. Do thou also draw from the side of Jesus sweet consolations for life, that thou mayst no longer live to thyself, but in him who was wounded for thee. Give him thy heart who opens his Heart to thee."[64]

GABRIEL BIEL, also a canon of Windesheim, was not merely "the last of the Scholastics"; he was an apostle of the Sacred Heart. In his writings and sermons, whenever he touches on the bitter Passion of our Lord, he is immediately caught up by the thought of the Redeemer's suffering Heart.

At the end of the Middle Ages one can notice in many monasteries and religious orders, despite all their deficiencies and recalcitrance, a happy note of spontaneous reform. This was

[64] *Orationes et Meditationes de Vita Christi* cap. XXXII, Op. V 197. Richstaetter, p. 190.

joined in many places to a revival of devotion to the Sacred Heart, for which the Carthusians of the 15th and 16th centuries were mainly responsible.

Among the Franciscans one must name St. BERNARDINE OF SIENA, who by his tireless preaching of the veneration of the Holy Name of Jesus became a guide to the Heart of Jesus. Times without number the theme recurs in his sermons, for instance in a famous Good Friday sermon, where he describes the opening of the side: "The opened side unlocks to us his Heart, that Heart which loves us even unto death. It invites us to enter into this unspeakable love. Let us go then to the Heart of Jesus, this deep Heart, this silent Heart, this Heart that forgets nothing, this Heart that knows all, this Heart which loves us, and burns with love. The might of love has opened the door, let us enter in!"[65]

Chief among the German Franciscans was the great mystic HEINRICH HERP (HARPHIUS). Before he took the habit of the Friars Minor, he belonged to the Windesheim Congregation of canons, and consequently shows the influence of Ruysbroek in his writings. In his *Theologia Mystica* he repeats much that earlier generations, especially Ludolf of Saxony, had said about the mystery of the Sacred Heart:

"God's will should be dear to us, in all and above all, for Christ's Heart was wounded out of love for us, that by our love we might enter through the opening of his side into his Heart, there to unite all our love with his divine love."[66]

Another strenuous worker for the devotion was the great Franciscan missionary DIETRICH COELDE. His *Mirror of Christians,* which is at once a catechism, a prayer-book, and a manual of devotion, is written in language that is simple, salty, and racy of the soil. It was republished in numerous editions.

---

[65] *Sancti Bernardini Senensis Opera* (Venice 1591), I 617.
[66] *Henrici Harphii Theologia Mystica* 15; Richstaetter, p. 210.

STEPHAN FRIDOLIN, who up to his death in 1498 worked in the Church of St. Clare in Nürnberg, is another Franciscan whose work for the devotion deserves mention. In a big folio volume of sermons, illustrated with wood-cuts from the school of Dürer, he gives a complete theological and ascetical exposition of the devotion to the Sacred Heart.

"To say nothing of the other blessings which we owe to the Sacred Heart, it has given us one gift in which all others are included; this is the Holy Ghost, the substantial gift of God. The Heart of Christ is the worthiest and purest of all the dwellings of the Holy Ghost, for he does not dwell there simply through the workings of grace, nor for a limited length of time, as with other men, but essentially, unceasingly, in the perfect exercise of all his operations and all his virtues, without the slightest imperfection. He dwells there always and for all eternity."[67]

Fridolin shows also the intimate connection between the Heart of Jesus and the Eucharist, and lets us penetrate deep into the sufferings of our Lord's Heart. He wrote two other small works to promote devotion to the Sacred Heart: *The Spiritual May* and *The Spiritual Harvest*.

Thanks to the Benedictines, the parish of St. Matthias in Trier became a focal point of the newly awakened devotion in the fifteenth century. This abbey initiated one of the oldest forms of consecration to the Sacred Heart; it also produced a prayer of reparation, the formulation of which can be understood only in the light of the reform movement within the Order. This had started in Bursfeld and led to severe struggles.

ST. FIDELIS OF SIGMARINGEN worked for the spread of the medieval devotion to the Sacred Heart in the period following the Reformation. The veneration of the Redeemer's Heart, born of a truly Franciscan devotion to the Passion, was one of the main supports of his spiritual life and of his striving for holiness.

---

[67] *Schatzbehälter oder Schrein der wahren Reichtümer*, p. 184.

The success of MARTIN OF KOCHEM in bringing the devotion to the man in the street was due largely to the raciness of his speech, which caught the imagination of a generation weak in faith. He was responsible for the republication of the prayers of St. Gertrude and Blessed Mechthild, and for several other writings. His large life of Jesus is especially rich in references to the Sacred Heart.

This roll can close with the name of the Silesian convert ANGELUS SILESIUS, a religious poet of tender sensibility and powerful faith. To him we owe one of the best Sacred Heart hymns in German, a hymn which re-echoes much of the *Summi Regis Cor, aveto* of Blessed Hermann Joseph. Here as a sample are the first and last of its twelve verses:

> Royal Chamber, hail to thee!
> Inn of mercy, house of grace;
> Whither weary souls can flee,
> Find in thee a resting-place.
> Hail to thee, most loving Heart,
> Sorely pierced by sorrow's dart.
>
> Let me enter, let me stay,
> Bound by closest ties to thee;
> Graft my heart in thine, I pray,
> That it live no more for me.
> This is my ambition's sum,
> Heart of thy Heart to become.[68]

Even before the time of St. Margaret Mary the young Society of Jesus showed a wide-spread devotion to the Sacred Heart, nourished principally from two sources:

First, it was in living contact with the best tradition of spirituality, which at the time of the Order's foundation was being diffused far and wide by the Carthusians of Cologne, even beyond

[68] Angelus Silesius, *Heilige Seelenlust* (1901), p. 77.

the frontiers of their own country. This tradition, understandably enough, was most vigorous in Germany. Father General Mercurian had even to prohibit the reading of the old mystics because, from his experience with Spanish and Portuguese mysticism, he feared it would result in a one-sided stress on contemplation to the detriment of the apostolate.

The other and more important source is to be found in the Spiritual Exercises. By them many Jesuits were led on to an intimate familiarity with the mystery of our Lord's Heart without in any way departing from their pristine spirit. Therefore the first venerators of the Sacred Heart in the Society of Jesus include some of the best interpreters of the authentic Ignatian spirituality.

Among the German Jesuits the first place is naturally held by CANISIUS. During his years of study at Cologne he came in contact with the Carthusian tradition, which brought him completely under its spell. Together with the Exercises, it formed the basis for a fervent devotion to the Heart of Jesus, in which he often made use of the prayers of the mystics. Here in Cologne he received the psychological preparation for the vision of the Sacred Heart which was to be granted him in Rome. It took place on the morning of his solemn profession, before his apostolic mission to Germany, at the altar of the Blessed Sacrament in St. Peter's. Here is his own description of that vision, from the *Testament*: "My soul fell prostrate before thee, my dull deformed soul, unclean and infected with many vices and passions. But thou, my Saviour, didst open to me thy Heart in such fashion that I seemed to see within it, and thou didst invite me and bid me to drink the waters of salvation from that fountain. Great at that moment was my desire that streams of faith, hope and charity might flow from it into my soul. I thirsted after poverty, chastity and obedience, and I begged to be clothed and adorned by thee. After I had thus dared to approach thy Heart, all full of sweetness, and to slake my thirst therein, thou didst promise me a robe woven of peace, love, and perseverance, with which to cover my naked soul. Having this garment of grace and gladness about me, I grew confident again that I should lack for nothing, and that all things would turn out to thy glory."[69]

The period of Catholic Reform produced many other Jesuits, especially in Cologne and Munich, whose lives were distinguished by a vigorous and effective personal devotion to the Sacred Heart. At least the more important names should be mentioned here:

FRIEDRICH VON SPEE has been likened to Suso and called the last of the German mystics. His *Golden Book of Virtues* abounds in allusions to the Heart of our Lord, and reveals a deep compassion with his exterior and interior sufferings: "On a certain Friday, a devout soul sat at the feet of the crucified Lord and cried: O Love, O Love, O fiery Love, my heart must surely perish! My love is Jesus. O Jesus, tell me that you love me. Ah, if I could only know that!" Then the sweet Jesus answered her and spoke thus to her heart: "My dearest child, I have buried you with a spear deep in my Heart. Now I cannot forget you for all eternity. When the soul heard this, she wept still more and said: O Jesus, truly you love me more even than a mother her child. In your Heart you must prepare for me a place of rest, in your Heart I shall rest day and night."[70]

"I know a soul which once spoke thus: Lord, take the bloody lance from your Heart and pierce my heart, that I may die of love. And when I am dead, bury me in your wounded side, that my dead heart may live for ever in yours."[71]

The song-book entitled *Trutznachtigall* gives us a number of simple yet profound and personal hymns to the Sacred Heart.

PHILIP KIESEL, one of the best Jesuit preachers in Germany, published in 1666 a four-volume collection of sermons, at least eighty of which treat of the Heart of our Lord. One whole

---

[69] Braunsberger, *Epistolae B. Petri Canisii* I 55–56; translation from J. Brodrick, *St. Peter Canisius,* London 1938, p. 125.

[70] Friedrich von Spee, *Güldenes Tugendbuch* II 18.

[71] *Ibid.,* II 14.

series, for the Bona Mors Confraternity, is devoted to the mystery of the Sacred Heart.

WILLIAM NAKATENUS was the author of a best-selling prayer-book which was translated into four languages and went through countless editions. It contains numerous prayers in honour of the Divine Heart of Jesus, among them a complete devotional exercise. The theme of the Sacred Heart runs right through the book and appears especially where he treats of the Passion of Christ. As an expression of his outlook, here is a simple hymn, which even today has not lost its appeal:

1

O Jesus mine,
O Lord Divine,
What will you have me give?
Unless you show,
I cannot know,
Nor ever peaceful live.

2

I give my heart,
And for my part
Beg your Heart in return.
This noble prize
Before my eyes,
All other gifts I spurn.

3

Do not, O love,
Deprive me of
This prize, my God, but deign
Your Heart and mine
As one may shine,
Afire with love's pure flame.[72]

[72] Wilhelm Nakatenus, *Geistliche Lieder* (Cologne 1903), p. 54.

With PHILIP JENINGEN we reach the age of St. Margaret Mary Alacoque. He was outstanding in his generation for his apostolate of the Sacred Heart; witness the words of his first biographer, Fr. Pergmayr, who wrote in 1763: "Fr. Jeningen's intimate converse with our Lord was distinguished especially by a fervent devotion to the Sacred Heart. He had set up his permanent abode in this most holy Heart, and could never do enough for its veneration. He sought every opportunity to spread this devotion among his brethren and among the faithful. In his letters especially he returns constantly to the devotion, as though no letter satisfied him in which he had not written of it." [73]

Pergmayr illustrates this with a whole series of quotations; here let one short extract testify to the love of this apostle: "O if one could only make it clear how precious and sublime is the Heart of Jesus! It is a fact quite manifest and, so to speak, immediately tangible to the soul, that in the Holy Sacrifice of the Mass we possess the Heart of Jesus, and that in this most holy Heart everything else is contained. It is here that we, banished children of Eve, have found our Father and our Father's House. In this Sacred Heart God finds his delight to be with the children of men. May the holy Heart of Jesus be ever praised and blessed, for not only does it surpass every other gift, but it bestows and communicates every gift. In this Heart we are in a place excelling Paradise itself, indeed without this Heart heaven would not be what it is."

"My heart is ready, my God; but by my heart I mean the Sacred Heart of Jesus, which affords more joy to the Heavenly Father than the whole court of heaven. O how good it is to dwell here! By my heart I mean too Mary's heart, under which the Heart of Jesus beat and began its life. Heaven has nothing more ravishing, earth nothing more worthy of love. O how good it is to dwell here, and humbly to contemplate the Most Holy!" [74]

Between 1549 and 1700, that is from the day on which Canisius,

---

[73] Jos. Pergmayr, *Vita Venerabilis Phil. Jeningen,* p. 117.   [74] *Ibid.,* p. 119.

strengthened by his vision in St.Peter's, walked once more on German soil, to the moment in which the mission of St. Margaret Mary became known, we know of at least twenty-five German Jesuits who proved themselves fervent devotees of the Sacred Heart in their own religious life and in their apostolate.

During these 150 years the other provinces of the Society of Jesus show a growing devotion to the Sacred Heart. Its development is always from the stage of fragmentary personal expressions to that of an ever more systematic exposition.

The first scattered signs are to be met in the spiritual diary of JEROME NADAL and in the spirituality of St. FRANCIS BORGIA; the latter has left us a moving prayer to the wound in our Lord's side. We can trace its gradual expansion in the theology of FRANCIS SUAREZ. The exegesis of CORNELIUS A LAPIDE, in a sweeping theological vision of history, gathers together all the prototypes of the pierced and streaming Heart in the Old Testament, from the creation of Eve out of Adam's side to the Prophet Ezechiel's vision of the fountain out of the right side of the Temple.

Writings on the Sacred Heart by the classical masters of the spiritual life become ever more abundant. The most important of them are the *De inquisitione pacis sive studio orationis* of JACOB ALVAREZ DE PAZ; ANTON LE GAUDIER's principal work, *De perfectione vitae spiritualis,* in which he frequently comes to speak of the Heart of our Lord, especially in connection with the Blessed Eucharist; and the writings of LUIS DE PONTE, who makes use of texts on the Sacred Heart from classical writers of all ages, from Augustine to Bernard and from Bonaventure to Gertrude of Helfta.

The spiritual writers of the Society in France, forming almost a separate school, and strongly influenced by Cardinal Bérulle, made the mystery of the Sacred Heart the centre of their piety. They include LOUIS LALLEMANT, and his disciples SURIN, RIGOLEUC and SAINT-JURE, ADRIEN LYRÉE, who wrote the solidly theological yet devotional *De imitatione Jesu patientis* (On the imitation of the suffering Jesus), and VINCENT HUBY, who together with BLESSED JULIAN MAUNOIR initiated a movement of missions and retreats to renew the religious spirit among the people. Finally there is the contemporary of St. Margaret Mary, JAKOB NOUET, who sums up in himself all the spiritual tendencies of his age.

With that we find ourselves at a turning-point in the history of devotion to the Sacred Heart; despite its spiritual worth and the blessings it brought in its train, it has hitherto been cherished and practised only by individuals. These individuals were undoubtedly very numerous at certain times and places; they did not have to seek alone the way to our Lord's Heart, but could follow trustworthy guides and the path marked by a long tradition.

From our present historical view-point we can see that by the end of the seventeenth century the ground was ready to receive a new seed. The time was ripe for the unfolding of the public, liturgical cult of the Heart of Jesus by the whole Church.

If one looks back over the eight hundred years of the medieval devotion to the Sacred Heart, one is faced with the question: What forces carried this development forward, and in what forms did it find expression?

If the history of Christian piety in Antiquity and in the early Middle Ages poses many unsolved problems, this much at least is clear, pace Richstätter and Hamon: that there was no "discovery" of the Sacred Heart in the twelfth century, preceded at most by a "dawn" of the devotion. On the contrary, medieval forms of piety leaned heavily on patristic traditions, to an even greater extent than we can demonstrate today. As for so much of our religious and cultural heritage, it is the Benedictine monks who here form the bridge of tradition. Naturally enough the patristic origin of the devotion shows itself most clearly at the period of transition to the early Middle Ages. From this beginning, so full of patristic thought, the great mystics of the Middle Ages received their most powerful stimulus; and the tradition passed on from them to the late Middle Ages and early modern times, gaining steadily in extension though frequently losing in depth.

All through the Middle Ages we encounter the salient patristic ideas about the Sacred Heart. In every century we find a vivid realization of the inexhaustible source of grace in the pierced Heart of the crucified Christ. The Church was always recognized as the Bride born from the Heart of Jesus. The sacraments were always seen as a seven-fold stream from the wounded side. And men never forgot Origen's explanation of the fountain of wisdom and of the profound knowledge of God to be drawn from the spiritual Heart.

St. John the apostle has an important place in this tradition and in the medieval devotion to the Sacred Heart. He was frequently invoked as the guide to that Heart on which he himself had been allowed to rest. He was in fact the patron of the medieval devotion, and men prayed through him for graces like to his. Consequently it would be quite reasonable to regard the picture of John resting on the Heart of our Lord as the typical representation of the Sacred Heart at the height of the Middle Ages. This too was an echo of the patristic tradition; Origen's interpretation of the person of St. John was in fact never forgotten; and a little later it was to help in shaping the liturgy for the feast of the apostle.

In explaining the Canticle of Canticles too, the Middle Ages learnt from the Fathers of the Church to apply the song to the nuptial mystery of Christ and the loving soul; hence the proliferation of commentaries on the Canticle in the early Middle Ages.

In spite of the vital dependence of one generation on another, the Middle Ages were nevertheless responsible for their own very effective development of the patristic heritage.

What exactly were the forces that fashioned medieval piety?

Probably the strongest of them was the contemplation of Christ, which was practised with a peculiar depth of emotion in the German-speaking countries: the fervent and, in the best sense of the word, "sincere" meditation on "our dear Lord", to which was added a profound understanding of the love and suffering of his interior life. The Heart, pierced on the Cross out of limitless love for us, revealed the inner life of our Lord, a life consumed with love and wounded by the sufferings of his Passion. Hence in these Middle Ages the widespread practice of meditation on the Passion combined with a certain genius for the interior life and with the mystique of the crusades to guide men to the mystery of the Sacred Heart and to its fervent veneration.

Moreover, devotion to the Blessed Eucharist, which developed more and more strongly after the introduction of the feast of Corpus Christi, exercised a strong influence on the cult of the Sacred Heart: men saw in the Eucharist the most splendid revelation and the most precious gift of the loving Heart of Jesus. Conversely devotion to the Blessed Eucharist suggested new modes and forms of expression to the cult of the Sacred Heart.

One can note also, especially in the late Middle Ages, the effect of mysticism in deepening and extending the cult of the Redeemer's Heart. This effect can be seen not so much in the content or forms of the devotion as in a surge of fresh vitality.

What were the most important forms of expression which the medieval devotion to the Sacred Heart fashioned for itself?

In the first place, both in time and in importance, stands prayer. Hundreds of prayers to the Sacred Heart have come down to us from the thirteenth century, and these are but a fragment; the greater part of this pious literature was lost in the storms of the Reformation, the Thirty Years War and the years which followed. The most ancient texts still extant go back to the twelfth century. In the thirteenth century they are already appearing in abundance. In the fourteenth and still more the fifteenth centuries they show a notable increase not only in number and range, but also in content and originality.

Many of these prayers are the fruit of personal experience and of mystical graces; hence their deeply emotional and intimate character. There is a danger that they may lose their meaning on the lips of men who have had no such experience, and so adulterate the devotion.

Prayers to the Sacred Heart appear at first as part of other devotions, but with the passing of time they stand more and more on their own. One of the most precious collections is the *Little Hours of the Glorious Heart of Jesus Christ,* from Cologne. With its profound thought, fervent enthusiasm and felicitous use of the Psalms, it has a unique value as a religious composition.

Up to the end of the Middle Ages men sought refuge in the Heart of Jesus increasingly in all the necessities of the Christian life: in tribulation and temptation, in prayer for God's mercy, for a happy death, for the sanctification of the priestly life, for the grace to preach the word of God as true apostles, and in anxiety for the threatened Church.

Another form in which devotion to the Sacred Heart expressed itself was the composition of poems, hymns and mystery-plays.

With this increasing publicity we find also the beginnings of a liturgical cult. The first liturgical celebration of the mystery of the Sacred Heart was the feast of the Holy Lance, which was granted by Pope Innocent VI in 1353 to be held throughout the Holy Roman Empire on the second Friday after Easter. The Heart of our Lord, pierced by the lance, is mentioned three times in the Mass and also in the hymn for Vespers and Lauds.

The feast of the Five Wounds, which was celebrated solemnly in the Dominican monasteries of Germany even in the Middle Ages, shows another approach towards a liturgical cult of the Sacred Heart. In the fifteenth century there is even a proper "feast of the Sacred Heart" at the Dominican monastery of Unterlinden in Colmar (Alsace).

The medieval picture of the Sacred Heart is, like the medieval devotion, strongly influenced by the mystery of the Passion, and indeed it grew out of this mystery: it shows the opened Heart of our Lord, surrounded by thorns, surmounted by a glowing cross and encircled by flames. This image, which was later to become the classical representation of Paray-le-Monial, showed a progressive development towards the end of the Middle Ages: from the original likeness of the crucified Christ the five wounds were isolated; then the most precious and glorious of these five, the wounded Heart, was itself detached and further elaborated by the artists.

We encounter also symbolic pictures, inspired by the Canticle of Canticles or by the thought of St. John resting on the Heart of our Lord.

The medieval devotion is movingly portrayed in a late Gothic wood-cut by Lucas Cranach. It shows the stylized Heart on a shield carried by four angels. The Heart itself frames a touching picture of the crucified Christ, to signify the inner sufferings of the Heart of Jesus. The Heart and the shield are cut in two by the vertical beam of the Cross. The left side of the shield is covered with drops of blood from the wounded Heart; above it, flames issue from the Heart, and glow within a crown of thorns. Under the shield kneels Mary, hands and eyes raised to the Heart of her Son, and John, holding his Gospel open at the description of this scene.

Thus did the greatest souls of the Middle Ages kneel before this picture of the Sacred Heart in reverent faith and generous love, pay homage to its mystery, and drink from its inexhaustible well-springs.

Josef Stierli

THE DEVELOPMENT OF THE CHURCH'S DEVOTION TO THE SACRED HEART IN MODERN TIMES

Ever since the Holy Spirit came forth from the Heart of the crucified Christ, he has been giving gradually clearer shape to the revelation of the Sacred Heart of Jesus. The mystery which was announced, under his inspiration, in the Old and the New Testament was later formulated in the exuberant theology of the Fathers and the early medievals: the Heart of Jesus was seen as the seven-fold fountain of grace. By the wonderful play of grace, the Holy Ghost called into being and sustained the rich medieval devotion towards the Sacred Heart. And now this flaming, tempestuous Spirit is pressing forward, by ways which are not always those envisaged by human planning, towards the latest phase of the devotion in the Church herself.

In grateful ackowledgement of her own birth from the wounded side of Christ, the Church uses her teaching office and her liturgical prayers and ceremonies to raise a hymn of praise to this grace-dispensing wound, and to the infinite love of the wounded Bridegroom; and by her sacrifices she shares in his work of atoning for the sins of the world.

It is impossible to give a detailed account of the modern devotion to the Sacred Heart in a short work of this kind. We can only record the salient facts of this complex history, and point out the main line of the development: the transition from the merely private practice of the devotion to its adoption into the public prayer of the Church.

The growing practice of prayer and song to the Sacred Heart naturally prepared the way for an official devotion of the whole Church. This tendency was clear even at the end of the Middle

Ages; witness the feasts of the Holy Lance and of the Five Wounds, and the isolated case in Alsace of a feast of the Sacred Heart.

As the Lesson for the feast of the Sacred Heart records[1], St. John Eudes set his heart on obtaining liturgical expression for the mystery of the Sacred Heart. Whatever his piety owed to historical influences was due to the school of Bérulle and to his knowledge, drawn from publications of the Cologne Carthusians, of the medieval devotion. His main concern was indeed with the veneration of the Immaculate Heart of the Blessed Virgin Mary. But besides this he worked zealously for the promotion of the devotion to the Sacred Heart of Jesus. Pius X could call him at his beatification *auctor, doctor et apostolus cultus liturgici Sacratissimi Cordis Jesu,* the initiator, teacher and apostle of the liturgical cult of the Sacred Heart of Jesus.

He devoted himself to establishing a solid theological basis for devotion to the Hearts of Jesus and Mary, which he saw in intimate union. He also attempted to secure a liturgical feast in honour of these two hearts. In 1672, just before the visions of St. Margaret Mary, he celebrated in the communities of his own order his first mass of the Sacred Heart, for which he had received ecclesiastical approval.

The fact that St. John Eudes alone composed no fewer than fifteen drafts for Masses in honour of the Heart of Jesus and the Heart of Mary, shows his uncertainty about the appropriate liturgical expression of the Mystery. Small wonder that his efforts found as yet no echo beyond the frontiers of France.

We know today that the devotion to the Sacred Heart was not established by the visions of St. Margaret Mary, but goes back beyond the Middle Ages to the patristic theology of the wounded side of Jesus as the source of grace. Nevertheless, since

[1] Brev. Rom. Fest. *Cordis Jesu,* II. Noct. IV. Lectio; see also 19th August, II. Noct. VI. Lectio.

Providence has called the Saint of Paray-le-Monial to play such a decisive role in the history of the devotion, it would not be right to minimise her significance for 'apologetic' reasons. The development of the devotion as it is taught and lived by the Church today is bound up for ever with her name. This humble nun, hidden in a Visitation convent, became God's instrument in the realization of his redemptive plans for our age. The words of our Lord recorded in the eleventh chapter of St. Matthew were fulfilled once again in St. Margaret Mary: just before his testimony to his own meek and humble Heart, our Lord said that it is to the poor in spirit and to little ones that the mysteries of the Kingdom of Heaven are disclosed.

To outward appearances, her life contains little of interest:

She was born on 22 July, 1647, the fifth child of a royal judge and notary in the County of Terreau. The family, while not particularly rich, had enough to live comfortably. But their fortunes were reduced by the premature death of the father, and the young widow was left to fend bravely against want, and to see to the education of her children.

Margaret records her own spiritual development in her autobiography:

"I was scarcely able to know myself when you showed me the hatefulness of sin and awakened in my heart such an abhorrence for it that I felt the smallest stain as an intolerable pain."[2]

"Without understanding what it meant, I felt myself constantly urged to repeat the words: My God, I consecrate to you my purity and make a vow of perpetual chastity."[3]

"The Mother of God always took a loving interest in me. I fled to her in every necessity and she shielded me from great dangers."[4]

---

[2] References in this chapter are to *Vie et Oeuvres de la Bienheureuse Marguerite-Marie Alacoque*, 2 vols., Paray-le-Monial 1878, II, p. 337–338.

[3] *Ibid.*, II, 338.

[4] *Ibid.*, II, 339.

After the death of her father, Margaret was sent to the boarding-school of the Urbanists (an offshoot of the Poor Clares) at Cha-rolles. Here she received her first Holy Communion and was filled with a craving for solitude, in order to be able to pray in peace. At the same time the longing for the religious life was awakened in her. But she soon fell into a serious illness, which put an end to her schooling and caused her four years of suffering. She was cured suddenly after a vow in which she consecrated herself for life to the Mother of God.

Until her entry into Paray-le-Monial she lived constantly with her mother. Together they had to suffer much from relatives who lived in the same house. "From then on, my whole love turned towards the Blessed Sacrament of the Altar. There alone I sought peace and consolation."[5]

Recalling the frequent quarrels at home, she confessed: "I wept at the feet of my crucifix. I did not understand that our Lord wanted to show me that he alone was the Lord of my soul, and that he wanted me to become like himself through suffering."[6]

Very soon a profound love for the Passion of Christ began to mature in her heart. "From this time forward, our Lord was continually present to me either in his crucified form or carrying his Cross as in an *Ecce Homo*. This awakened in me such a compassion and such a love of suffering that all my pains seemed light in comparison with the wish to suffer in order to become like my suffering Jesus."[7]

The time came when Margaret, with her sensitive heart and radiant gaiety, found herself beset by enthusiastic young men, and overwhelmed with proposals of marriage. Now there raged in her heart the struggle between her own first choice of undivided love for Christ and the wish to please her relatives and marry according to her rank. The ideals of the religious life

---

[5] *Ibid.,* II, 339.   [6] *Ibid.,* II, 345.   [7] *Ibid.,* II, 342.

attracted her soul more and more powerfully, and she undertook the most severe penances in atonement for her own unfaithfulness and for the sins of the world. At the same time there awoke in her heart a compassionate and recklessly generous love for the poor. The thought of the scourging of her Lord embittered all the worldly pleasures for which her nature craved.

"You wish for pleasures?" Our Lord once said to her. "I never sought any, but delivered myself up to every kind of suffering for love of you and in order to win your heart. And now you want to dispute it with me."[8]

On 20 June, 1671, when she was almost twenty, she entered the Order of the Visitation at Paray-le-Monial, and from the first she was utterly convinced of the "duty to be holy, cost what it may", and to give herself to God "entirely and without the least reserve"[9].

On 25 August of the same year she ended her first probation and took the habit. Her noviceship was rich in extraordinary graces, which she concealed as far as was possible; but she had to endure at the same time a series of difficulties and humiliations arising in part out of these very graces.

In the notes on her Profession Retreat she wrote: "Here are the resolutions, which are to last all my life, since my Beloved himself has dictated them. After I had received him into my heart, he said to me: Behold the wound in my side, where you must take up your abode now and for ever: it is there that you will be able to preserve the robe of innocence with which I have clothed your soul, in order that you may live henceforth by the life of a Man-God; live as if no longer alive, so that I may live perfectly in you."[10]

She wrote the act of oblation in her own blood: "I, poor, mean, and worthless creature, promise my God to submit myself and to suffer all that he desires of me, sacrificing my heart to the

[8] *Ibid.,* II, 346.   [9] *Ibid.,* II, 364.   [10] *Ibid.,* II, 388.

accomplishment of his good pleasure, regarding no other interest but his greater glory and his pure love, to which I consecrate and abandon all my being and every moment of my life. I belong for ever to my Beloved, I am his slave, servant and creature, since he is all mine, and I am his unworthy spouse, Sister Margaret Mary, dead to the world. All from God and nothing from myself; all to God and nothing to myself; all for God and nothing for myself."[11]

On 6 November 1672 she made her simple religious profession, and her intimacy with our Lord grew ever closer from that moment.

On 4 October 1673, shortly before the revelations of the Heart of Jesus, St. Francis of Assisi was given her as a guide: "On the feast of St. Francis, our Lord let me see in prayer this great saint, clad in a garment of light and unspeakable brilliance. He had been raised above the other saints to an extraordinarily high degree of glory, because his life was so like that of the suffering Redeemer who is the life of our souls and the love of our hearts. His glory was the reward of his great love for the Passion of our Lord, a love which rendered him worthy of the sacred stigmata and made him one of the great favourites of Jesus' Heart. By a very special favour he had been given great power in applying to the faithful the merits of the Precious Blood, a power which made him in a sense the mediator of this treasure."

"After I had seen all this, the Divine Bridegroom, as a token of his love, gave me St. Francis as my soul's guide. He was to lead me through all the pains and sufferings which awaited me."[12]

Shortly after this the great Visions began, in which our Lord revealed to her the services she was to render to the cult of his

[11] *Ibid.*, I, 71.
[12] Cf. A. Hamon, *Vie de la Bienheureuse Marguerite-Marie*, Paris 1909, p. 125 f.

Sacred Heart. The first apparition can be dated with fair certainty to the feast of St. John the apostle, 27 December, 1673. St. Margaret Mary recounts it herself:

"One day as I was praying before the Most Holy Sacrament and had a little more leisure than usual—normally the tasks I was given did not leave me much time—,I was completely invested with the divine presence, so completely that I utterly forgot myself and where I was. I surrendered myself to this divine Spirit and abandoned my heart to the force of his love. He made me lean for a long time on his divine breast, whilst he revealed to me the marvels of his love and the inexplicable secrets of his Sacred Heart, things which he had hitherto always hidden from me and now disclosed for the first time. But he did it in so plain and effective a manner as to leave me no room for doubting it, such were the results that this grace produced in me, who am always afraid of deceiving myself with regard to what I assert to take place within me.

"He said to me: 'My divine Heart is so inflamed with love for men, and for you in particular, that it can no longer contain within itself the flames of its ardent love, and must needs spread them by your means, and manifest itself to men and enrich them with the precious treasures that I will reveal to you. These treasures contain the graces of salvation and sanctification necessary to draw men out of the abyss of perdition, and I have chosen you, as a very abyss of unworthiness and ignorance, for the accomplishment of this great design, in order that all may be done by me.'

"Then he asked for my heart, which I implored him to take, and having done so, he placed it within his adorable Heart, showing it to me as a little atom being consumed in a glowing furnace; and then withdrawing it thence like a burning flame in the shape of a heart, he replaced it whence he had taken it, saying: 'Behold, my beloved, a precious pledge of my love, which is inserting in your side a tiny spark of its most fiery flames, to serve as your heart and to consume you until your last moment. And as a sign that the great favour I have just done you is not imaginary, but the foundation of all those that I still have to bestow upon you, although I have closed the wound in your side, the pain of it shall ever remain with you; and though hitherto you have adopted the name of my slave, I now give you that of the beloved disciple of my Sacred Heart.'"[13]

Henceforth the first Friday of every month was marked by special proofs of favour but also by searing pains.

The date of the second vision of the Sacred Heart cannot be fixed any more precisely than the year 1674. Here is Margaret's account: "This divine Heart was shown me on a throne of flames; it was more resplendent than the sun and transparent as crystal; it had its own adorable wound, and was surrounded by a crown of thorns, signifying the stings caused by our sins, and there was a Cross above it, implying that from the first moment of the Incarnation the Cross was planted in it . . .

"He showed me that the ardent desire that he had of being loved by men and of rescuing them from the path of perdition, where Satan brings them in crowds, had made him form the design of manifesting his Heart to them, with all the treasures of love, of mercy, of graces, of sanctification, and salvation, which it contains, in order that he might enrich all who were willing to render to it, and procure for it, all the love, honour and glory in their power, with the profusion of these divine treasures of the Heart of a God from which they spring. He told me that this Heart was to be honoured under the form of a heart of flesh, the picture of which he wished to be exposed and worn by me on my heart, in order to impress its love upon my heart, and fill it with all the gifts with which his Heart is full, and so destroy all irregular movements within it. He said that wherever this holy picture should be exposed to be honoured, he would lavish his

13 *Ibid.*, II, 379–380.

graces and blessings, and that this blessing was a last effort of his love to favour men in these latter times with a most loving redemption, to deliver them from the thraldom of Satan, which he intended to overthrow, that he might place us under the gentle liberty of the dominion of his love, which he wished to reestablish in the hearts of all those willing to practise this devotion."[14]

The narrative of the saint continues with an account of the third vision, equally indefinite in date, from the year 1674: "On one occasion, whilst the Blessed Sacrament was exposed, I felt wholly drawn within myself by an extraordinary recollection of all my senses and powers. Jesus Christ, my gentle Master, presented himself to me, all resplendent with glory, his five wounds shining like so many suns. From his sacred Humanity issued flames on all sides, especially from his adorable Breast, which resembled a furnace, and which was open, disclosing to me his most loving and lovable Heart, the living source of these flames. It was then that he discovered to me the unspeakable wonders of his pure love, and to what excess he had gone in loving men, from whom he received only ingratitude and neglect, 'which I feel much more', he said, 'than all that I suffered in my Passion. If only they made me some return for my love, I should think but little of all that I have done for them, and should wish, if it were possible, to do yet more. But they have only coldness and rebuffs to give me in return for all my eagerness to do them good. Do you at least give me consolation by making up for their ingratitude as far as you are able.'"

'In the first place you will receive me in the Blessed Sacrament as often as obedience will allow you, no matter what mortifications and humiliations may result to you, but they must be regarded as pledges of my love. Moreover, you will receive Holy Communion on the First Friday of each month, and every Thursday night I will make you share the heavy sorrow that it was my

---

[14] Letter to Père Croiset, 3rd November, 1689; cf. A. Hamon, *op. cit.,* p. 156f.

will to feel in the Garden of Olives. This sadness will bring you, without your comprehension, to a state of agony, harder to bear than death. In order to be with me in that humble prayer which I then offered to my Father in the midst of my agony, you will rise between eleven o'clock and midnight, so as to lie prostrate with me for an hour, with your face on the ground, both to appease God's anger and to ask mercy for sinners.'

'But listen, my daughter, and do not lightly believe or trust every spirit, for Satan is eager to deceive you. Wherefore do nothing without the approval of those who guide you, in order that, having the authority of obedience, you may not be misled by him, for he has no power over those who are obedient.'"[15]

The new Superior of Paray-le-Monial, Mother Saumaise, to whom Margaret opened her soul as far as possible, believed, on the strength of clear criteria, in the supernatural character of the messages. But she held it advisable to have them tested by learned theologians. Margaret submitted obediently to this examination, though it only increased her interior trials and exterior embarrassment.

Then our Lord sent her FR. CLAUDE DE LA COLOMBIÈRE, to whom she unburdened herself with full confidence. Providence used the father to strengthen her on her way and assure her of the authenticity of the extraordinary apparitions and commissions.

Prepared in this way, she received the last and greatest revelation, which asked for a liturgical celebration of the mystery of the Sacred Heart. It was in the octave of Corpus Christi, 1675, but the saint does not fix the day any more precisely. It lay certainly between the 13th and 20th of June.

"As I prayed before the Blessed Sacrament one day during the octave of Corpus Christi, I received from my God excessive tokens of his love, and felt myself desirous to make some return and to render him love for love; then he said to me: 'You cannot

---

[15] *Vie et Oeuvres,* II, 381.

make me any better return than by doing what I have so often asked of you.' Then revealing his divine Heart, he said: 'Behold this Heart which has so loved men that it has spared nothing, even to exhausting and consuming itself, in order to give them proof of its love, and in return I receive from the greater number nothing but ingratitude, contempt, irreverence, sacrilege, and coldness in this sacrament of my love. But what I feel still more is that there are hearts consecrated to me who use me thus. Therefore I ask of thee that the first Friday after the octave of the Blessed Sacrament shall be kept as a special feast in honour of my Heart, to make reparation for all the indignities offered to it, and as a Communion day, in order to atone for the unworthy treatment it has received when exposed upon the altars. I also promise that my Heart shall shed in abundance the influence of its divine love on all those who shall thus honour it or cause it to be so honoured.' "[16]

Then everything was quiet again.

The following period was marked for Margaret Mary by bodily and spiritual sufferings, by humiliations from her sisters in religion, and by an abundance of often painful graces. But for ten years the visions were veiled in silence.

At the beginning of the year 1685 Margaret became mistress of novices and took advantage of the celebration of her own patronal feast on 20 July to pay her first outward homage to the Heart of our Lord. Skilfully she directed the celebration which had been devised for her towards the Heart of her beloved master:

"I found as yet no means of spreading the devotion to the most holy Heart, although this was my greatest wish. Let me tell of the first opportunity which his kindness offered me. As the feast of St. Margaret fell on a Friday, I asked our novices, who were at that time entrusted to my care, to pay to the most Sacred Heart of our Saviour Jesus Christ all the little honours which they had prepared for my patronal feast. They did this gladly, set up a little

[16] *Ibid.*, II, 386.

altar, put a small picture on it, a pen and ink drawing, and we endeavoured to render him all the honours that his divine Heart inspired in us. This brought down many humiliations, contradictions, and complaints on me and on the novices, for I was accused of wanting to introduce a new devotion."[17]

Margaret is referring to the storm of indignation which this little celebration aroused in the sisters' community. But only a year later, on 21 June, 1686, the whole convent celebrated the first feast of the Sacred Heart. What had happened in the meantime?

In 1684, that is two years after the death of Fr. Claude de la Colombière, four volumes of his sermons and one of his retreat notes were published in Lyons. In the notes on the spiritual exercises which he made in London in 1677, he spoke of a favoured soul whom he had met and who had received from our Lord himself in a vision the commission to promote the devotion to the Sacred Heart. Even though neither name nor place were mentioned, the references were immediately understood in Paray-le-Monial, where the book was read at table. The authority of Fr. de la Colombière, who had died with a reputation for holiness, broke down the prejudices of the community and overcame all opposition. Paray-le-Monial became the first home of the "new" devotion to the Heart of Jesus.

It was as though a stone had been thrown into a calm, expectant pool: the ripples spread further and further, first in the convents of the Visitation, then in their spiritual orbit. Margaret put all her remaining strength at the service of her mission. The prayers and sacrifices of the years of waiting gave place now to apostolic activity. Her letters went out in all directions to awaken and promote the cult of the Sacred Heart as she saw and understood it in her visions.

She herself, however, was still standing in the way of her mis-

[17] *Ibid.*, 269–270.

sion; the commissions of our Lord were so closely bound up with her own person that it was impossible to separate one from the other. As long as she was still alive, men could not speak freely in public about the privileged "disciple of the Heart of Jesus".

God himself removed the obstacle by calling the saint to himself on 17 October, 1690. The grain of wheat had fallen into the earth. Its seed could now spring up and bear fruit.

Since the time of St. Luitgard of St. Trond there have been many visions of the Sacred Heart known to us from all centuries. But in St. Margaret Mary Alacoque we have something new: the centre of her visions is not a personal grace meant primarily to deepen her own holiness and bring her nearer to Christ, but rather a mission to the Church. That is why we thought it only right to recount in some detail these visions and the saintly life which formed their setting and their context.

Just as the visions were aimed beyond the saint towards the whole Church, so their content has moulded the main external forms of the Church's devotion to the Sacred Heart today: the First Friday and Communion of Reparation, the Holy Hour on Thursday in memory of our Lord's Agony in the Garden, a special liturgical feast of the Sacred Heart on the Friday after the octave of Corpus Christi, and the strong emphasis on consecration and on vicarious reparation. This fact, taken together with the canonization of the visionary, constitutes the strongest evidence for the Church's belief in the authenticity of these experiences in the quiet convent of Paray-le-Monial.

At the end of Margaret's life indeed, it seemed as though nothing had been achieved, apart from the blossoming of the devotion in her own surroundings. She had done all that she could; but the goal was too distant to be reached in her life-time, and the forces of opposition went far beyond her powers.

Is not this apparent fiasco one more voucher for the genuineness of her message? Christ too at the end of his earthly life had little to show of external achievement.

In the visions of Paray-le-Monial, as in the first and fundamental revelation of the Incarnation, our Lord disclosed the mystery of his Heart to a woman. But then the men of the Church were called into the service of the divine mission. Their success too was small, measured by earthly standards; but they launched a movement which nothing could check.

Three names in particular are linked for ever with the providential mission of the simple nun of Paray.

Blessed Claude de la Colombière

His life was as simple and short as the story of that soul for whose sake Providence sent him to Paray-le-Monial. He was born on 2 February, 1641, entered the Society of Jesus in 1658, and was ordained priest in 1671. During a tertianship that was rich in graces and in decisions, he found for himself the way to the Heart of our Lord, and bound himself by a heroic vow to observe his rule with perfect fidelity.

In 1675 he came as superior to the small Jesuit residence in Paray. The short year which he passed there enabled him to become the helper and collaborator of St. Margaret. As extraordinary confessor (visiting the convent at Quarter Tense) he met Margaret Mary at the climax of the revelations. Our Lord himself had told her to expect this faithful servant of his, and from the first meeting a holy friendship joined the two kindred souls, which can be paralleled only by that between Francis de Sales and Jane Frances de Chantal, or between Brother Francis and Sister Clare. Fr. de la Colombière confirmed the genuineness of the visions and commissions in their every detail. For himself, by the consecration of his life to the Sacred Heart on 21 June, 1675, he took a personal share in the allotted task.

In 1676 he was transferred to London as Court Chaplain to the Duchess of York. Among the down-trodden Catholics of London he exercised a fruitful apostolate, and worked tactfully but with a clear purpose for the devotion to the Sacred Heart.

At the same time he continued the work which he had begun in Paray by helpful letters of advice to Sister Margaret and still more to Mother Saumaise, who was now a staunch champion of the new devotion.

At the fresh outbreak of persecution in England, he was arrested, and escaped the death sentence only through the intervention of the French Ambassador. He was expelled from the country and returned to France in 1679, but his health was completely broken. He stayed for a while in the scholasticate at Lyons, and there he successfully planted the seeds of the devotion among the young students of the Society. Finally he returned to Paray-le-Monial, to die there on 15 February, 1682.

That was not to end his work for the devotion to the Sacred Heart. The publication of his retreat notes, which not only disclosed his own spirituality of the Sacred Heart, but at the same time mentioned the visions and the mission of the unknown nun, opened the way in the convents of the Visitation, and in the circles which they influenced, for the acceptance of the revelations made by our Lord in the years 1673–75.

JEAN CROISET

A few years after the death of Father de la Colombière, his younger confrère Jean Croiset inherited the task of helping Margaret Mary Alacoque by his advice and active assistance. During his studies at Lyons he made the acquaintance of Father de la Colombière, and later of St. Margaret's early writings, and he threw himself enthusiastically into this mission.

In the year 1689 he published a booklet on the veneration of the Sacred Heart in the sense and spirit of the visions, and included an extract from the retreat notes of Father de la Colombière. The work quickly went through three editions.

He kept up a lively correspondence with Margaret, and together they planned how they would further the devotion and turn the wishes of the Sacred Heart into reality. The nun, enclosed within the narrow walls of her convent, was grateful and over-joyed to find such a fearless champion of her cause, and she dis-closed to him all the secrets of her soul.

Croiset soon expanded his sketchy booklet into a larger work, *La Dévotion au Sacré-Coeur de Notre-Seigneur Jésus-Christ.* It was just ready for the press when Margaret died, so Croiset was able to add to his book a short account of her life and her visions. The work was first published in 1691 and ran rapidly through many editions and printings. Friends and foes were free with their opinions on it. The author had to endure attacks and opposition even from the ranks of the Society. But the Provincial, convinced of the genuine character of the revelations, covered Fr. Croiset's enthusiastic apostolate with his full authority.

In 1694, however, with the change of Provincial, his opponents got the upper hand. A commission of theologians investigated Croiset's teaching and gave a verdict against him. He was deposed from his professorial chair at Lyons and removed from the college, in order that he might not be able to influence the young Jesuits. But his former Provincial and some other prudent and influential fathers entered the struggle on his side and after some time ob-tained his rehabilitation. Always obedient to his superiors, he retained an unquenchable enthusiasm for the devotion, and his life was consumed in its service.

But misfortune struck him again. In 1704 one of the many editions of his book found its way onto the Roman Index of for-bidden books, though the diffusion of the work was not thereby held up. It has never been possible to establish satisfactorily the reasons for this censure. Fr. Galliffet, who had access to the archi-ves in Rome, looked into the question, and ascribed the censure to " the novelty of the devotion, certain errors in the manner of its presentation, the play of human weaknesses and the work of the devil." This edition of the work remained on the Index until 1887.

Joseph François Galliffet

In Father Galliffet we meet the third and perhaps the most influential helper of St. Margaret in the realization of her mission.

He had entered the Society of Jesus in 1678, and in 1680, when he was studying philosophy in Lyons, he had come under the spiritual direction of Fr. de la Colombière. It was there, as he himself records, that he was first initiated into the spirituality of the Sacred Heart.

The seed planted at Lyons took ten years to germinate. During his tertianship he was caring for the sick in a hospital—one of the prescribed "experiments"—when he caught an infection so dangerous that the doctors despaired of his life. Then Fr. Croiset vowed in Fr. Galliffet's name that if his life was spared, the sick man would consecrate himself to the spreading of the cult of the Sacred Heart. Fr. Galliffet did in fact recover from his mortal illness and accepted the vow made by his confrère as valid and binding.

In the many offices which he held in the Order, mainly administrative positions as rector in various houses, then as Provincial, and finally in Rome as Assistant to the General, he kept his vow faithfully. The sojourn in Rome offered him many contacts and openings for working in the interests of devotion to the Sacred Heart and of our Lord's charges to St. Margaret Mary Alacoque.

He composed an exhaustive work *De cultu Sacrosancti Cordis Dei ac Domini Nostri Jesu Christi* (On the veneration of the Sacred Heart of our God and Lord Jesus Christ), in which he investigated the devotion from the points of view of theology, philosophy, psychology and history. The weakest point is the psychological section, where he defends the untenable thesis that the bodily heart is the seat and centre of the emotional life. His opponents, who included not merely Jansenists but also truly religious men and solid theologians, concentrated on this weakness as a starting-point for an attack on the whole work and on the cause it defended.

Despite all his efforts, Galliffet too was denied any real success; Rome answered his petition for the realization of the demands of Paray-le-Monial, especially for the introduction of a special feast of the Sacred Heart, with an unequivocal "No".

The story of these three men is sufficient indication that the commission of St. Margaret Mary Alacoque could reach fulfilment only after a lengthy and weary struggle. The opponents came not merely from the outside, from the Jansenists, Gallicans, and philosophers of the Enlightenment; they were to be found even in the bosom of the Church and in the hierarchy itself. It was to take almost a hundred years for the cause of Paray-le-Monial to win its first victory in the Church, and yet another hundred before its definitive success.

The ecclesiastical and theological opponents were united by the catch-cry that the devotion was "new" and could therefore claim no place in the spirituality of the Church; but this "novelty" was understood in various ways. There were certainly subordinate officials in the Curia who knew nothing of the broad and deep devotion to the Sacred Heart in the Middle Ages or of its survival among Catholics in the seventeenth century. To them the whole devotion inevitably seemed an inadmissable innovation in the Church.

But when important figures in Rome, even pious and learned popes, laid their veto against the "new devotion", that was not a fundamental rejection of the cult of the Sacred Heart. These same shepherds of the Church gave lavish encouragement and fatherly support to the vigorous movement of Sacred Heart confraternities in the first half of the eighteenth century, by generous grants of indulgences and other privileges. In the years 1690–1740 alone, the nadir of the fortunes of the "new devotion", approximately seven hundred such Sacred Heart confraternities were founded and given ample proofs of Rome's favour. The promoters of the confraternities came principally from the ranks of the Society of Jesus, and Fr. Galliffet was conspicuous for the

126

number which he founded and for the zeal and love with which he promoted this new form of the devotion.

The fact that Rome was at the same time greeting the "new devotion" with a blunt *Non expedit* should not be taken as a blow at the veneration of the Sacred Heart. This negative answer referred only to the actual form of the devotion demanded by the visions of Paray-le-Monial. On the one hand Rome was not yet completely convinced of the supernatural character of the apparitions, and felt itself in no way obliged to act upon them. On the other hand there were many theological and liturgical questions regarding the "new devotion" which had found as yet no adequate explanation: for instance Fr. Galliffet's untenable psychological thesis, that the physical heart is the central organ of the whole emotional life. Indeed the most valuable function of the ecclesiastical opposition was that it necessitated an ever deeper consideration of all the relevant problems, and in this way it ministered, though unconsciously, to the cause of Paray-le-Monial. Moreover this reserve on the part of Rome has its parallels in the processes of canonization and in the investigation of miracles and apparitions. The measure of the reserve corresponds to the extent of the demand; at Paray-le-Monial these demands went so far beyond the normal framework that the Church was obliged to measure and examine them by the most rigorous standards.

Let us trace the most important stages of this process of clarification. On 30 March, 1697, Rome uttered its first "No" to the request for a general feast of the Sacred Heart. Benedict XIII showed himself equally cautious towards the repeated petitions of the years 1726–29, in which Fr. Galliffet took part. Prosper Lambertini, later Pope Benedict XIV, was at hand to ventilate all the doubts and difficulties touching an ecclesiastical devotion to the Sacred Heart, and with his theological acumen he pulled Fr. Galliffet's book to pieces. Naturally there was no hope of further progress during his pontificate.

It was through these intensive theological discussions of all the questions connected with the new cult that devotion to the Sacred Heart progressively shed its dependence on a mere private revelation and found its roots in the soil of Holy Scripture and the Church's teaching, without thereby jeopardizing the significance of St. Margaret's visions as commissions and pointers. Nothing of their content was to be sacrificed; but the discovery of a basis in Scripture and theology justified their unequivocal imperative.

So we owe equal thanks to the men who, in company with St. Margaret Mary, toiled untiringly for her mission, and to those who from the heart of the Church offered it stubborn resistance. It was only through the clash of opposing parties that the essential features and the liturgical form of the devotion to the Sacred Heart, as it is publicly practised by the Church, could be partially clarified. Even then they reached no definitive and completely satisfactory result, as is clear from the variety of Masses and Offices which were later to be permitted or prescribed.

Finally, in the year 1765, that is almost a century after the visions, Rome gave its first blessing to the cause of St. Margaret Mary. For the Church it was a moment of crisis; the forces of absolutism and of the Enlightenment had all but immobilized her. The message of Paray-le-Monial had meanwhile been propagated far and wide: in France and Poland especially, but also in Spain, Italy and Germany and in the foreign missions. The numerous petitions for the granting of a liturgical celebration of the devotion to the Sacred Heart were crowned by a well-reasoned and solidly theological memorandum of the Polish bishops. Clement XIII granted a special Mass and Office of the Heart of Jesus, at first restricted to Poland and the Visitation Order. It was a posthumous triumph for Fr. Galliffet: the Pope had belonged to one of the many confraternities of the Sacred Heart founded by this pioneer, and had learnt there to value the message of Paray-le-Monial; moreover he knew from his own experience the devotion of the people to the Sacred Heart, a devotion which had never been quenched.

Now began a period of liturgical experiment, which helped further to fix and refine the shape of the devotion. The years that followed brought a profusion of Mass-formulas, an unconscious reflection of the two basic tendencies in the patristic theology of the Sacred Heart: the one objective and sacramental, as in the Ephesian and Johannine tradition, the other more spiritualist, as in the theology of Origen and the Alexandrian school.

In 1856 Pius IX extended the feast of the Sacred Heart to the whole world. Leo XIII raised it in 1899 to a double of the first class, and consecrated the whole world to the most Sacred Heart of Jesus. The immediate incentive for this action came from Sister Maria Droste zu Vischering, of the Good Shepherd Convent at Porto, whose visions were recognized as genuine by a commission of theologians.

The encyclical *Miserentissimus Redemptor* in 1928 brought this chapter to a close. The feast was raised to the highest liturgical rank, with a new Mass and Office for the whole octave.[18] Pius XI's encyclical gives a short summary of the theology of the Sacred Heart, in which the central position of the devotion is emphasized. The two principal acts of consecration and reparation, now spoken in the name of the whole Church, are shown in their full meaning and value. The Mass and the Office form a classic epitome of the priceless riches of the devotion and of its historical development.

In this way our Lord's mandate to St. Margaret Mary was fulfilled officially by Pius XI in the name of the entire Church, while at the same time the precious heritage of two thousand years' theology and spirituality was bequeathed to the generations of today and tomorrow.

This history of the devotion to the Sacred Heart has revealed

[18] See above, p. 1, note 1.

much of the secret history of the Church herself. It was an eventful and variegated journey, which began with the solemn testimony of the apostle John to the fountain of graces opened in the side of the crucified Lord, and it led through patristic theology and the heartfelt piety of the Middle Ages to the prayer and the teaching of the Church herself. In all the forms and aspects of this theology and piety we meet the mystery of the life-giving love that wells up in the Heart of the Pierced One. The teachings of theology concerning the Heart of Jesus, and the loving reparation and devotion to this Heart in all the centuries of the Church's history, are themselves part of the stream of graces from the fountain of the Saviour. So the living history of the devotion is, in part at least, a fulfilment of Ezechiel's lofty vision: the mighty surge of the fountain from the right side of the Temple.

The year 1928 marks at once an end and a beginning. With the fulfilment of our Lord's charges to Margaret Mary, the Sacred Heart devotion of the Middle Ages and the Sacred Heart theology of the Fathers have reached a certain consummation; the devotion has achieved its definitive form as part of the spirituality of the universal Church. We stand before a new beginning and a new responsibility: our *modern age,* the time of the great apostasy from God, has been given the devotion to the Sacred Heart as a sign and a path of salvation. The worldwide apostasy should be countered by a worldwide dedication of hearts to the Heart of the Redeemer; the immense sin of the world should be expiated by the members of Christ's Body with vicarious reparation, in union with the dedicated Heart and atoning death of our Lord on the Cross.

KARL RAHNER

SOME THESES ON THE THEOLOGY OF THE DEVOTION

THIS chapter does not attempt to give a detailed and balanced theological basis for the cult of the Sacred Heart. Such an attempt would claim too much space, and repeat too much of what has been well and thoroughly explained elsewhere. The intention here is to discuss briefly (hence the "thesis form") something of what has been said already but seems to need further clarification and definition.

1. PRELIMINARY QUESTIONS

We are not examining abstract dogmatic principles to discover what devotion to the Sacred Heart could be, especially from reference to its object. We are asking rather what is actually meant by this devotion, in the doctrine and practice of the Church.

In the course of its history and in our own day, the devotion, in the doctrine and practice of the Church, has shown many aspects and forms. So it would be neither right nor reasonable to impose on anyone a one-sided notion or practice of the devotion, by narrowing it down to one or other of these forms.

An understanding of the things of the heart presupposes a certain attitude and disposition in the person who is being instructed in them. If the discussion of the Sacred Heart devotion strikes anyone as obscure or extravagant, that man should ask himself whether he is humble, reverent and loving, whether he is really awe-struck at the wonderful and ineffable mystery of a God who, in Christ, wished to love us sinners with his most personal and intimate love. It is obvious from the beginning that only such a man, the man of love and prayer, can understand a discussion of the Sacred Heart.

131

The meaning of a word can be determined correctly only if we first note its general underlying assumptions, and ascertain the ambit within which the word is employed. The doctor, for instance, who understands by "heart" (at least primarily) the cardiac muscle as an organ of circulation, should recognize that he has accepted the unspoken limitations of the viewpoint of a physiologist, who sees the body as a material mechanism. This apriori notion may be permissible under certain circumstances, but it is an arbitrary and limiting one. There can be no question of adopting it here.

In the original (and not the subsequent, derived or metaphorical) sense, "heart" is a primal word. It is not susceptible of a proper definition by the joining of better known concepts. Since it has this primal character in so many cultures[1] (Semitic, Graeco-Roman, Western, Mexican etc.), it is clearly such a word as could be easily employed in the vocabulary of a world religion. It falls into the category of words for the whole man; that is, it signifies a human reality predicable of the whole man as a person of body and spirit, a reality which is therefore prior to any possible distinction between body and soul (really made on subsequent reflection).

Other such words, which form part of the basic vocabulary of mankind, are "head", and "hand" (for blessing, defending, threatening) as opposed to "hand" as the body's instrument for gripping. It is misleading to ask whether "heart" denotes primarily a physiological organ or something spiritual. No matter what answer we get, it must lead to unsatisfying consequences, which can be averted only by resorting to wearisome and forced hypotheses. Words like "heart", "head", "face", and "fist"

---

[1] Cf. Kittel, *Theologisches Woerterbuch zum NT* III, col. 60 ff. (*Heart* in the Old Testament; in the Greeks, in Hellenistic and Rabbinical Jewry). — A. Guillaumont, *Les sens des noms du coeur dans l'antiquité,* in: *Le Coeur,* Études Carmélitaines 1950, p. 41–81. The same volume contains studies on the concept of heart in ancient Egypt, India, in Mohammedan piety, in Mexico etc.

denote realities which lie beyond the distinction of body and soul. In other words, their formal source is the original, concrete, ontological unity of body and soul. Since man in his entirety is a bodily being, the concept of "heart" includes the idea of bodiliness, and therefore includes also the bodily heart. Not for its own sake is the bodily heart thus included; still less is it taken as a merely external symbol for something else, for what we really mean. It is rather one of the notes which constitute this primal human concept.

"Heart", taken in this primal sense, denotes that centre which is the origin and kernel of everything else in the human person. It is here that the whole concrete "nature of man, as it is born, blossoms and spends itself in soul, body and spirit, . . . is crystallized and set; here it is, as it were, anchored" (H. Conrad-Martius). Here is the focal point of a man's primal and integral relations with others and above all with God; for God is concerned with the whole man, and in his divine actions it is to man's centre, his heart, that he addresses his graces or his judgements.

It is therefore by no means inevitable nor a matter of course that "heart" should imply love. The fact that our Lord freely wished the centre of his Person to consist of "love for us" is just the incomprehensible thing in our experience of him. (Hence we are justified in using special symbols for it, the heart-wound, blood and water, the rays, the cross, the crown of thorns.) For a heart could be loveless and evil, its love merely peripheral. To find that the innermost core, the ultimate reality of a person is love, is something we experience only in the Heart of our Lord.

The representation of the physical heart is a symbol, not a likeness, of this personal centre. It is however a natural, not an arbitrary, symbol. The very nature of man as a creature of body and soul gives the body a symbolic character; and for the centre of this composite creature, the most obvious symbol (this is partly a matter of psychological experience) is the heart.

Because the image of the physical heart as such is only a

symbol, not a likeness, of the inmost centre of man (not simply of his soul), it can and should be stylized, it should not aim at perfect physiological "accuracy", and it can be supplemented by other symbolic appendages (crown of thorns, cross, rays, position in the geometrical centre of the man), especially if the love of the heart is to be symbolized. A likeness of our Lord with his Heart shown as far as possible true to nature, so that we are looking as it were into the physiological "centre" of the man, misinterprets the idea of the symbol, and distracts attention from its symbolic character. Representations of Christ's Heart by itself are, it is true, not permitted on altars. They are forbidden by the Church because the altar must display the Person of Christ as the object of worship. Apart from that, however, they lack neither sense nor suitability.

The primal concept of "heart" together with its graphic symbolization, on account of its basic, non-conventional character, is what the depth-psychologists call an "archetype"[2]. This alone is sufficient reason for refusing to abandon it in favour of some more abstract term (such as "personal centre", "interior", or "love").

There is one point we must watch in interpreting the historical records of the cult of the Sacred Heart, as indeed in every description of spiritual or religious practices: we must distinguish between the actual cult and the description born of subsequent reflection on it. The former can be genuine, lively and profound while the latter is wanting in many points of accuracy, originality and theological precision; or it may reflect a phase of spirituality which is in some aspects dated, and not such as should necessarily impose its norms on us.

In accordance with the general rules for the interpretation and judgement of private revelations, this distinction between

---

[2] I have attempted to treat in a simple way of the ascetical significance of such archetypes in *Geistliches Gespräch über den Schlaf,* in: *ZAM* 23 (1950), p. 1–12.

fact and description must be invoked wherever the devotion to the Sacred Heart props itself on private revelations which can be accepted as authentically from God.[3]

If we should eventually come to adopt such historical forms of the devotion, their modes of expression, their language and their style, there is something further to be noted: that there are, especially as regards the use of language and the incidence of certain ideas, several devotions to the Sacred Heart. There is that of the mystic, that of the soul redeemed in fear and trembling, that of the genuine everyday piety of the "ordinary" Christian. One form of the devotion shows creative originality, another is moulded by tradition, another may even be a more or less spurious form, perhaps merely tainted with artificiality, perhaps really pseudo-religious (through "cramp", self-deception or counterfeit fervour). A discretion matured by sound religious training should mark these differences and mark also the type of person to whom the devotion is to be presented.

This power of discernment must be exercised especially in regard to differences of sex, age and national mentality. Children are generally too immature for a special devotion to the Sacred Heart. Some of the more highly-charged emotional phrases in prayers to the Sacred Heart will not agree with the taste of all peoples, and should be abandoned where they do not appeal.

We must distinguish clearly between the veneration of a person and that of a thing (e. g. a picture, relic, institution, material circumstance in a person such as his official authority, his moral code etc.). Ultimately the veneration of a person is determined by the nature of personality in general and the concrete individuality of the particular person being venerated.

In the veneration of a person, one consideration is crucial. A

---

[3] Cf. K. Rahner, *Ueber Visionen und verwandte Erscheinungen*, in: *ZAM* 21 (1948), p. 179–213.

person has not only innate, unalterable "qualities", but also "attitudes" towards himself and others; and these attitudes are free, time-bound, actual, transitory and unpredictable; they can be empirically "experienced" but not metaphysically deduced.[4] These attitudes of a man to others (to God, to other persons and reflexively to himself), show a multiplicity, under which there exists, or ought to exist, a formal unity, joining together the attitudes of a person into an articulate, meaningful whole. This process of free, formative unification takes place in the concrete, living person. His innate qualities, if we can imagine them prior to this process, are taken over by this free and formative act of self-understanding, they are "understood" (in one way or another), and actuated. Therefore they can produce reactions in others only in so far as they are understood in this way. A man's qualities, therefore, cannot be honoured except in the concrete, in so far as he by his attitudes has stamped these innate qualities with a definite existential character, a personal colouring, so that they have become an intrinsic constituent of his attitudes.

That which constitutes the original form-giving unity of a person's attitudes is the heart, in the general sense which we explained above. Only a person can have a heart, that is, a centre of "existence"—animals have a cardiac muscle; a person's attitudes are "cordial" in the sense that they spring from a common inmost centre, which unites them all and impresses on them their ultimate meaning.

What then is involved in honouring a person? It means leaving oneself open to the impact of his personality, and giving a positive recognition and a loving response to his concrete reality as one experiences it, and to his attitudes which, as we said, are free, transient, and unpredictable. In honouring his

---

[4] Cf. K. Rahner, *Theos im NT,* in: *Bijdragen* 11 (1950), p. 212–236; 12 (1951), p. 24–52 (especially 230–236 and 24–35).

heart, one honours the original, innermost, formative centre of his attitudes.

In the devotion to the Sacred Heart the proper and adequate "object" is always the Person of our Lord (cf. Denzinger, 1561, 1563). The basic structure of this cult is therefore that of *latria*, because the Person of our Lord claims adoration. Sacred Heart prayers in the proper sense include therefore such as are addressed directly to the Person of our Lord (with a mention of his Heart) and not merely prayers addressed immediately to his Heart, for instance Pius XI's prayer of reparation for the feast of the Sacred Heart. The latter type of prayer is however quite legitimate; it follows the practice of the Church and a usage common even in secular speech. A lover, for instance, will call his beloved "dear heart".

Ultimately, however, these prayers refer simply to the Person of Christ, especially since what we beg for from the Heart are actions of the person—"have mercy on us". As utterances of the very highest fervour, they must be used comparatively seldom, and with discretion, if they are to be genuine prayers.

In the devotion to the Sacred Heart it is therefore the Person of our Lord that is worshipped, "under the aspect of" his Heart, that is, of his primal, innermost, formative centre (centre of the whole man, body and soul, and of his Person, human and divine). His Heart is the source of all his attitudes and all his behaviour towards us, of all that we have experienced of him in the history of our salvation. And our ultimate discovery is that this centre (this "Heart") is possessed by a free, unfathomable love. This love, as the inmost "essence" of God himself, is bestowed on us as a free grace.[5] And it is this love that characterizes and unifies all the attitudes of our Lord. Since the aspect under which our Lord is worshipped in the devotion is precisely the Heart as the inmost centre of his Person, the objection that it would be just

[5] Cf. the article cited above in: *Bijdragen* 12 (1951), p. 28–35.

as good to venerate some other "part" of Christ's person (his face, blood, hands etc.) is obviously mistaken from the start. Even where these other cults are meaningful, even where they are approved by the Church, they are essentially different from the devotion to the Sacred Heart. The "aspect" of this veneration of the Person of our Lord is the innermost formative centre of all his attitudes.

Dogmatic theology normally distinguishes in this devotion between the *objectum (materiale* and *formale) partiale* and *totale*. In this particular case the distinction seems to us to have neither language nor fact to recommend it. It is an unhappy distinction as regards the "material object": it makes (unintentionally) too strong a verbal division between the Heart and the Person of our Lord; it fails in fact to understand the peculiar character of the "heart", which is not simply a piece, but the primal, unifying centre of the whole. The distinction misses the peculiar indivisibility of the person, which is different from and more radical than that of things. In the person, the "part", because it is taken over and "understood" by the personal centre, can be seen correctly only in the whole, and the whole person can be judged adequately only from its "heart-centre". We might put it this way: in devotion to the Sacred Heart, "heart" denotes the "whence", the "whither", the "aspect", under which the Person of Christ is adored. The veneration of the Sacred Heart might be defined then as "the latreutic cult of the Person of Christ under the aspect of his Heart in so far as this is governed by the prodigal love of God for sinful men, the love in which God gives himself to the sinner". Consequently the devotion is not confined to the form in which the heart itself is personified and addressed.

The practice of distinguishing the formal object within itself (into total and partial formal object), and from the material object, is open to the same criticism. We come to know the "Heart" of Jesus in its most determinate sense precisely through our experience of the free and prodigal love in which God communicates himself, and not merely his created gifts, to the lost world. In this case, therefore, the object of our adoration is in fact identical with the reason for its adorability, both the absolute reason and the reason relative to us. The love of God, pouring itself out from the personal centre of Christ, is adored, and is itself the reason why it is adored. In explaining the object of the devotion, there is therefore no didactic reason for a detailed distinction of the formal object in itself and in its relation to the material object.

2. THEOLOGICAL BASIS OF THE DEVOTION

Theology can and must show that the devotion to the Sacred Heart is materially contained in Scripture and in patristic and medieval tradition. It must show this to be true both as regards the precise object of the devotion (the general concept of heart; biblical references to the Heart of the God-Man; his Heart as the fountain of life, as the origin of the Church etc.), and as regards all that we might call veneration of this Heart.

Nevertheless this abstract dogmatic argument and the indication of a precedent will not provide sufficient basis for the present devotion to the Sacred Heart. For this we must appeal to the "private revelations" of Paray-le-Monial, or, if you wish, to the Church's acceptance (historically occasioned by the revelations) of the present devotion, which certainly did not always exist in its present form. The Church's approval and appropriation of the "Paray" devotion did not imply merely the formal blessing of something that had been at all times a possibility. It meant the new creation, from the perennially valid material of the faith, of something that was demanded at that precise moment by the actual historical circumstances of the Church. It is not hard to justify this assertion. The present devotion to the Sacred Heart, in spite of its continuity back as far as the Bible, has not always existed in the form in which it exists today (think for instance of the Church's liturgical cult of the Sacred Heart, of the concentration of definite dogmatic notions under the rubric and archetype of the Heart, of the clearly defined forms of the devotion today, of the emphasis on reparation in and with Christ). What is the cause of these extra features? It is not enough to say that they were always a possibility. What caused the actual realization of this possibility? It is a question which of its nature cannot be answered fully by dogmatic theology from its limited sources of Scripture and tradition.

A private revelation[6] as a commission to the Church implies not so much a statement of fact, communicating some new doctrine or information, for this would be hard to reconcile with the fact of its being directed to the *Church*. It implies a command. It reaches the Church in a definite historical situation, faced with several possible lines of action, all of which could be reconciled with the general public Revelation. The private revelation points out the one path which the Church must with all urgency take. What is new is not the matter of such a revelation but the placing or shifting of the emphasis within the ambit of what is legitimate for Christians. Such an imperative is possible because, while we may know from our faith that many things are simultaneously good and true, we cannot as believers accomplish all that is true and good at the same time, in the same measure, and with the same intensity. The private revelation could be understood then as heaven's reading of, and injunction for, the actual situation of the Church. It answers the question: Granted the general principles of the faith, what line of action is at this time most urgently required in the Church? The private revelation in the Church's life has a parallel in the life of the individual. It is the contingency which St. Ignatius Loyola in the Spiritual Exercises calls the first and second time for an election, when theoretical

[6] Cf. K. Rahner, *Les révélations privées. Quelques remarques théologiques,* in: *Revue d'Ascétique et de Mystique* 25 (1949), p. 506–514 (Mélanges Marcel Viller), and K. Rahner, *Der Einzelne in der Kirche,* in: *Stimmen der Zeit* 139 (1947), p. 260–276.

consideration of the general alternatives can narrow down the field of choice but cannot (on principle at least) settle the will unequivocally. Consequently the decision is made not on purely theoretical considerations, but by a kind of inspiration of grace.

In interpreting such a private revelation one must therefore take account both of the general principles of mystical theology, and of the historical situation of the Church and the world into which the heavenly message was spoken.

What was the situation into which the message of Paray-le-Monial was addressed as a compelling imperative? It cannot be described exclusively nor even principally in terms of Jansenism. Not only was Jansenism and its range of ideas too ephemeral a phenomenon to provoke such an answer, but the message only became effective in a period no longer swayed by Jansenism. In view of the way the message did actually take effect and of the guidance of the Church by the Holy Ghost, that explanation is untenable.

The message must therefore be intended for the modern situation in general, which properly began only with the French Revolution. This period is characterized, and that in ever increasing measure, by the secularisation of life (of the state, society, economy, science, art). The religious values of Christianity are being progressively eliminated from modern life, and the burden of belief is resting more and more exclusively on the personal decision of the individual. The Christian world, which could once carry a man almost independently of his own decision, is subject to unceasing attenuation. Every man must live, irrespective of whether he decides for or against Christianity, in a situation marked by the outward, and therefore also inward, "absence of God", a situation which corresponds to Golgotha and Gethsemane in the life of Jesus (Mk. 14, 32ff.; 15, 32ff.), where life is to be found in death, where abandonment implies the deepest proximity to God, and where the power of God parades itself in weakness.

This is the perspective in which one must view the message of Paray and its relevancy in the historical situation of the Church, even down to such everyday manifestations as the Holy Hour. It emphasizes the *interior life, faith* in the love of God, present even when it seems furthest away (in consequence of the growing sin and godlessness of the world, from which believers and unbelievers alike suffer), and *reparation*. And these three notes, which undoubtedly characterize the historical devotion of Paray, become easier to grasp and interpret correctly when seen in this perspective.

Interior life is not the selfish luxury of religious introversion. The interior man is rather he who, by the power of God, believes and loves in spirit and in truth, in a world where the love of God has grown cold, or at least has almost ceased to project itself into 'exterior' life. Interior life means the strengthening of man in faith and love without the props of an externally Christian society.

The second characteristic is *faith in the love of God* in spite of his judgements. It has a special meaning in our day, when God, the Lord of history, appears as an angry judge, when the hour of darkness seems to have overtaken human history, and the historical situation of the world reflects mysteriously the interior state of souls.

Reparation means the endurance of this godless situation with and in the Son, in Gethsemane and Golgotha, and fellowship in Christ's apparently fruitless love for the sinful world.

We are now in a position to decide if the devotion is really 'dated'.

a) Many elements in the traditional presentation of the devotion do carry clear signs of their age; the limited viewpoint from which they have been presented can only be explained from the theological and religious background of the seventeenth century. For example, this form of the devotion has no ordered connection with the doctrine of the Blessed Trinity; in this respect the Ignatian theology of the Spiritual Exercises is really broader and deeper. Moreover one misses in the devotion a lively awareness of the dogma that Christ is our mediator with the Father, that he stands from the beginning essentially on our side, so that the characteristic tendency in our religion and preaching should be, not to Christ, but with him and in him, in the fellowship of his life and death, to the Father. But these "period" failings are not essential to the devotion and can be supplied without undue difficulty.

b) All the ingredients of devotion to the Sacred Heart are borrowed from dogma, and in this sense the devotion is valid for all ages of Christianity. These elements are themselves so important and suggestive, and they fit so naturally under the concept of the heart, that one can truly say: Just as there always has been a certain devotion to the Heart of Jesus, since the earliest days of the Church, so will there always be one.

c) The devotion in the strict sense, as it issued "new" from Paray-le-Monial and was appropriated by the Church, especially by the encyclical *Miserentissimus Redemptor* of Pius XI, is in a very positive sense the product of circumstances. But since, as was indicated above, these circumstances are still with us and show no sign of changing, indeed are only now revealing all their breadth and gravity, the cult of the Sacred Heart can only become more and more seasonable. If the devotion, understood in its proper and most profound sense, has suffered a reverse in very recent times, this is not because it is ill adapted to our age. Such a reverse is rather itself a sign that "charity has grown cold". Or perhaps it results from a faulty preaching of the devotion, which has arbitrarily neglected to supply the deficiencies mentioned under a); or perhaps the devotion has been indiscreetly presented to men who have yet to learn the rudiments of Christianity, and are unready yet for the strong nourishment (which is at the same time the most delicate) of the mature.

d) Whether or not this phase of the devotion will last till the end of time, is not given to us to know. We are not asked to prophecy, but rather to entrust ourselves in this our day to the guidance of the Spirit in all humility and good will. Anyone who has this humility and good will can be an active apostle of the devotion to the Sacred Heart and at the same time innocent of any opinionated claims to having the "last word" in spirituality.

3. THE PLACE OF THE DEVOTION IN CATHOLIC PIETY

Devotion to the Sacred Heart, in so far as it venerates our Lord, the author and substance of our salvation, under the aspect of his Heart, well deserves the title given it by Pius XI' *Totius religionis summa*. This Heart does in truth hold a central position, as the point through which everything passes to the ultimate centre, the Father. To this extent, devotion to the Sacred Heart is not simply a special devotion among other such, limited to certain clearly defined prayers and practices, which one might set aside at will or replace by some other "devotion".

Still it would be wrong to think that devotion to the Sacred Heart and the spiritual life are one and the same thing. That is not true even if one extends the meaning of this cult beyond any special "devotion" and beyond any set of prayers and practices limited in their object and their appeal. The heart is the origin and centre of, but it is not identical with, the whole religious life. We men do not start from the centre but are only slowly making our way towards it. So it is only natural that we cannot begin to understand this unifying centre until we have to some extent taken possession of the whole structure in its various parts and aspects. We must be constantly assimilating anew the many different realities of the faith in their details and in their synthesis, and learning the inner structure and relative importance of the various sentiments, attitudes and virtues of the Christian life. Without this, the devotion can scarcely advance beyond vain abstractions and the cult of vague sentiments of piety.

The aim and ultimate goal of the devotion (logically at least, if not chronologically), is to attain this *summa* of which Pius XI speaks; and this supposes that we have first made our own all the different elements which compose it. But when we attain to this centre and sum of our religion, it is not to rest there. If we genuinely possess it, we shall be constantly driven forth to perform the works of love, and to share in the life of our Lord by drawing closer to his mysteries, by the service of his Church and the love of our fellow men, and by living the life and accepting the sufferings which God has allotted us. All this is connected with the Heart of our Lord, and if one wanted to give the name of 'devotion to the Sacred Heart' to all this activity, then the devotion would be conceptually and materially identical with Christianity. But that could only be harmful to the devotion. It would become so "general" and "broad" that its own peculiar character would be lost in a vague immensity and it could no longer promise any special contribution or blessing for the spiritual life.

From the first two paragraphs of this section it follows that an explicit, conscious, and all-embracing concentration of the whole spiritual life round devotion to the Sacred Heart, a sort of Montfortism[7] transferred to the Sacred Heart devotion, is certainly possible (provided one remedies the "period" deficiences indicated above). But such a concentration is not part of the devotion as recommended to every Christian. In this matter we must leave every man free to travel, under God's guidance, by his own path and at his own speed. The same is true even when it comes to "dosing" the spiritual life with an occasional explicit reference to the Heart of our Lord. No man is ever going to realize in his spiritual life the whole religious reality in all its manifold intricacies, much less realize it all at once. It is impossible to set up any objective and accurate norm which will decide for all men just

[7] i. e. a parallel ambition to that of Grignion de Montfort, who strove to establish an actual and conscious reference to the mediation of Mary as far as possible in all activities of the spiritual life.

which truths they are to assimilate consciously into their spiritual life and with what intensity they must realize them. We must take care that every Christian believes and grasps certain fundamental truths and realities of the faith, beginning with those which must be explicitly believed whether from their own nature, or on account of God's command. On this foundation one can build a worthy Christian spirituality, which will include devotion to the Sacred Heart. But such a spirituality allows of an endless variety of forms, and within it devotion to the Sacred Heart can appear in the most various shapes and degrees of intensity. Obviously, then, the devotion may never be identified for every man with the complete spiritual life.

4. THE OBJECT OF THE DEVOTION

The general concept of "heart" which we explained above is valid also in the Church's official devotion to the Sacred Heart. Both in Scripture[8] and in the documents of the Church, "heart" is understood in the uniquely human sense as the primal and innermost centre of the human person, composite of body and soul.

The object of the devotion to the Heart of Jesus is therefore our Lord under the aspect of this his Heart. Look at the theories on the object of the devotion in the light of this definition. Some are partially inadequate (the merely physical heart as the "symbol" of love), some too abstract (seeing in the heart merely the "interior life of Jesus"). The notion of heart from which these theories start is either merely physiological, instead of being wholly human; or it is abstract and metaphorical, and contains therefore the tacit assumption that "heart" is properly a physiological term and must be "metaphorically" transferred to the interior life of the soul.

All our Lord's attitudes towards us are unified and informed by a redemptive love, in which God makes us the free gift of his

[8] Cf. Kittel, op. cit. III, col. 609–611; 614–616.

146

most intimate life in the Holy Ghost. With this gift our Lord's love enters into the history of this sinful world and wins its victory by enduring unto death the sin of the world and its own rejection by sinful men. All this outpouring of love is a revelation of his Heart.

"Heart" cannot be reduced to any of the natural component parts of man or of a God made man. It is the centre of the whole person. Consequently the love which gives unity and form to the Person of our Lord is not merely the human love of Christ, in which a potentiality of his human nature was realized, but the love of the God-Man.[9] The divine love of the Eternal Word has become incarnate in the human love of Christ, has fashioned itself a place in history and cast itself for an unmistakable role in the sinful world; and thereby it has guaranteed that love, and not righteous anger, is God's first and last message to the world.

5. THEOLOGY OF REPARATION

In the cult of the Sacred Heart we worship our Lord under the aspect of the Incarnate Word's redemptive love. Consequently the devotion must necessarily include reparation, which is a participation in this redemptive love, and a sharing of its fate.

What does reparation mean in the actual economy of salvation? Sin has been overcome by the Cross of Christ, on which our Lord won his victory by a loving and obedient endurance of the consequences of sin, namely separation from God, and death. Reparation for the sins of the world, both one's own sins and other people's, must then consist primarily and essentially in a freely accepted participation in the fate of our Lord, and in bearing with faith, love and obedience, the manifestations of sin in the world: suffering, darkness, persecution, separation from God, and death.

Our protestations of reparation, our acts and prayers, and the

[9] Cf. Philippe de la Trinité, *Du Coeur du Christ à l'Esprit d'amour,* in: *Le Coeur,* Études Carmélitaines 1950, p. 379–389.

reparative "works of supererogation", though they are useful and to some extent indispensable for every Christian, are really only a preparation. They are the rehearsals of the believing and willing heart for its allotted share in the fate of our Lord, who "became sin" and as the Lamb of God takes away the sins of the world.[10]

Every reparation, since it gives us a share in the fate of Christ, is thereby a participation "in Christ Jesus" in the fate of his Mystical Body, and works for the salvation and blessing of the whole body.

Every good action performed in the course of our life in "this body of sin", has a penal and therefore an expiatory character. It has this character automatically, from the mere fact that a man in grace accepts with faith and love his share in the sufferings of Christ. He need not explicitly intend to make reparation; in fact it is sometimes better that he should not think about it. It is sometimes necessary for a spiritual director to guard against a pseudoreligious introversion and an exaggerated sensitiveness to pain and effort in a certain type of "victim soul", by keeping the formal notion of reparation in the background of their consciousness. The same caution should be used with all persons who are still taking their first steps in the exercise of the virtues. Reparation, like charity, can be considered as the "form" of all the virtues. But that does not mean that reparation, any more than charity, can replace or absorb the other virtues. These must be understood and practised in themselves. Here too, devotion to the Sacred Heart must not be allowed to engross the whole spiritual life.

The reparation of Christ as man and of men in Christ is offered to the Father, or rather to the Triune God. In this sense we can and must affirm, in the language of metaphysical theology, that the reparation of Christ in his human nature is also offered to Christ as the eternal consubstantial Word of the Father. Dogmatic theology has developed this doctrine of the double "moral"

[10] Cf. K. Rahner, *Passion und Aszese,* in: *ZAM* 22 (1949), p. 15–36.

subject in Christ, who is agent and recipient of his own reparation. Dogmatically and metaphysically, therefore, there is good reason for the language of the devotion to the Sacred Heart (for instance in Pius XI's prayer of reparation: "We offer to thee [Christ] the satisfaction which thou didst offer to thy Father on the Cross"). But is this to be recommended for preaching or teaching? We expect more from the language of prayer, especially if it is to be the everyday prayer of Christians, than that it should be dogmatically sound. It should also be as simple and intelligible as possible, so as to show clearly the decisive lines and fundamental notions of the faith as we live it. It is, for instance, dogmatically true that Jesus as man can and does adore the Eternal Word of the Father; nevertheless it is hardly proper to speak in our everyday preaching and prayers of Jesus adoring himself.

The type of language illustrated above sits awkwardly in our prayers, and in any case it is not an essential constituent of the devotion or of its prayers of reparation. It will almost inevitably produce a false impression in the simple Christian: as though the reparation which Christ offers to his Father is being arbitrarily taken and transformed into the reparation which should be offered to Christ. Moreover it is almost certain to obscure the simple Christian's awareness that Christ stands over against the Father on our side as our Mediator, and that it is only with him and in him that we can render atonement for the sins of the world. And without this awareness, participation with Christ in the work of reparation is impossible.

The notion of reparation is essential to devotion to the Sacred Heart. But we are doing it sufficient justice if we preach and pray on these lines: Christ, who is our Mediator, has atoned for our sins to the Father, the holy and eternal Majesty of God, through his Passion and death, the ransom of sin; but he wished us to have a share in his expiatory sufferings. We may and we must continue his suffering and death in the Mystical Body of his Church to the end of time, by sharing in the fate reserved for his love in the world. In our prayers of reparation, we assure him that in deed and in truth we wish to enter into the sacrifice which he offered to his Eternal Father; that strengthened by his grace, we desire to unite ourselves in life and in death with the immolation of our eternal High Priest, and with the offering of his loving Heart, obedient unto death.

6. Consoling Our Lord

There is an idea and a practice dear to the devotion to the Sacred Heart (especially in connection with the Holy Hour), of wishing through our compassion to "console" our Lord in Gethsemane, and all through his Passion, for the human sorrow which he felt at the sin and ingratitude of the world that spurns his love. If we are to lay the widespread psychological and religious objections to the devotion, we must give this practice a particularly careful scrutiny, and an interpretation that is both dogmatically and pedagogically sound.

If the spiritual life is to develop fully and inform one's entire existence, one of its most important and indispensable practices must be meditation on the sufferings of Christ (as distinct from prayer directed exclusively to our Lord as glorified); and for this meditation we must bring our suffering and dying Saviour as vividly as possible before our eyes. This contemplation naturally tends to annihilate the distance in time between the contemplative soul and the Passion of Christ, and psychologically it has every right to do so. (We leave out of consideration here the forms and effects of this annihilation of time in a strictly mystical vision.)

What is the true theological and religious meaning of this time-vaulting representation of the Passion of Christ? In general terms, it does *not* imply a wish to be a fellow-actor within the imagined happening, to be, for instance, one of the persons whose actions affected Christ. That would be merely a fictitious play of the imagination, which is not to be rejected on principle, but should be valued for what it is: a psychological and, if properly employed, inoffensive help towards the representation of the mysteries of Christ's life, which is the real objective. The true theological and ascetical meaning of this vivid contemplation is rather that it gives the soul a clear grasp of those historical (and as such, past) events which made our Lord what he now is, and but for which he would not be our Lord ("the Pierced One", the "Lamb who is slain", "he who has learnt obedience by suffering": all epithets with a present sense). Secondly, in the Passion of Christ, and only there, we can read the "law" which should inform our life and claim our ready obedience, for it is the fresh pattern of growth implanted in us by the grace and life of Christ.

The lively contemplation of the life and Passion of Christ not only permits of being joined with a prayer to the glorified Lord, but its whole orientation leads naturally towards such a prayer. This glorified Lord is no mere abstraction, a God-Man untouched by history. In him the original source and the ultimate fruit of his life-story, namely his Heart, is eternally living and present.

Prayer to Christ cannot find a theological basis in a make-believe. It cannot prescind from the fact that he is now glorified, or that we are living centuries after him, in order to come closer to his Passion. Whatever psychological paths this prayer may follow in order to transcend our narrow consciousness, we may not make it our positive ideal to forget that objectively our prayer is directed to the glorified Christ. A prayer "to the suffering Redeemer" is, theologically speaking, a prayer to Christ who *has* suffered; only we must remember and realize that this "having suffered" refers to a very real present state of Christ.

It may be, then, that by representing the Passion of Christ to ourselves, especially in a visual way, we receive great psychological stimulus to offer active consolation to our suffering Lord, more stimulus, in fact, than we get from the theological considerations which are adduced to justify this practice. Nevertheless such comforting, in the sense of alleviating his sufferings by sharing them, must look elsewhere for its theological justification.

151

The theory most commonly held today, and that propounded by Pius XI in *Miserentissimus Redemptor*, runs as follows. Our Lord in his Passion, by virtue of his immediate vision of God and of his infused knowledge, knew of the reparation and satisfaction, and therefore of the compassion, to be offered by men at all times, even in the generations still unborn; and from this knowledge of men's love and compassion he was able to draw comfort for his own human Heart. Consequently any sympathy we offer him today was even then a comfort to him. But before declaring ourselves satisfied with this explanation, we must look a little closer.

a) Instead of assuming it as self-evident, we should take the trouble to show explicitly that our Lord in his Passion was in fact comforted by this knowledge, which was beyond question at his disposal. We must show, in other words, that he, guided in his human nature by God, did allow the comforting action of this knowledge to work on his consciousness. This is not proved exegetically by an appeal to the strengthening angel. One might ask whether the terrible immensity and depth of his interior suffering at this sinful world's estrangement from God did not tend to obstruct the comforting vision of his victory (which alone makes our 'consolation' possible and real), and whether his vision of the poverty and ambivalence of our "good works" did not cause him almost as much suffering as the vision of our sins. Is it not in a certain sense a disappointment for an infinite love even when it is accepted and answered in a very limited way?

b) If anything really "comforted" our Lord in his Passion, then it was obviously *all* the actions and intentions marked by his grace and love, in proportion to their supernatural dignity and existential depth, and not only those which were accompanied by a conscious intention of comforting the suffering Christ. If he permitted himself any consolation, it was from the sharing of his sufferings in obedience and love by all the men who in all times and all places have lived or are living in his grace, and not simply from the sentiments and protestations which had this for their explicit aim. Indeed the aim was better attained by the former than by the latter. The fellowship in suffering attained in the brutal routine of everyday life is the most genuine and perfect imitation of Christ, and claims the whole man with all the resources of grace and of his heart; and often enough it will of itself keep a man from referring to the temporal and psychological effect of these his sufferings on the suffering Christ. In order to comfort our Lord, therefore, it is not essential to have the express intention of doing so.

c) Moreover it is surely doubtful whether the ordinary Christian, in his normal (as opposed to mystical or visionary) life of prayer, can or should disregard the real object of his prayer. In fact, even when meditating on the Passion, he is praying to the glorified Lord; and he can no longer have the intention of comforting the glorified Christ, even though he may know that the good work which he does now was in fact a consolation to Christ in Gethsemane. Is that not imposing on the average Christian a complicated mental process which he can carry through only with difficulty, and the result of which can be attained just as effectively by a simpler path? What ultimately concerns us is not compassion in the sense of a sympathetic wish to console[11], but rather the generous and unselfish willingness to accept the law of Christ's life, which is the law of voluntary self-sacrifice. Fundamental to the Christian life is its historical character; the Christian submits obediently to being planted in his time, without attempting to transcend it mystically or imaginatively or in any other way. Is it then ever right in prayer to disregard the fact that we are standing before a glorified Lord, who, even though he

---

[11] Cf. St. von Dunin Borkowski, *Leiden mit Christus,* in: *Stimmen der Zeit* 116 (1929), p. 390–391. This short note is instructive at least as regards the psychological inhibitions which are in fact experienced by pious men of good will who are by no means "rationalistically" inclined.

has known suffering, has no need of consolation now as we pray? Not that we are trying to comfort our Lord as he is in his present state. Nobody would maintain that. But when we are praying with the glorified Christ, as he is at present, before our eyes, it is extremely difficult explicitly and formally to direct our consolations to a moment in his past, which as a time of suffering has really and truly passed away.

From what has been said it follows at least that the explicit intention of consoling our Lord in his sufferings should not be reckoned one of the essential elements of devotion to the Sacred Heart, nor should it be exacted of every devotee. How then should one explain the exposition, in the encyclical *Miserentissimus Redemptor,* of the theory we have just discussed? First, it is a proof of the objective fact that Christ was truly consoled by the "compassion" of his Mystical Body; and secondly, it shows a possible way of explicitly intending to console our Lord, if one can practise it with genuine devotion. It does not follow that every man can or should strive to do so.

This will in no way jeopardize the essential features of the Holy Hour: meditation on the Passion of Christ as the law of our life, prayer for and exercise in the grace of suffering with Christ, the rehearsal and practice of reparation in and with Christ. So we attain, in a more simple way, the goal of the practice we have been discussing: that the Head of the Church even in his earthly life, both in sorrow and in comfort, had a share in all that has been done and will be done for him through the whole course of history by the members of his Body.[12]

7. The Promises of Paray-le-Monial

The promises of Paray-le-Monial are subject to the normal rules for the interpretation of private revelations. This means in practice that even if, taken as a whole, they are recognized as

[12] There is a suggested plan for such a Holy Hour by K. Rahner in A. Trescher's *Heilige Stunde und Passionsandacht* (Innsbruck 1949).

having a supernatural origin, one is still justified in treating them with a critical caution, and the possibility of errors and inaccuracies in the transmission of the heavenly message by the holy visionary is not excluded *a priori*.

Taken in their entirety, these promises affirm and offer no more than our Lord himself promised in the Gospel to absolute faith (Mt. 17, 20; 21, 21 f.; Mk. 16, 17 f.; John 14, 12 f.). What is new in these promises is therefore not their content, but the circumstances of their fulfilment, the fact that what has already been promised in substance in the Gospels is now attached precisely to devotion to the Sacred Heart. To anyone with a proper grasp of the devotion, who practises it in the deep and unconditional faith that it demands, this "new" element in the promises will offer no special problem.

Taken as a whole, these promises should be interpreted in the same way as those made in the Gospel to the prayer of faith. In neither case are we dealing with a technique or recipe for gaining a hold over God and the unconditioned sovereignty of his inscrutable will. The promises are made to man only in the measure in which he surrenders himself in unreserved faith and unquestioning love to the will of God, which is absolute, and for us unfathomable, love.[13]

For the interpretation of the so-called "Great Promise", which is bound up with the nine First Fridays, one should consult what reputable authors have to say. Those who believe that this promise, in the form in which it is pronounced, contains nothing to contradict experience or the principles of dogma, should take care, when preaching it, so to present it that it does not become for many men the occasion, at least after they have made the novena of First Fridays, of sinning in irresponsible presumption on God's mercy.

[13] Cf. on the problem of the prayer of petition: K. Rahner, *Von der Not und dem Segen des Gebetes* (Innsbruck 1950), p. 78–94.

RICHARD GUTZWILLER

NOTES ON SOME OFFICIAL TEXTS
OF THE CHURCH'S DEVOTION
TO THE SACRED HEART

THE scope of this chapter is defined by its title. It is concerned with texts from the Church's devotion to the Sacred Heart.
They are to be ecclesiastical in two ways: first, in that they are
prescribed or at least approved by the Church, and therefore
exclude the private formulas of saints, theologians, mystics
and religious writers; and secondly, they are to be texts used in
the public worship of God, and consequently exclude prayers
which are merely for private use. Not all such texts will be discussed, but only a selection of the most important. And they
will be the subject of certain "notes"; there is no question of
a complete theological or ascetical analysis of them. Yet even
from this simple framework some important findings emerge.

Here we wish to speak briefly about the formularies of the
Ecclesia Sacrificans and the *Ecclesia Orans,* in other words, about
the Mass and the Office for the feast of the Sacred Heart.

The fact that the Mass in use today is the fourteenth to be composed, is evidence of a certain hesitancy, a cautious probing on the
part of the Church, but it shows too the care with which she
chooses and tests her official prayers. A comparison of the last
three formularies, which are still to be found in some of our
Missals, is most instructive.

The first is the Mass *Miserebitur.* Its text shows a marked
veering of the Sacred Heart devotion towards the interior
sentiments of Jesus, especially towards his sentiments of mercy.
Already in the Introit the word *misereri* occurs three times. The
Collect speaks of the *beneficia caritatis.* The Epistle, from Isaias

157

XII, praises the mercifulness of God: "Thy wrath is turned away and thou hast comforted me. I will deal confidently and will not fear." The Gradual stresses the disposition of the suffering Jesus, his love even to the end, his meekness and humility. In the Gospel the pierced Heart of the crucified Christ is shown as a symbol of mercy. And the same thought recurs in the Offertory, which speaks of the *retributiones Christi,* the kindnesses of Christ: "He satisfies thy desire with good things." The Secret too looks to our interior dispositions; it prays that we be filled with the flames of divine love. The Preface is that of the Cross. The Postcommunion is likewise concerned with interior sentiments; it portrays Christ as meek and humble of heart, and from him we should learn to despise the vain pomps of the world.

In the whole Mass, therefore, the Heart is understood as the interior disposition of Jesus. The element of reparation is completely absent from these texts.

Still more striking is the difference between the second Mass, *Egredimini,* and the one now in use. The former is not only taken up with interior dispositions, but it is pervaded by an atmosphere of joy. The Introit speaks of "the day of espousals, the day of heart-felt joy". In the Collect we beg "to become like unto him, to be clothed with his virtues and inflamed with his love". The keynote of the Gradual is joy: "The king of mildness will not be mournful nor disturbed." The Gospel is taken from our Lord's farewell talk: "Abide in my love—that my joy may remain in you and your joy may be full." The same note rings through the Offertory: *Laetus obtuli universa,* I have joyfully offered all these things — *cum ingenti gaudio,* with measureless joy. The Secret prays that we be inflamed with the fire from the Heart of our Lord. Even the Preface is full of joy; it is the Preface of Christmas: "That while we recognize God made visible, we may be taken up through him into the love of the invisible." The Communion sustains the thought: *Suavis est Dominus,* "The Lord is sweet." And the Postcommunion too speaks of his *suavitas cordis*. Everything here is set in the key of joy, love and gratitude. Not a word about reparation.

This is in marked contrast to the Mass now in use, *Cogitationes cordis eius*. Here the idea of reparation holds the foreground, and a deep solemnity pervades the whole Mass. The Introit speaks of death and famine, which are overcome only through the thoughts of God's Heart. The Collect emphasizes that it was our sins that wounded the Heart of our Lord, and that therefore our homage should be a "worthy offering of satisfaction"; the stress is laid therefore on sin and reparation. In the Epistle (to the Ephesians) we beg to be rooted in the love of Christ. But in the Gradual the theme of the sinners recurs. The contrasts between the Gospels of these Masses we have been considering are very significant. The Gospel of the *Egredimini* Mass differs completely from that of the other two, which both take their text from St. John's account of the Passion. But whereas in *Miserebitur* the account is broken off at a critical point, the present Mass goes on to include St. John's demonstration of how the sacrifices of the Old Testament find their fulfilment in the Cross. In the true lamb of sacrifice no bone will be broken; and the prophecy of Zacharias is fulfilled, "They shall look on him whom they have pierced." Here too the central idea is that of sacrifice, indeed of the atoning sacrifice of the Lamb and of the immolated King. The Offertory, with its words *improperium* (reproach), *miseria* (misery), *consolantem me quaesivi* ("I sought for one that would comfort me"), is again eloquent of sin and reparation. The same is true of the Secret prayer, for it describes the sacrifice as "expiation for our sins". The Communion hints at the mystical meaning of the opened side of our Lord. The Postcommunion once again demands that we should learn "to despise earthly things and love those of heaven". The Preface, written specially for the feast, is a complete innovation. Its main theme is, not the interior sentiments of our Lord, but the objective mystery of the pierced Heart, which remains open even for sinners. And even the "floods of mercy and grace" are seen not as an expression of our Lord's disposition, for at the moment of the lance-thrust he was already dead, but rather as the sign of an objective happening, a mystery of grace.

These texts are concerned therefore with sin and reparation. The three Masses show a development from the idea of our Lord's love to joy at this love, and finally to the serious demand for a return of reparation. A study of the encyclical *Miserentissimus Redemptor* reveals that this progressive elaboration of the idea of reparation was a fully conscious process.

The texts of the Office for the feast of the Sacred Heart and for its octave[1] combine a great richness of thought with deep religious inspiration. Whereas the present Mass is essentially set in a serious key, and in fact voices our joy at our Lord's love only in the Epistle, the note of joy is to be heard more often in the texts of the Breviary.

That is true even of the antiphons. In the First Vespers and Matins all the antiphons have a joyful ring. They speak first of the mild dominion of our Lord: "With your mild yoke rule, Lord, in the midst of your enemies." Then comes the thought of mercy: "The merciful and gracious Lord gave food to them that feared him." The Lord is not only our food, but also our light: "In the darkness a light has arisen for the faithful, the mild and merciful Lord." All this awakens joyful gratitude: "What return shall I make to the Lord for all that he has given me?" Even the *De Profundis* breathes confidence in God's mercy: "With the Lord there is mercy, and with him there is plentiful redemption."

The antiphon of the Magnificat speaks of the fires of God's love: "I have come to cast fire on the earth; and what else do I want but that it be kindled?"

There is an echo of this in the antiphon of Matins: "From

[1] See above, p. 1, note 1.

160

generation to generation God's thoughts are of gracious mercy." The Lord is the fountain of life, he is a torrent of joy: "In thee is the fountain of life: with the stream of thy joy thou wilt give us to drink, O Lord."

The Second Nocturn begins in the first antiphon with the idea of Christ the King: "God is king over all the world; he will rule over all peoples." The dominion of God gives security even to the fearful soul: "When my heart was fearful, you set me up on a high rock." Even in pain, comfort and joy are not absent: "The greater the pain of my heart, the more did your consolations delight my soul."

In the Third Nocturn, the first antiphon begins with love: "You who love the Lord, remember his holiness and praise him." Then it goes over to the idea of salvation: "All the ends of the earth have seen the salvation of our God." And it ends on a note of joyous fulfilment: "I shall praise you among the peoples, for your mercy is higher than the heavens." The antiphons of Lauds and Second Vespers begin by recalling the mystery of the piercing of the Heart on the Cross. Then the voice of our Lord himself is heard: "If any man thirst, let him come to me and drink.—Come to me all you who labour and are burdened and I will refresh you.—My son, give me your heart, and your eyes will look on my paths." And in the middle of it all, the great antiphon of grace: God has loved us with an eternal love and therefore, raised above the earth and full of mercy, he has drawn us to his Heart. Joy at his merciful love and at the riches of grace is therefore the characteristic of the antiphons.

There is an obvious development in the hymns. In the First and Second Vespers, sin and reparation hold the foreground. Even the first verse speaks of the *superba criminum cohors*. In the second verse it comes out with all clarity:

> *Vibrantis hastam militis*
> *peccata nostra dirigunt—*

161

> The soldier's lance that pierced thee through
> Was wielded by our sins.

The third and fourth verses point to the reparation performed by our Lord:

> And from the opened Heart there came
> The Church of Christ, his bride.
> The gate was opened here for all
> To find true life inside.
>
> From this the stream of grace will flow,
> The seven-channelled flood;
> The Lamb invites us here to wash
> Our sins in his own blood.

The fifth verse recommends reparation, in which man must share by turning back from sin to love.

In the hymn of Matins this mystery of love is shown to us in all its grandeur, as the mystery of Creation, of Incarnation and Redemption. Then it passes to the real aim, which again is reparation:

> *Percussum ad hoc est lancea*
> *Passumque ad hoc est vulnera,*
> *Ut nos lavaret sordibus*
> *Unda fluente et sanguine —*
> For this he bore the lance's thrust,
> The blows, the wounds, the pains,
> That blood and water from his side
> Might wash away our stains.

The hymn of Lauds is filled with the idea of sacrifice. The Heart of our Lord is shown as the true Ark of the Covenant, in which lies not the law of the ten commandments, but the law of love. It is the new temple of the New Testament, the new curtain which renders the new Holy of Holies not less but more accessible. Above all, the pierced Heart reveals the disposition of

Christ the High Priest, who immolates himself in the bloody sacrifice of the Cross and the unbloody sacrifice of the Mass. He calls for a return of love: "Who will not render love for love?"

The hymns lead therefore from the thought of our Lord's atonement and love to a reminder of his sacrifice and an appeal for the response of man, who is to be wholly drawn into the mystery of this love.

The lessons for the feast of the Sacred Heart are taken, in the First Nocturn, from the prophet Jeremias: the prophet unfolds to the bowed and humiliated people the mighty vision of the home-coming, the new covenant of a new people with new hearts. It is in the Church, the spiritual Israel, that this new heart is to be found, as the Heart of our Lord.

The lessons of the Second Nocturn sketch the history of the devotion to the Sacred Heart, spreading out over the several days of the octave the most important passages from the Sacred Heart encyclical *Miserentissimus Redemptor*.

A special interest attaches to the choice of the lessons for the Third Nocturn, which the Church has taken from the various commentaries on St. John's account of the opening of our Lord's side. They are texts from the fourth, fifth, twelfth, thirteenth, fourteenth, fifteenth, and sixteenth centuries, and they lead us to the heights and depths of mysticism. The two texts for the feast itself are ascribed to St. Bonaventure. According to the first, Christ's side was opened in order that the Church might be granted the Sacraments in blood and in water. "A living spring leaping up to eternal life" (John 4, 14). The second passage from St. Bonaventure is a bold one. It sees the opening of our Lord's side as the digging up of the hidden treasure in the field of Christ. The precious treasure is "the invisible wound of love". And the passage introduces the phrase which is to be echoed in the hymn to the Sacred Heart: "Who will not render love to him who has so loved us?"

On the second day of the octave the text is from the fifth homily

of St. John Chrysostom. Once again the objective mystical significance of the Johannine account of the Passion is emphasized:
blood and water gave birth to the Church and in particular to the
Sacrament of love, the Blessed Eucharist. Therefore men should
drink from the chalice of the altar "as though you were drinking
from his side." On the third day there is no special lesson, because the Sunday's Gospel takes its place. On the fourth day
Laurentius Justiniani writes that the birth of the Church from
the side of Christ on the Cross happened in the same way as the
creation of Eve from the side of Adam. Through the water the
Church is cleansed from sin, through the blood the way to heaven
is opened to her. The preacher for the fifth day is Bernardine of
Siena. According to his exposition, the opening of Christ's side
is like the heavens being opened, not this time for the waters of
the deluge, but for "the deluge of love". It is moreover a revelation of love. "The secret hidden from all eternity—now
disclosed by the opened side." Finally "the opening of the side
is an image of the opening of the eternal temple." The sixth day
brings lessons from various writings of another Father of the
Church, St. Peter Canisius. The first is taken from one of his
domestic instructions, in which he emphasizes that here we have
the fulfilment of the word of our Lord: "If any man thirst, let
him come to me and drink." The second passage comes from his
meditations on the Gospel, and explains that the word of the
prophet is here realized: *Haurietis aquas in gaudio,* "you will draw
waters in joy"; here we can nest secure in the hollows of the rock.
The third passage, likewise from his meditations, has rather a
moral and ascetical character: "In every temptation flee lovingly
to the amiable Heart of Christ, and cast your sins with confidence
into the abyss of his love."

On the seventh day, Cyril of Alexandria insists that the flow
of blood and water is an image and an inauguration of the
Eucharist and Baptism, *imago quaedam atque primitiae.* The lessons
end with some remarkable texts from St. Augustine's commen-

tary on St. John. Just as the door, through which alone men could escape the deluge, was built into the side of Noah's ark, so men must enter through the opening in Christ's side, by Baptism and the Eucharist, into the interior of the Church, in order to escape the deluge of sin. The Crucified with the pierced Heart is the true lamb of sacrifice, and, at the same time, an earnest of Christ's second coming: "They will look on him whom they have pierced; which is a promise that Christ will return in that flesh in which he was crucified."

These passages offer inexhaustible matter for meditation and preaching. In the Offices for the octave the thoughtful reader will find much to provoke his thought and stimulate his prayer; for the source of this Office is the pure theology of the Fathers and mystics. Biblical texts and theological reflections, ascetical exhortations and loving contemplation, here merge into one truly Catholic prayer. This is the prayer which was familiar to the saints, and to which the Church invites us on this solemn feast of the Sacred Heart of Jesus.

Litanies are an old form of prayer which has always been cherished by the Church. Even Israel had a kind of litany, in its 135th Psalm. From the abundance of contemplation invocations stream as from an overflowing fountain. They mount like tongues of fire from glowing flames. Litanies might be likened to windows opening in all directions and offering ever fresh prospects, or to a cathedral in which new details are constantly attracting the visitor's astounded eyes. The multiplied invocations are like the glittering facets of a cluster of jewels.

The litany of the Sacred Heart is still young. In 1691 Fr. Croiset put together 23 ejaculations for his private use. Seventeen of them were embodied into the litany of the newly-founded Sacred Heart confraternity in Marseilles, which contained in all twenty-seven ejaculations. In 1721 when the plague broke out in that city and the Archbishop held a public procession of prayer and penance, he made use of this litany. In 1898 it was approved by the Sacred Congregation of Rites and increased by six invocations, so that there were altogether 33, in memory of the 33 years of our Lord's life on earth. In 1899 the litany was approved for the whole Church in this form, which is still the official one today, and it was this form which Leo XIII used in his consecration of the world to the Sacred Heart. The logic of its composition does not extend to its every detail, but one can distinguish three groups of invocations.

The first group sketches the relation of the Heart of Jesus to God, and first to the Blessed Trinity. It is the Heart of the eternal Father's Son. It is the Heart formed by the Holy Ghost in the womb of the Virgin Mary. And it is the Heart substantially united with the Word of God. The consequences of this relationship to the Blessed Trinity are drawn in the following invocations; the Heart of Jesus is of infinite majesty, a temple of God, a tabernacle of the Most High, a house of God.

The second group shows the riches of this Heart in itself. It is a burning furnace of charity, an abode of justice and love, and full of kindness and love. It is the abyss of all virtues and therefore worthy of all praise. This royal Heart is the king of all hearts. In it rest all the treasures of wisdom and knowledge, for the fullness of the Godhead is here incarnate. Consequently it is in this Heart above all others that the Father is well pleased.

The third group stresses the relations of the Sacred Heart to men. From its fullness we have all received. It fulfils the longing of the Old Testament, is full of mercy, rich unto all who call upon it, and a source of life and holiness. Finally there are eleven invocations which emphasize reparation, so that this thought, which was brought into the foreground again by the encyclical, is of special and striking import in the litany. The last invocation summarizes them all: Heart of Jesus, delight of all the saints. It is worth noting the unmistakably biblical character of the litany of the Sacred Heart, if only to refute any idea of a discrepancy between this devotion and the thought of the Bible. Nineteen titles

166

of the litany are quotations from Holy Scripture, and several others contain allusions to scriptural phrases.

We possess several official prayers of consecration to the Sacred Heart. The first of them goes back to St. Margaret Mary Alacoque. "I give and consecrate to the Sacred Heart of our Lord Jesus Christ my person and my life, my actions, penances and sufferings, not wishing for the future to make use of any part of my being except in honouring, loving and glorifying that Sacred Heart . . ." This act of consecration glows with deep sincerity and a holy ardour of love. But it is strongly personal, subjective and individualistic in its outlook. It speaks constantly of "I", "me", and "mine". This lends the whole prayer a certain note of intimacy, but it imposes too a bias and a limitation. It is striking that this act of consecration says not a word about reparation.

The formula of consecration published by Pius XI in connection with the encyclical *Quas Primas,* of 11 December, 1925, is completely different. It begs that our Lord may rule over the lost sons, over those who have been led astray by false doctrines, or separated by schism, over the heathens, over Islam and the Jews; that he may bestow on his Church freedom and security, and procure peace and order for all peoples. This prayer of consecration breathes the spirit of worldwide catholicity, it is permeated by an apostolic sense of responsibility, and it broadens the horizon of the "I" to include the community of all men, of all peoples and of all mankind. In this way the two acts are complementary. The first ministers rather to a personal piety, the second to the service of God in the Communion of Saints. But this second formula too makes no mention of reparation. It is no longer recited on the feast of the Sacred Heart, but has been transferred to that of Christ the King.

In its place the same Pope Pius XI has given us, in connection with the encyclical *Miserentissimus Redemptor,* a new prayer of consecration, a prayer concerned with reparation and proper for recitation on the feast of the Sacred Heart and on the first Friday of the month. It speaks of the forgotten and despised love of Jesus, for which we should by our outward homage make some reparation. The prayer asks that atonement be made for the shamelessness and licentiousness of men, for the desecration of Sundays and Holydays, the blasphemies against God, the neglect of the sacraments. This prayer is of a more sombre, serious and affecting character. Its approach too is unusual in that we make to Christ the reparation which he himself once made. "We offer thee the reparation which thou didst once make on the Cross to the Father." Christ is at once the dispenser and the receiver. He speaks in the name of sinful mankind and is at the same time the God who is addressed. In this formulary too, Mary is mentioned for the first time, though without reference to her immaculate heart. The act is offered simply "in union with the reparation which thy Virgin Mother once made", and again "through the intercession of the most Blessed Virgin Mary, our Mediatrix in the work of reparation." Everything is centred round the idea of reparation.

Besides these three prayers, we have a special formula for the consecration of families, composed by Pope Benedict XV. However it is not intended for public devotions and can therefore be omitted from our considerations. St. Pius X's act of consecration for priests is penetrated with the priestly spirit, with apostolic zeal, love for souls and deep piety. But since it too is not destined for popular devotions, a more careful analysis of it lies outside our scope.

We possess then three formulas for public devotions, which complete one another to some extent, and which progress from the consideration of individual needs and aspirations to those of the community, and from Christ's reign of love in the community to his work of reparation for it. Only the future can tell whether the present formula is the definitive one, or whether the living growth of the liturgy and of the worship of God will produce still further acts of consecration, which will take into account contemporary attitudes and the religious sensibility of succeeding generations.

In any case, the prayers of the Church offer us a great wealth and variety of thoughts and suggestions. If we survey the whole range of them, we can draw the following conclusions.

In the Church's official prayers, the main emphasis is laid on the objective element of the devotion. The liturgical texts are based, not on those passages of Scripture which describe the interior sentiments of Jesus, but rather on the account of what happened on the Cross.

What happened on the Cross was primarily the slaying of the Lamb: not the execution of Jesus so much as the bloody achievement of his sacrifice. The Pasch was fulfilled. Man as the first-born of creation was redeemed through the blood of the First-Born of all creatures. By insisting that "no bone of him was broken" St. John stresses the allusion to the flawless, spotless lamb of sacrifice—flawless in the Johannine sense of "transparency", the absence of all sin.

The emphasis falls especially on one element in the accomplishment of this sacrifice: the flow of blood and water. In the blood the Church sees a symbol of the Eucharist, which is an unbloody continuation of the bloody sacrifice. The flow of blood from the heart implies that separation of body and blood which is symbolized in every eucharistic sacrifice by the separation of the species of bread and wine. So every Mass is an *anamnesis,* a recalling of the death of our Lord.

The water from the side of Christ is on the one hand a symbol of Baptism, in which men receive new life by reason of the sacrificial death of Christ. And it is too a sign of the effusion of the Spirit. Moreover in the opening of our Lord's side, the Church is born as the new Eve from the side of Christ, the new Adam.

Finally, the text of Zacharias, "They shall look on him whom they have pierced", points to the Second Coming of Christ.

These three ideas, namely the realization of the figure of the Paschal Lamb, the flow of blood and water, and the piercing of the King who brings salvation, show, by the reference in each case to the heart (for the lance is thrust through the heart and the blood springs from the heart), that Christ offers himself out of love, a love that carries him to the extreme even of death on the Cross. And this thought suggests the other, the subjective element of devotion to the Sacred Heart.

When we speak of the subjective element, we think primarily of the subjective dispositions of Jesus himself. We understand "heart" as his interior sentiments, the centre of his Person; and we say that the real centre of Jesus' Person is love. No text is more pertinent in this context than that from the Epistle to the Ephesians, where St. Paul speaks of the dimensions of Christ's love.

When we come to speak of the opening of Christ's Heart, we mean that this love is revealed and rendered visible. The union of the subjective and objective elements, that is, the union of the sacrifice of Christ and the love which brought him to that sacrifice, discloses this self-sacrificing love as the essential mystery, the very core of the history of our salvation.

The subjective element of the devotion looks also to the dispositions of men, whose sins have caused the death of Christ. For though the rejection of him must be imputed first of all to Israel, yet the whole pagan world, through Pilate and the Roman soldiers, shared in that guilt; and just as the second sin of humanity is the work of Jews and Gentiles, so the reparation offered by the sacrifice of Christ embraces both Jews and Gentiles. But the rejection of Christ is continued even after the completion of his sacrifice by the indifference of the masses, the tepidity of the faithful and the mediocrity of the elect. Consequently the continuation of the sacrifice of the Cross in the daily Mass is a perennial renewal of this act of reparation. Here a further factor in the subjective element of the devotion is disclosed: the atoning sacrifice of Christians is drawn into Christ's great act of atonement; for the Christians' sacrifice, like Christ's, is supported by love, and can therefore expiate the want of love in other men.

In devotion to the Sacred Heart all these lines converge on one point, on the love of the King of the world, who gave himself in sacrifice for all mankind, and draws into his great act of atonement all the love of self-sacrificing men. The mystery of the pierced Heart is disclosed as the centre of history. Only at the end of time, when Christ appears, "a lamb as it were slain", will this central mystery appear in all its grandeur. Then the devotion to the pierced Heart of our Lord will reach its final perfection.

ON THE BIBLICAL CHARACTER
OF THE LITANY OF THE SACRED HEART

MOST of the invocations in the litany of the Sacred Heart consist of literal or almost literal quotations from Holy Scripture. Other titles clearly allude to biblical phrases, and the remainder are biblical in inspiration. The connections of each invocation of the litany with the Bible will be indicated in the pages that follow.

Every litany begins with the invocation of the Blessed Trinity. The litany of the Sacred Heart follows this by indicating the relation of the Heart of our Lord to God as the Father, the Holy Ghost and the Son.

Heart of Jesus, Son of the Eternal Father: The revelation of the Father is the essential message of the New Testament. In the Old Testament God is called father, but only as father of the people, not as father of every man. The good news that God is the father of all men was first brought by Christ. He alone is the true Son of God by his very nature (Mt. 11, 27), and consequently when he is praying or teaching, the word "Father" carries on his lips a very special overtone. But through him, the Son of God, we too have become sons, not indeed by our nature, but by grace. He has taught us to pray to God as to the Father: "Thus shall you pray: 'Our father, who art in heaven'" (Mt. 6, 9). His Heart is filled with an extraordinary love for the Father. So we, as sharers in the sonship of God, should share also in a confiding love for him. One of the favourite phrases in the epistles of St. Paul is "God, the father of Jesus Christ"; Saul, the Jewish doctor of the law, grasped in a special way what the fatherhood of Jesus means, and as Paul the apostle of Jesus he gave it unique expression (Rom. 1, 4;

173

I Cor. 1, 9; II Cor. 1,3; Eph. 1, 3; Col. 1, 3 etc.). The doctrine that God is our Father is based therefore on the Old Testament, fully developed in the Gospels, and handed on enthusiastically by St. Paul.

Formed by the Holy Ghost in the Womb of the Virgin Mother: This invocation is a theological formulation of the scene of the Annunciation as described in the first chapter of St. Luke's Gospel (Lk. 1, 26f.). The Holy Ghost, Third Person of the Blessed Trinity, awakens life in the womb of the Virgin. That generative act by which man shadows forth the creative power of God, is here effected by the prototype, the creative Spirit of God himself. The creative action of the spirit, who moved over the deep in the beginning, here overshadows the womb of the Virgin and forms his masterpiece, the Heart of the Incarnate God. Mother and virgin, bride of the Holy Ghost, Mary is all these because in her womb this Heart was formed, and in it and from it our Lord has taken his origin. No scene of the Bible reveals more clearly the personal grandeur of soul of the Virgin Mother: her attitude of readiness and openness towards God, her prudent consideration of the word of God, and the *Fiat* of her obedience.

Substantially United with the Word of God: After the Father and the Holy Ghost, the litany turns to the Word of God. The invocation is a clear echo of the prologue to St. John's Gospel, which tells how the Word was made flesh (John 1, 14). The Heart of Christ belongs to his human nature, which is joined to his divine nature in the one person of the Logos. The title recalls in its undertones the christological struggles of the first centuries. In Nicaea the essential equality of the Son with the Father was solemnly defined against Arius. At Ephesus it was proclaimed as an article of faith that the union of the humanity of Jesus with the Second Person of the Blessed Trinity was not merely a moral but also a physical one. And at Chalcedon this human nature was asserted in its full humanity against the doctrine of Eutyches, who taught that it was absorbed by the divine nature.

In Jesus Christ there are two natures, but only one person. This doctrine is no more than the conceptual elaboration of the first chapter of St. John's Gospel. Scripture and theology blend in this invocation of the litany. They lay the basis for the adoration and veneration of that Heart which through the hypostatic union with the Logos is the very Heart of God.

These three ejaculations convey, then, the splendour of the Gospel message, the beauty of the first chapter of St. Luke, and St. John's absorption in the mystery of God.

Heart of Jesus, of Infinite Majesty: Here we draw the consequences of the first three invocations. The majesty of God is a favourite theme of the Bible, especially of the Old Testament. The 71st Psalm proclaims that the whole earth shall be filled with the majesty of the Lord (Ps. 71, 19). In the book that bears its name, Wisdom is called the unspotted mirror of God's majesty (Wis. 7, 26). This *Sapientia,* which is personified in the Old Testament, appears in the New as a real person, the Incarnate Wisdom, who displays, as in a mirror, the majesty of God. According to the first chapter of Colossians, our Lord is the image of the invisible God (Col. 1, 15), and therefore "the brightness of his glory" (Heb. 1, 3). We read in Ezechiel that the majesty of the Lord went into the temple (Ez. 43, 4). And the second book of Para-lipomenon tells how the majesty of God filled the temple (II Par. 7, 1). The Heart of God made man is this temple, which is completely filled with the majesty of God. That majesty and glory which once rested on the Ark of the Covenant dwell now in the Heart of our Lord, as the true Holy of Holies of the New Covenant. All that awe which in the Old Law enveloped the representative of Israel, the High Priest, as he went through the outer courts to the Holy Place, should be found in the New Testament in every man of prayer. *Majestas* here implies that the Lord is always greater than any imagination or concept which man can make of him. The title recalls St. Ignatius' eloquent *magis* in the Spiritual Exercises. This infinite majesty is still hidden, is visible only to the eyes of faith; but the Son of Man will come again in majesty (Mt. 16, 27; 26, 64). In the Parousia the *majestas infinita* will blaze out before the whole world.

Holy Temple of God: A special importance attaches to the Temple in the Old Testament. The construction of the Temple of Solomon is described circumstantially down to the smallest detail. At the fall of Jerusalem no blow was felt more keenly by the people than the destruction of the Temple. The rebuilding under Esdras, the feast of the consecration of the Temple, the renewal of the sacred fire under the Machabees, and the construction of the Temple of Herod the Great, were historic events for Israel. But this Temple was razed to the ground at the conquest and destruction of Jerusalem in 70 A. D. The stone temple was only a symbol of the living temple of the Body of Christ. Our Lord himself said: "Tear down this temple: in three days I will raise it up again." (John 2, 19.) And he spoke, as the Gospel emphasizes, of the temple of his Body. In this living temple the Heart is the Holy of Holies, for it conceals the mystery of God's love. Paul calls every Christian and the entire Christian community a holy temple of God. That is all the more true of Christ himself. He is a "holy temple of God" in the full sense of the Pauline phrase. When our Lord told the Samaritan woman: "The hour cometh and now is, when men shall adore neither in the temple at Jerusalem nor on mount Garizim, but the true adorers shall adore in spirit and in truth" (John 4, 23), he was defining true worship. It is a cult which implies not merely an external rite and external sacrifice, but the interior homage of the spirit and the heart. And it is worship in truth, in reality, not merely in Old Testament symbols. Interior devotion and the fullness of reality are therefore the essential notes of Christian piety. The Heart of our Lord, as the fulfilment of the figures of the Old Law and the perfect expression of the interior life, demands that our piety should also be interior and realistic.

Tabernacle of the Most High: In the middle of the Israelite camp on its journey through the desert stood the tabernacle, the sign of the Lord's covenant and of his sovereignty over Israel. Now the carnal Israel has given place to the spiritual, the synagogue to the Church. It is a pilgrim Church, making its way over the earth down through the centuries, towards the promised land of a new heaven and a new earth. And in this spiritual Israel, Jesus, the Word of God, has "set up his tent amongst us" (John 1, 14). Incarnation means that the tabernacle of God has been set up in the midst of mankind. St. Peter in his second Epistle calls his body a tent which is to be broken (II Pet. 1, 13–14). Thus was the Body of Christ broken. But he lives on, body and soul, in the mystery of the Eucharist. That is why the Church gives the name tabernacle to the place where our Lord dwells under the sacramental species. Finally the Epistle to the Hebrews says that Christ, after accomplishing his great sacrifice, entered into the true tabernacle of God, built not by human hands but by God himself, the tabernacle of heaven (Heb. 9, 11). Thither he bears the expiation of our sins, his own blood in the sacrificial vessel of his Heart. So this invocation of the litany brings us from the pastoral people wandering in the desert to the earthly tabernacle of the Body of Christ, thence to the dwelling of Christ in his holy Church, especially on her altars, and leads finally to the true tabernacle of God in the glory of heaven.

House of God and Gate of Heaven: In the book of Genesis (Gen. 28, 17) Jacob's dream is described. The patriarch sees heaven opened and the angels of God going up and down. Seized with astonishment, he cries out on awakening: "Here is the house of God and the gate of heaven." He sets up a memorial stone on the spot and anoints it with oil. Christ applied this text of Genesis to himself when, after calling the first disciples, he told them: "You will see heaven opened and the angels of God ascending and descending on the Son of Man." (John 1, 51.) He is the head of the twelve apostles, who are to take the place of the twelve tribes of Israel. Through him heaven, once shut by sin, was reopened, and through him the angels of God ascend with the prayers of men and descend with the graces of God. He is the great memorial stone, to whom we can apply in this context the phrase of St. Paul: *And the rock was Christ* (I Cor. 10, 4). He is the "anointed" memorial stone, for he is the Christos, in a unique sense the anointed one. His human nature is bathed in the anointing oil of the Godhead. Jacob received at this vision the promise of the Lord: "Thy seed shall be numerous as the dust of the earth. Thou shalt spread abroad to the west, and to the east, and to the north, and to the south. And in thee and thy seed all the tribes of the earth shall be blessed." This promise is effectively fulfilled in the spiritual posterity of Christ and the blessing of the Lord which rests on them, and these blessings have their origin in the love of our Lord and therefore in the Heart of the Incarnate Lord. Here is the perfect realization of all that Jacob foreshadowed when he spoke of the house of God and the gate of heaven.

The litany's second group of invocations shows the riches of the Heart of our Lord in itself.

Burning Furnace of Love: There is frequent mention in the Bible of the "burning furnace". It is either a crucible, in which silver and gold are purified (Prov. 27, 21; Wis. 3, 6), or a furnace, like the one in the book of Daniel, which was intended to burn and consume the three young men, but in which they were preserved through God's grace, and raised their song of praise in the midst of the flames (Dan. 3).

Our Lord's Heart is called a burning furnace because in the fires of his love all is purified, and it is a love which neither consumes nor burns but moves men by the flames of charity to sing the praises of God.

Vessel of Justice and Love: This title presents two of the central ideas of biblical thought. *Justice:* the man of the Old Testament has little thought for a future judgement; rather he knows himself to be here and now, at every moment and in every place, before the judgement-seat of God. One question preoccupies him: whether he can survive this judgement of the just God, who judges all men in justice. The man of the Old Testament believes that he can face this judgement if he has been scrupulously observant of the Law, this constitution which formulates the justice of Yahweh. But in fact he cannot observe all its precepts, and therefore suffers from feeling himself unjust before the justice of God.

In the New Testament, especially in the Epistle to the Romans, this question of justice and judgement is taken up and carried to a definite solution. Man is indeed an unjust creature, and cannot face the judgement of God. He is not acquitted but condemned; for he is in truth a sinner. If he is pardoned, it is because God is gracious, and grace takes the place of justice. Yet God is not thereby unjust, nor does he renounce his rights. Justice is satisfied by the Incarnate Son of God, who takes upon himself our sins and expiates them. In view of this reparation God makes just men of sinners, and his justice is vindicated (Rom. 3, 26). God's pardon of the sinner is therefore not only a moral act by which he remits the guilt of sin, but an operation which touches the inmost being of man: by the justice of God the sinner is transformed into a just man. The formal cause of this justification is the justice of God. Our Lord's Heart, symbolizing his atoning death no less than his love, is, as it were, a junction, where we unload our sins, and whence we emerge as just men. The longing of the Old Testament is here abundantly fulfilled, for man receives a share in the very justice of God; the sinner becomes a saint.

Love: The New Testament insists on love rather than on justice; for it is the love of God, made visible in Jesus Christ, that puts justice second to grace. And it is love which, again according to the Epistle to the Romans, is poured out in our hearts through the Holy Spirit who is given to us (Rom. 5, 5). The love of God for men, the love of God in men, and the love

179

of men for God, are the work of Christ, or, more exactly, the work of his Heart's love.

Full of Goodness and Love: The first invocation in this series spoke of charity, the next of love, and this one of goodness; every nuance of love is thus attributed to Jesus. This invocation suggests the Gospel picture of Christ, and depicts our Lord as the man of great love. He will not extinguish the smoking flax nor will he break the bruised reed. He does not condemn the adulterous woman nor refuse pardon of her sins to the sinner who anoints him. He heals the sick, eats with publicans and sinners, lets the little ones approach him, and has a word of forgiveness for the thief on the cross. He feels pity for the people, and like a good shepherd he goes after the lost sheep. Goodness and love are also the law which he preaches: "A new commandment I give to you, that you love one another" (John 13, 34–5). And he makes the verdict of the Last Judgement depend on the works of practical love that men have performed. His Church is the work of his love. His sacraments are inventions of his love. And the call to participation in his glory leads to the perfection of love.

Abyss of All Virtues: In the original biblical sense the abyss is the immeasurable and unfathomable primal deep. The biblical picture of the world shows the earth surrounded by the sea, vaulted by the firmament, and floating on the primal deep. "Who has measured the depth of the abyss?" (Ecclus. 1, 2). The word abyss is therefore the expression of a depth without base or bottom, of something inexhaustible; and now it is applied to Christ. All that there is of beauty or goodness, all that can adorn the soul of man, is to be found in him in a wealth and abundance that is simply immeasurable and inexhaustible. The extent of our Lord's riches in the world of the spirit is as limitless as was the primal deep in the material world. We never reach the bottom, for his treasures are unfathomable. We never run ashore, for his greatness is unbounded. We never reach an end, for his love is infinite.

Worthy of All Praise: In the Old Testament, praise is on the one hand the jubilation of creation, which for example breaks out in the psalms, and on the other hand the praise of man, who acknowledges and extols the glory of God. In the New Testament, the song of praise is raised especially in the Apocalypse. In the fifth chapter Christ is greeted with the paean of jubilation: "Thou hast redeemed us to God in thy blood out of every tribe and tongue and people and nation: and hast made us to our God a kingdom and priests. And we shall reign on the earth" (Apoc. 5, 9). Hence the outburst of sevenfold praise: "Worthy is the Lamb that was slain to receive power and divinity and wisdom and strength and honour and glory and benediction."

The litany asserts that the fullness of this praise is due especially to the Heart of our Lord. In fact, our Lord with his pierced side is the "lamb as it were slain", so that the apocalyptic jubilation which is rendered to the lamb should be applied above all to the pierced Heart of Christ. For he attained his victory by death: *Victor quia victima.*

King and Centre of All Hearts: We can catch here the echo of a deeply significant truth of Scripture. Ezechiel (11, 19) and Jeremias (32, 39), speaking of the future realm of the messianic King, say that God will give a new heart to his people. Now it is not so easy to see how this prophecy was fulfilled in the men of the New Testament. The best of them suffer from the fact that their heart has not been renewed. Yet the word of the prophet was fulfilled, in Christ. He has the new heart; and others have it in so far as they have part with him, or, as St. Paul would say, in so far as they "live in Christ". His new heart, his royal heart, is the centre of all hearts. From him the force of love streams out on other men. He is the centre of attraction, the source of their stability. The New Covenant is only inaugurated, it has not yet reached its completion. It has begun in Christ, and so the new heart is given to us in the Heart of Christ. It will be completed one day when all men live in love and possess a new heart. In the meantime, that is now, between the Then and the Hereafter, the new heart which the prophets promised is ours only through and in and with Christ, the King and Centre of all hearts.

In Whom are All the Treasures of Wisdom and Knowledge: This title is a quotation from the Epistle to the Colossians (Col. 2, 3), where true wisdom is contrasted with deceitful philosophy. This philosophy has its source here below, in human thinking and human tradition. The true *Sophia,* which is to be found in Christ, springs from above, from God. The Word of God is the real wisdom, and in Christ the Word of God is incarnate. He embodies in himself the fullness of wisdom.

In the Epistle to the Colossians knowledge is opposed to the false gnosis, the root purpose of which is to degrade divine revelation to the level of mere human knowledge. While promising a deeper knowledge of the faith, in reality it empties it of all content.

The attribution of true philosophy and perfect knowledge to Christ shows the very broad sense in which the concept of heart is understood in the litany: that it has an intellectual connotation embracing the whole life of the spirit. On the other hand it intimates that true philosophy and wisdom cross the boundaries of love and find there the secret which is the key to everything. Finally, besides this objective element there is a hint of the more subjective one, namely that the heart, or more precisely the love of man, discovers realms of knowledge which are closed to the naked intelligence. *Le coeur a ses raisons que la raison ne connaît pas.*—Pascal was alluding to a knowledge which is not the work merely of the understanding, but which engages the whole man; for ultimately it is not the intellect that knows, but the man.

When finally this invocation of the litany speaks of the "treasures" of wisdom and knowledge to be found in Christ, it is comparing these treasures with gold and silver hidden deep in the earth. We must drive galleries into the rocks and dig shafts into the earth in order to win its riches. The thrust of the soldier's lance into the Heart of our Lord brought these treasures to the surface. For the riches of our Lord's love have been laid open for all men.

In Whom Dwells All the Fullness of the Godhead: This invocation is also a quotation from the Epistle to the Colossians (2, 9). The *Pleroma* is not something intermediary between God and the world, but it is the full measure of the Godhead, and it dwells in the man Jesus. According to St. Paul it dwells in him bodily, therefore not merely in a moral sense, as Nestorius thought. Divine and human nature are joined in the unity of the person, and one can say that the Godhead dwells in Jesus in all its fullness. Therefore, as St. Paul emphasizes to the Colossians, it is not necessary to seek support elsewhere, and to rely on the "elements of the world", for we possess in Christ not merely godlike elements but the plenitude of the divine nature. These two titles of the litany of the Sacred Heart convey something of the riches, the grandeur and the abounding fullness of the Godhead which lies hidden under the shell of Christ's human Heart. A human form in its poverty bears riches that are divine. God is no longer far away, behind the barred doors of an iron-girt heaven, but close at hand, in the loving Heart of our Lord.

In Whom the Father is Well Pleased: The public life of Jesus is set between two solemn scenes, in which he is presented as the Son in whom the Father is well pleased: the baptism in the Jordan and the transfiguration on Tabor. At the Jordan (Mt. 3, 17) the Trinity becomes visible; for it is the Spirit that hovers over him in the form of a dove. The man Jesus is drawn into the fiery stream of the triune God. He is the well beloved Son. God's displeasure weighs on men, his lost sons. But on the Son of Man, who leads the lost ones home, rests God's good pleasure. Where he ranks himself with sinners and takes their sins on himself, in the baptism of penance, there alone is the good pleasure of the Father made known to the world.

On Tabor, where Moses and Elias, the Law and the Prophets, bear testimony to our Lord, Christ begins to speak more clearly of his "end", that is of his Passion and death. But before he enters into his Passion, we enjoy for one moment an anticipation of his glory, as in the antiphon of a psalm. His human form is irradiated and glorified by the Godhead; and again the voice is heard which calls him the Son in whom the Father is well pleased (Mt. 17, 5). Through him men regain the good will of God, and become sons again through the Son. That is why the angels sang at his birth of the peace which is brought to men who enjoy God's good pleasure (Lk. 2, 14).

It is clear, then, how biblical in thought and phrase is this second part of the litany of the Sacred Heart.

The first invocation of the third part forms a link: "Of whose fullness we have all received." The words come from the prologue to St. John's Gospel (John 1, 16). In him, as the only-begotten Son of the Father, is the fullness from which we have all received "grace for grace". The Gospel says further that it is concerned here with two things: "grace and truth". For he is full of grace and truth. The more man feels the agony of his own emptiness and the more he empties himself, as is said of Christ (Phil. 2, 7), the more ready a receptacle will he become for receiving of the fullness of Christ, who is the overflowing well-spring, the never-failing fountain of graces.

Desire of the Everlasting Hills: The phrase is a quotation from the Vulgate translation of the book of Genesis (49, 26). Jacob prays that the blessing he is bestowing on Joseph may endure till the coming of the desire of the everlasting hills. The phrase is therefore taken in a messianic sense. The meaning of the Hebrew text is somewhat different: "The blessings of thy father are richer than the abundant blessings of the everlasting mountains and the beauty of primaeval hills." The phrase goes back to the pastoral people's meditation on nature. These men living close to the soil, seeing the constant flow of fertilising waters into their valleys from the mountains and the heights, recognize there the source of the blessings which sustain themselves and their herds in the plains. Moreover, since they are nearer to heaven than the plains, the heights have been from antiquity the sites of sanctuaries; so nature and religion agree in recognizing that help comes from the mountains, to which men therefore raise their eyes (Ps. 120, 1).

Consequently Mount Sion is the holy mountain, for on it stands the temple. But both the material blessings of springs and the divine blessings of sanctuaries are only symbols of the God-Man, from whom, as from a towering mountain, benedictions flow into the valley. The Vulgate translation, though not literal, possesses therefore a deep meaning of its own. In Christ the Messias it sees the blessing which was promised by the Patriarch Jacob, the blessing for which all the sons of Israel have sighed, and which has now become reality. Because every blessing issues from the grace and love of our Lord, the Heart of our Lord is called the fulfilment of this desire.

Patient and Most Merciful: The phrase is found for the first time in the book of Exodus (34, 6). The Lord there shows himself to Moses in a mysterious vision, and says of himself that he is gracious and of great mercy, for he bestows his grace even to the thousandth generation.

Moses himself, in speaking to God, appeals to this phrase and to God's gracious nature (Num. 14, 18). The Psalmist in sore distress reminds men that God is patient and of great mercy (Ps. 85, 15). In the 144th Psalm (v. 8) this patience and mercy of the Lord form a special motive for praising him. The Prophet Joel exhorts: "Rend your hearts and not your garments, and turn to the Lord your God: for he is gracious and merciful, patient and rich in mercy" (Joel 2, 13). So this phrase which the Lord used of himself was taken up by Israel with joy and gratitude. Its real fulfilment is to be found in the Incarnation of God, for now God is not merely patient in the moral sense, but he has become the great *Patiens,* who suffers in patience, and makes this his suffering stand sinners in good stead. His patience is therefore the cause of his mercy; and conversely he endures all that befalls him because he has pity on the people. Between his patience and his mercy there exists a mysterious reciprocity.

Rich to All Who Invoke Thee: The phrase comes from the Epistle to the Romans (10, 12). Jews and Gentiles, says St. Paul, must indeed confess themselves guilty and hold their peace before God; but if they cry to him, he will listen to them, whether Jews or Gentiles, because he is rich unto all that call upon him. God's predilection is no longer confined to one single people. Christ is the Saviour of the world. The national synagogue is replaced by the Church of all peoples. Wherever men call upon Christ, they find a hearing. The invitation is universal because God's love knows no frontiers. So the Heart of our Lord, which brings us this infinite love, is the ultimate reason for the infinity and catholicity of grace. God gives without counting. All who invoke him can draw from his riches.

Fountain of Life and Holiness: This invocation originates in the psalm-verse: "Thou shalt make them drink of the torrent of thy pleasure: for with thee is the fountain of life" (Ps. 35, 10). Bubbling fountains and flowing water recur constantly in the imagery of the Bible. The first page of Holy Scripture mentions the stream of Paradise. Isaias (12, 3; 49, 10; 55, 1) wrote of the future messianic kingdom, that men would draw water in joy from the fountains of the Saviour. Every year on the feast of Tabernacles the procession went from the Temple to the pool of Siloe, there to draw water and recall the help of the Lord, who in the desert made water flow from the rock, and at the same time to prefigure the living rock in the desert of time: *"And the rock was Christ"* (I Cor. 10, 4). Jeremias calls God the fountain of living water (Jer. 2, 13) in contrast to the dried-up cisterns of human wisdom; and Ezechiel (47, 1 ff.) describes the torrents of water flowing down to the right side of the temple in the new Jerusalem. Jesus himself spoke to the Samaritan woman at the well of Jacob about the living water which he would give (John 4, 10); and at his public appearance on the feast of Tabernacles he cried out: "If any man thirst, let him come to me, and let him drink, who believes in me" (John 7, 38). At the crucifixion the soldier struck with his lance, as once Moses with his staff, at the seemingly closed rock of this dead Heart, and out flowed the waters of salvation. These waters, of which the prophets spoke, are the abundant graces of the messianic era (Joel 2, 28). So the water which issues from the Heart of our Lord is a sign of his spirit, which he will pour out over his own. At this point the themes of Christ's death and the effusion of the Spirit to revivify the Church, merge into one. When the Messias comes again and his Kingdom reaches its perfection, he will lead his own to the "fountains of life" (Apoc. 7, 17) and give them to drink "water out of the fountain of life" (Apoc. 21,6). A spring will gush forth and flow through the middle of the new Jerusalem as a "stream of life" (Apoc. 22, 1), and make the new earth into a Paradise. So this invocation shows the progressive realization of the Old Testament promise through Christ, leading to its perfect fulfilment at his Second Coming. It is clear that the secret of the history of salvation is the love, and therefore the Heart, of our Lord. Man should thirst for this love as the hart for the fountains of water (Ps. 41, 2).

Propitiation for Our Sins: This phrase from the first Epistle of St. John (2, 2) focuses attention on the idea of reparation. The gracious God was antagonized by the sins of men, but the propitiation of the God-Man made him favourable to us once more. This reparation is made through his death on the Cross (Rom. 3, 25; Eph. 1, 7). Christ marks the turning-point in world history from reprobation to redemption, the revolution which brings the apostates back to God, makes them friends instead of strangers, turns curse into blessing, rejection into predilection. Sin becomes the *felix culpa*—the happy fault; and all this is brought about by the love of our Lord's Heart, which is stronger than hatred, so that his reparation overcomes "not alone our sins, but the sins of the whole world" (I John 2, 2).

Heart of Jesus, Filled with Reproaches: This text from the book of Lamentations (Lam. 3, 30) is true primarily of the man who conforms to God's will, and then of the humiliated people of Israel. But Christ, as the son of David, gathers up in himself the greatness and the history of this whole people, and is the consummation of that history in his lowliness as in his exaltation. He is the one filled with reproaches, despised by his own, rejected by the chosen people, cast out by the sons of the household. He who alone truly glorifies God is condemned as a blasphemer. The author of life is delivered over to death. The 21st Psalm draws a terrifyingly vivid picture of the Christ laden with ignominy.

Heart of Jesus, Bruised for Our Offences: This phrase is taken from one of the mysterious "servant of Yahweh" hymns (Is. 53, 5). "He has borne our infirmities and carried our sorrows ... he was bruised for our sins." This prophecy too was fulfilled in Jesus. The anointed king and the Son of God has become a servant, and takes on himself the fate of a slave, to be beaten and bruised because he has charged himself with the sins of Israel and of all mankind. Two themes run through the messianic prophecies, the one describing the royal grandeur of the Messias, the other his abasement to the rank of a slave. Both these prophetic themes are fulfilled in Christ. Therefore over the Cross on which he was executed as a slave stood the inscription: *King of the Jews.*

Obedient unto Death: In this text from the Epistle to the Philippians (2, 8) Paul has resumed the whole life and activity of our Lord under one short formula. Christ as the Word of the Father is essentially something spoken, therefore a listener. In the Incarnate Word this listening becomes an obedience, and in particular an obedience to the divine command that he surrender and sacrifice his whole life: an obedience therefore unto death (Heb. 5,8). When the Father wills that this death should be death on the Cross, the acquiescence of obedience is the deepest possible humiliation, but at the same time an elevation to the heights of glory: "For which cause God also has exalted him." Christ emptied and dispossessed himself so far as to endure the nameless death of a slave. Yet in him that is not an emptiness but a fullness. Hence the swift ascent from abasement to glory. The slave becomes Lord, the obedient Christ is given all power. The Word is not only spoken but speaking. And now he is no longer uttering simply the word of creation, and calling the world out of nothing into existence, but a word of grace, which gives life to the dead of soul, and calls the new world of grace into existence (Rom. 4, 17).

Heart of Jesus, Pierced with the Lance: The lance which pierced the side of Jesus (John 19, 34) opened a retreat where souls can take refuge, as birds find asylum in the clefts of the rock (Cant. 2, 14). This piercing is an opening, *latus eius aperuit,* and consequently a revelation, a disclosure of our Lord's love. It was the lance that pierced the Heart of Christ, but it was love that made this mortal thrust the beginning of salvation, and turned the Cross into

"the tree on which true Life expired

and life for us through death acquired."

God, who permits evil in order that from it he may draw good, shows that his bleeding Heart has become, through the power of his love, the salvation of all hearts.

Source of All Consolation: This title of the Sacred Heart recalls the second Epistle to the Corinthians (1, 3), where Paul speaks of the "God of all consolation". Christ is not seeking but dispensing consolation. We do not come to him to comfort but to be comforted. That does not call in question the type of comforting of our Lord expounded in the encyclical *Miserentissimus Redemptor;* but the litany speaks of Christ only as the source, not as the object of consolation.

For he is the "Consolation of Israel" (Lk. 2, 25). That is why, in the Sermon on the Mount, he called the mourners blessed; for they will be comforted. They will find in him, the Saviour, their only consolation in the comfortlessness of sin and of bodily and spiritual death; for his death brought life. In the desolation of his abandonment by God he uttered the dying word: "My God, my God, why hast thou forsaken me?" in order to call us all to the presence of God and so into the kingdom of consolation. Through the surrender of his life he has given us his Spirit, the *Consolator Optimus* of the sequence for Pentecost.

Our Life and Our Resurrection: This was the claim of Jesus himself, as he spoke to Martha at Lazarus' grave: "I am the resurrection and the life" (John 11, 25). Just as he called Lazarus out of the grave, so he was himself called out of the grave by his Father on Easter morning, and became the "first-born from the dead" (Col. 1, 18). With this he pushed open the portals of life for us and opened the womb of the earth so that one day we may all enter, through him and with him, to the light of eternal life. He is therefore not only our resurrection from the death of sin and our new life in grace, but also our guarantee that we shall not fall prey to the second death (Apoc. 20, 6). Instead, through the resurrection of the flesh and the eternal life of the soul, we shall share in that glorious life which is his in all its plenitude.

Our Peace and Our Reconciliation: "It pleased God" says St. Paul, "to reconcile all things to himself through Christ ... making peace through the blood of the cross" (Col. 1, 20). This mention of peace and reconciliation implies that through sin a state of war arose between men and God, but that Christ as the *Rex Pacificus* has restored peace. *In terra pax hominibus* is the first song heard at his birth in Bethlehem (Lk. 2, 14). "Peace be to you," is the first word that the risen Lord speaks to his disciples (John 20, 19). His life is set between greetings of peace, but the price of this peace is the Heart's blood which he poured out on the Cross.

Victim for Our Sins: When Jesus spoke of "my blood that is poured out for the remission of sins" (Mt. 26, 28), he showed himself as the fulfilment of the blood-offerings of the Old Testament. Sin demands bloody atonement, and this was rendered for sinners by the Sinless One, who thereby triumphed over sin and Satan. This title of the Sacred Heart recalls the ninth and tenth chapters of the Epistle to the Hebrews, where St. Paul contrasts the greatness and power of the sacrifice of Christ with the inefficacy of the Old Testament offerings, which had to be constantly repeated, and effected only an external, legal purification, leaving sin quite untouched.

Salvation of Those Who Hope in Thee: The notion of salvation runs through the whole of Scripture; for the message of the Bible is that men lost salvation through sin, but are saved and sanctified by the Saviour Jesus Christ. The name Jesus means "Yahweh is Salvation". Jesus is therefore salvation incarnate; he is salvation for all those who set their hope neither on themselves nor on men, but on him, and who count on his present help and his future Second Coming.

Hope of Those Who Die in Thee: In the Epistle to the Colossians (1, 5) St. Paul asserts that hope is laid up for us in heaven. This hope is nothing other than Christ himself; for in the same letter (1, 27) Paul reveals that the real secret of his writing and of all his activity is the presence in our midst of Christ, the "hope of glory". He himself is in glory; if then he is in our midst, we already have in him the beginning of glory. If we abide in him we shall have the fulfilment of glory; and the passage to that fulfilment is death. So Christ is truly the hope of those who die in him.

Delight of All the Saints: One is reminded of the bride in the Canticle of Canticles "flowing with delights, leaning upon her beloved" (Cant. 8, 5); for the man who relies entirely upon our beloved Lord receives from him a profound peace. Or again one thinks of Ezechiel's phrase, *In deliciis paradisi Dei fuisti* (Ez. 28, 13); for this garden of delights is to be found wherever God, the source of all joy, is present. So the saints found the paradise of their soul and of their life in the company of Christ, the Incarnate God. In the Book of Proverbs (8, 31) divine Wisdom declares that it is her delight to be with the children of men; this word of Scripture, astonishing though it be, finds its fulfilment in Christ, the incarnate Wisdom of God. And if he delights in the company of the

191

children of men, then all the more is his presence among them their greatest joy, at least for those who penetrate in faith and love into the mystery of his Heart.

The litany of the Sacred Heart, which has spoken so explicitly of sin and reparation, closes here with an allusion to the Paradise with which mankind's story opened, and with which the new earth will begin. The beginning and the end here come together in the joy and delight of the Lord.

It may seem strange that the invocations of this litany, permeated as they are with the language and thought of the Bible, are addressed not simply to the Person of Christ, but to his Heart; but that should serve to recall us constantly to the objective mystery of Christ's bloody immolation on the Cross, and the subjective mystery of the infinite love which inspired his sacrifice. And none will appreciate this litany more keenly or draw more copiously from its treasures than the readers of the Bible.

THE DOGMATIC AND RELIGIOUS VALUE
OF THE DEVOTION
TO THE SACRED HEART

THE object of this chapter is to indicate the spiritual power and value of devotion to the Sacred Heart. This has indeed already been discussed indirectly. The true riches of the devotion can be best gauged from its own nature and from its history, though an adequate appraisal of them would require not only an intuitive grasp of the whole realm of theology and popular devotion, but also that vision which only God enjoys, of the secret history of men's hearts; for no human eyes can see nor earthly words describe the intimate encounter of man's heart with God's.

Here we wish to review the most important and widespread advantages of the devotion, the fruits which are so closely linked to the genuine practice of the devotion that they invariably accompany it. Naturally this in no way credits the devotion with a monopoly of these advantages, as though they were to be found in no other form of Christian life. These claims are meant in a positive not an exclusive sense. True religion, wherever it is found, springs from the heart and returns to the heart, even if it does not use the language and imagery of devotion to the Sacred Heart. Our intention in these last pages is simply to show how the devotion, both in theory and in practice, is a mighty force capable of meeting the great and inescapable demands of true religious life.

A Catholic's religious outlook should be formed not merely by personal experiences, but by objective truth and objective values. In other words, our piety should be founded on dogma. It should take its shape from faith and Revelation. The more deeply the religious life is rooted in the central truths of dogma, the richer will be its development along the lines of organic growth.

So we must ask first of all for the dogmatic credentials of the Church's devotion to the Sacred Heart. It must be confessed that in the devotion as commonly practised, men are by no means fully aware of these riches; at this point piety has often parted company all too radically with theology. This fact should not, however, dampen genuine devotion to the Sacred Heart, but should be taken as an urgent challenge: our teaching and preaching should expose the dogmatic foundations and connections of the devotion more clearly and effectively than they have hitherto done. In showing here the central position of a "Sacred Heart theology", we do not rule out the possibility of developing dogma from some other angle, and building just as vigorous a spiritual life round some other key idea. Nevertheless it is worth asking whether the theology of the Sacred Heart does not lead us into the very centre of dogma.

The Cross of Christ is the hub of world history and of human history: it is here that grace brings God and man together, and that man surrenders his whole self to God. But the centre of this central Cross is the pierced Heart of our Lord. In this mystery, if we take it in all its breadth and depth, all the important lines of Catholic dogma converge. All the great truths touching the Blessed Trinity and our own salvation are linked to the mystery of the Sacred Heart.

With its vertical beam the Cross points out beyond itself into the mystery of the Triune God, who is infinite love. The spectacle of the crucified Christ and of his pierced Heart taught us, as no words, not even the words of Revelation, could teach, that God is love. For this Christ who is raised up on the Cross with an emptied Heart is the "image of the invisible God". "Who sees me, sees the Father." If his pierced and streaming Heart symbolizes his utter self-surrender, we can recognize through it the prodigal love of God himself. And just as this Heart, pierced in token of its love, is the centre of Christ's figure on Golgotha, so the boundless love which it symbolizes forms the very centre of the mystery of God himself. That is the first dogmatic message of the Heart of Jesus: God is infinite love, love in himself, and love for us.

But it is above all in the mystery of love that this infinitely loving God is a trinity, Father, Son and Holy Ghost; and the most arresting revelation of this mystery is again the image of the crucified Christ, with the pierced and streaming Heart.

Let us attempt to make this truth a little clearer. This pierced and streaming Heart discloses to us, in a manner surpassing even the miracle of the Incarnation and its subsequent development and completion, the prodigal love of the Father. "God so loved the world that he not only did not spare his only-begotten Son," but had him assume a human heart, and had it, the very Heart of God, bleed to death to prove his fatherly love for men. At a deeper level, by surrendering his Son to the death of the Cross and the draining of his Heart's blood, the Father figured forth the "mission" of the Son, which began in the bosom of the Trinity and terminated in the world; in that "procession" the Son went forth to shed his Heart's blood "outside the camp" (Heb. 13, 12).

The Sacred Heart reveals too the Son's loving surrender to his Father's will. The morning prayer of the incarnate God is completed in this evening sacrifice: "See, I come to do thy will. Thy law is set in the midst of my heart." The obedience of Jesus' life, rooted in a Heart "obedient unto death", is but the extension into the world of the Son's union with the Father within the Godhead. The will of the Father is his one love, his only passion.

The pierced Heart holds then a double revelation for us: first, of the man Jesus surrendering his Heart to his heavenly Father; secondly, at a deeper level, of the eternal Son's perfect union with his Father in the mystery of the Blessed Trinity. The Son's gift of himself springs from his Heart, from the inmost centre of his Person, and therefore from the purest love; whether it be offered in the historic sacrifice of the Cross or eternally in the timeless life of the Trinity.

As the loving relationship between Father and Son in the mystery of the triune life, the Holy Ghost proceeds from all eternity as the "fruit" and the "gift" of God. If it is true that the essential relation within the Godhead between Father and Son becomes visible in the symbol and the reality of the pierced Heart on the Cross, then this Heart should show us the Holy Ghost; and so in fact it does. The Holy Ghost compasses in himself all the treasures of Redemption, and as such he is symbolized in the blood and water streaming from Jesus' Heart. The prophets of the Old Testament saw the messianic riches of salvation under the image of flowing waters. Jesus himself employed this image, and during the symbolic and prophetic water-procession at his last feast of Tabernacles, he spoke about it: "If any man thirst, let him come to me, and let him drink who believes in me." St. John adds in explanation: "This he said of the spirit which those were to receive who believed in him. For there was not yet spirit, because Jesus was not yet glorified" (John 7, 37–39). According to Jesus' own words (John 12, 28; 13, 31; 16, 5; 17, 4–5), that hour of glory was to come with his crucifixion on Golgotha and the completion of his sacrifice in the resurrection. On Good Friday, when the Passion is over, the waters of salvation break out from the depths of the triune life. Ever since that hour "the Holy Ghost has been poured out upon all flesh."

If then we see what happened on the Cross not simply as a passing event but as a symbol which points deeper, if we savour its full significance, we can glimpse there the features of the Blessed Trinity; through the pierced Heart of the crucified Christ we see with the eyes of faith into the mystery of triune love.

It is a pity that these deeper implications are largely ignored in the popular cult of the Sacred Heart, which generally stops short at Christ, often indeed at his humanity. It is a pity; for all the love that comes down to us from above must spring from the Heart of the Father and pass to that of the Son, there to become (through the mediation of the Virgin Mary, image of the Church) the heart of the world, and so to touch our own hearts. Conversely all our love for God, every ascent of our heart, must be carried by the Holy Ghost through the Heart of the Son to its goal in the Heart of the Father.

If we understand all the necessary reserves and qualifications, we can say that the plan of Redemption is to make of us all a single heart, the Heart of the Son in the presence of the Father. That is the ultimate meaning of all consecration to the Sacred Heart and of all the mystical experiences of an exchange of hearts: with Christ and through Christ and in Christ, one with his Heart, we unite ourselves with his perfect surrender to the Father.

Because the whole Christ, no part excepted, is a Mediator, his Heart too is entirely devoted to the task of mediating between the Heart of the Father and the hearts of men. When the veneration of the Sacred Heart becomes more conscious of its essential basis in the Trinity, it not only enriches itself, but also harmonizes more naturally with the Liturgy, which is sustained and guided by this doctrine of the mediation of Christ.

The vertical beam, showing the way to the primal mystery of the Blessed Trinity, is not the only pointer on the Cross. For the tree of the Cross is rooted in our earth, which is soaked with blood from the Redeemer's Heart; consequently all the lines of the Christian doctrine of salvation converge in the mystery of the pierced Heart of Christ. This Heart was offered up for the salvation of us all. As it is the source of all redemptive graces, it is also the central point of all the good news of salvation. Our understanding of the central position of the Sacred Heart in the scheme of Redemption will be considerably enlarged if we glance at the doctrine of the Fathers and the central notions of their theology of the Sacred Heart.

The mystery of the Sacred Heart presents the most compelling witness to the true and integral Incarnation of God for the salvation of men. This is not a *post factum* interpretation, reading back an alien emphasis and meaning into the Heart of Jesus. St. John himself wished by his Gospel to defend the awful reality of the Incarnation against all the spiritualizing tendencies of the gnostics. That is why the climax of his book (chapter 19) records the piercing of the Heart of Christ. This is his testimony to the two truths, the Incarnation and the Redemption.

First as to the reality of the Incarnation: was it just the appearance of a body that suffered—with apparent, not real sufferings? No, the body that was delivered up to death was a real body with a physical heart. In his first Epistle St. John develops this thought, to stress the reality of our salvation. We are redeemed not merely by the Spirit, but by the flesh of the Incarnate God, by this body of Christ which was delivered up to death on the Cross, by the blood of this dedicated Heart (I John 5, 6).

The mystery of the Sacred Heart displays the plan of the Incarnation in the light of a Redemption from sin. The crucified Christ with the pierced Heart is the Lamb of God, who frees us from the sins of the world by taking them upon himself; his Heart is wounded for the crimes of our hearts. He is the great expiatory victim which, as Jeremias had prophesied, was plighted and forfeited as a pledge for us all (Jer. 30, 21). The mystery of the pierced Heart manifests, in a manner more profound and arresting than any other image or mystery, the true character of the Redemption. It shows the love and obedience of Christ's Heart atoning, and more than atoning, for the sinful rebellion of our hearts. St. Paul (Phil. 2, 5–10) placed the central mystery of Redemption in that *kenosis* by which Christ emptied and dispossessed himself, and of this *kenosis* there is no more eloquent symbol than Christ's Heart, pierced, and emptied of every drop of blood.

This image of the pierced Heart bears a mark which characterizes the whole economy of Redemption, the mark of apparent frustration: the love which has given itself to the last receives in return—at least to all outward appearance—only abuse and ingratitude, coolness and indifference, so that the blood appears to have been spilled and the Heart surrendered in vain. Here we are faced with the most arresting image of helpless love. Nothing could be more exposed than the defenceless heart of a crucified man. But it is precisely in this way that the innermost secret of the Redemption appears: God gives his pierced Heart to those who have pierced it. This is how the Redemption will be achieved: the helplessness of the heart, which is delivered up and exposed to every abuse and maltreatment, must finally bend our proud hearts and inflame our cold hearts.

Now a third mystery is presented to us: the Incarnation of Christ and the Redemption of the world are prolonged in space and time by *the Church*. Therefore the Church too is intimately linked to the mystery of the pierced Heart. The Fathers of the Church, with the penetrating gaze of faith, discovered a double connection between the Church and the Heart of Jesus: birth and marriage. Both connections are based on Holy Scripture.

On the Cross, the Church issues from the Heart of Jesus in a mysterious birth. That which was once foreshadowed in the creation of Eve from the side of Adam is here fulfilled: from the opened side of Christ, the second Adam, sleeping in the death of the Cross, his holy bride, the virgin Church, is born. This was a central doctrine of patristic theology and it has never since been forgotten. We can still catch an echo of it in the hymn for the feast of the Sacred Heart:

> *Ex corde scisso Ecclesia*
> *Christo iugata nascitur —*
> From Jesus' opened Heart is born
> The Church, the bride of Christ.

The theme recurs at least five times in the Lessons of the Breviary during the octave[1] of the feast, and is echoed in texts from the patristic and medieval tradition.

The notion of the Church's birth is connected with that of her marriage to Christ, her bridegroom-in-blood; for the hour of her birth is also the hour of her marriage. Red and white is the bridal dress, blood and water from the Heart of the bridegroom. Our Lord gives the Church his own Heart, in order to receive from her the heart of redeemed mankind.

So the Church is a mystery which was born of the pierced Heart of Christ; the thought should deepen our notion of the Church, which is too often one-sided and legalistic. The mystical body of Christ is nourished from the source of living water in Christ's Heart.

The theology of the Redemption leads us on from the Church to the mystery *of the seven Sacraments*. One sometimes hears the complaint that in our preaching the Sacraments have been materialized, and presented almost as automatic vehicles of grace. But we have seen the beginnings of a movement to stress their close connection with Christ and the Church. Theology considers the Sacraments as an afterglow and extension of the Incarnation, as means of the Redemption and channels of the grace merited by the great Sacrament of the Cross. Now if we link up this theological consideration with the mystery of the Sacred Heart, both the Sacred Heart devotion and the spirituality of the Sacraments will profit by it.

Just as the Heart of Jesus and the Church form an intimate unity, so the Sacraments have a close connection with both. They represent at first sight the maternal fecundity of the Church, the bride of Christ, who never ceases to bear and rear children, heal and strengthen them, and lead them to their maturity; but Mother Church draws all her vitality from the Heart of Jesus.

The stream of blood and water from the Heart of Jesus is a sym-

---

[1] See page 1, note 1.

bol of the seven Sacraments. The imagery of water immediately suggests Baptism, through which men are washed clean from the guilt of the first Adam and incorporated into the second Adam. The blood symbolizes the Blessed Eucharist, to which the other Sacraments are subordinated, for it is noblest of them all. As the death on the Cross appears in patristic theology as a marriage, so the Eucharist is essentially a nuptial Sacrament, the highest earthly participation of the soul in the marriage between Christ and his Church. Because it is a nuptial Sacrament, it is also preeminently a Sacrament of the heart.

All the fullness of the seven Sacraments is contained in the two chief Sacraments, Baptism and the Eucharist; the seven channels of grace flow in an unbroken stream from the pierced Heart of the crucified Christ, and fulfil the promise which he made at his last feast of Tabernacles. This notion is essential to the Church's theology of the Sacred Heart; witness the liturgy for the octave of the feast, in which the idea of the Sacred Heart as the source of the Sacraments recurs on nine different occasions.

Through the Sacraments the Church lavishes upon us all the graces of the Sacred Heart; and with this we have reached the final element of this doctrine of salvation. The blood and water from Christ's Heart stand ultimately for the stream of all the graces of the Cross, the stream which is sweeping us along to *eternal life;* one day it will be transformed into the river of the new Jerusalem, foretold by the Apocalypse and by Jeremias in his vision of the stream from the right side of the temple.

The Heart pierced by a lance (John 19, 34) and the Lamb that was slain (Apoc. 5, 6) represent in this way, for time and eternity, the source of divine life for redeemed mankind. As long as we are pilgrims here on earth, we drink the new life from the Heart of Jesus crucified. In the heavenly Jerusalem we shall be given to drink from the inexhaustible fountain of the immolated Lamb.

It may be possible to gather even from these slight indications how the dogmatic consideration of the Sacred Heart is the point on which the great truths of Revelation and the fundamental facts of our Redemption converge. All the great dogmas which should shape our Christian life radiate from the Heart of Jesus and lead us back to it.

Though a distinction was made between two groups of dogmatic truths, the doctrine about God and the doctrine about salvation, the two themes intersect in the mystery of Christ's Heart. It is in this Heart, delivered up for us, that the mysterious love of the Trinity breaks in upon our unregenerate world and saves it. This Heart is the open door to a blessed community of life with our Lord; it points our way home to the Triune God, who folds us to his Heart in eternal love.

So the dogmatic consideration of the mystery of the Sacred Heart reveals a universe unimaginably broad and deep. But it has still more to offer; we complain today of the estrangement between piety and dogma. It is a charge to which devotion to the Sacred Heart, at least in many of its popular forms, must plead guilty. Yet the estrangement is far from being inevitable. The dogmatic foundations are ready at hand, and history shows us that before ever the devotion was practised, the Fathers of the Church had established a theology of the Sacred Heart. If we wish to make our modern devotion more effective, we must draw freely from this centuries-old tradition. It will teach us what a vital force theology can be, and what depths of theology lie behind the Church's cult of the Sacred Heart.

A truth properly grasped will always bring practical results. So the dogmatic riches of the mystery of the Sacred Heart cannot but show themselves in a revitalized religious life. We wish in the remarks which follow to pick out some of the essential elements, in order to demonstrate in them the practical value of the veneration of the Sacred Heart. Again we are claiming no

202

monopoly. Every one of these advantages can surely be found in other approaches of Catholic piety; we shall not discuss whether they are to be found elsewhere in such abundance and such harmonious unity as in the devotion to the Sacred Heart. For we are concerned only with showing positively the real benefits of a genuine and deep devotion to the Sacred Heart.

The devotion is centred on the inner life of our Lord, with all its riches of love for the Father and for men. It teaches us not merely to study his words and his actions, but to trace them back to their well-springs in the inmost centre of his Person. The object of the devotion is itself a constant incentive to a deepening of our interior life.

It is true that the proper understanding of the Heart of Jesus is possible only to the man who wishes seriously for a deeper interior life. It is beyond the capacity of characters which are by nature superficial or markedly extrovert or egocentric. But the man who recognizes and appreciates spiritual values will, through meditation on the Heart of Jesus, reach a mature, interior piety of the heart, as opposed to a merely verbal devotion. It is hardly necessary to prove at length the need for such a deepening of one's piety, not only from the very nature of the religious life, but also on account of the specially insistent demands of our time. We live in an atmosphere of restlessness and hurry, with all the fibres of our hearts we are drawn outside ourselves, and even with the greatest good will we find it difficult to achieve interior peace and recollection. This strong centrifugal tendency calls for a still stronger force to draw us back to the interior. There can be no doubt that a genuine devotion to the Sacred Heart does exercise a magnetism of this sort, restoring order and calm and a taste for the interior life. There is no greater threat to the apostolic activity of priests and laymen than absorption in the outside world, so that their work degenerates into mere activism, organization and routine. We forget too easily the springs from which all apostolic activity draws its life, namely prayer, meditation and the other sources of grace itself.

The relationship between devotion to the Sacred Heart and the apostolate is not confined to their link with the interior life. The mystery of the Sacred Heart carries within itself forces which powerfully stimulate the apostolate. No believing heart can think about the Heart of Jesus consuming itself for others down to the last drop of its blood without feeling a strong urge to a similar unselfish sacrifice in the service of souls. Conversely, a man's zeal for the apostolate is a reliable criterion for the genuineness and depth of his devotion to the Sacred Heart. A devotion which in no way urges a man to apostolic work, even if only in the form of loving service, prayer, and sacrifice, should arouse our suspicions.

The great apostolic virtues are movingly portrayed in the Heart of Jesus: humility, obedience, zeal for souls, and confidence in God.

Devotion to the Heart of Jesus is surely the most effective remedy against the "modern heresy of action" (Pius XII) in that particular form which infects the apostolate. At the centre of the Redemption stands not an action (in our modern activist sense) but a sacrifice. So a genuine apostolate requires an equilibrium between action and suffering (or passion, in the etymological sense of the word). If there is a "passive" note of this kind in devotion to the Sacred Heart, it should be seen as a reflection of that redemptive work which gave Christianity its character, the Passion of Jesus on the Cross.

In her devotion to the Heart of Jesus the Church lays a strong emphasis not only on sacrifice but also on the primacy of grace. This primacy is of course something that every believing Christian and every genuine spirituality will acknowledge; grace infinitely surpasses in value all natural goods, and it is absolutely necessary for salvation, transcending in importance all merely human efforts. The Church has condemned the opposing opinions in the heresies of Pelagianism and Semipelagianism. Yet for all these condemnations there have always been quite a number of Pelagians and Semipelagians who, in practice at least, attach too great an importance to man's natural powers and activity, and relegate grace to the subservient role of facilitating or embellishing human action.

The devotion to the Sacred Heart opposes this misconception with a solemn revelation of the sovereignty, the riches, and the fruitfulness of divine grace. This is immediately clear if we think of the dogmatic truths which are bound up with this mystery, of the supernatural view taken of the Church and of the whole plan of salvation, or of the significance of the Sacraments in connection with the Sacred Heart. But besides its dogmatic connections, the devotion reaffirms the primacy of grace in its practical demands for sacrifice and reparation.

A further advantage of devotion to the Sacred Heart appears when we consider it on the psychological level: the devotion harnesses the forces of the emotions for the benefit of the whole spiritual life.

In the devotion as practised in our day, the emotional elements have undoubtedly been overemphasized, and its prayers and hymns have often betrayed a counterfeit sentimentality. But the abuse of these valuable powers should not prevent us from trying to employ them in the proper way. The findings of depth psychology have put us in a better position for appraising and valuing properly the power of the emotions than the rationalistic generation which preceded us.

For us there is no difficulty in submitting to the demand that true piety must be based on well-established facts and on a will fully conscious of its goal. A knowledge of the faith, and an ascetical effort that involves mortification and the conscious cultivation of Christian attitudes, form an essential part of the spiritual life; but they are not everything. Man is not made up simply of intelligence and will. The more highly gifted a man is, the deeper his emotions. Consequently the man who cultivates only his understanding and his will must inevitably cripple himself, particularly in his spiritual life. One fine day the repressed and thwarted forces of his emotions will take a fierce revenge.

Now though devotion to the Sacred Heart is based on the solid truths of faith and on a powerful appeal to the will and to a man's zeal for holiness, it also arouses and directs certain of his emotional forces. It helps him to be completely human in his most fundamental relationship, in his dealings with God. The emotional forces so extensively cultivated by devotion to the Sacred Heart are no mere baroque embellishments of the religious life, with which we could easily dispense. If we extend our notion of heart to include all our emotional and affective life, we are admitting that the heart reaches to depths far beyond the range of the conscious faculties of intellect and will.

At a time when the increasingly mechanical and utilitarian attitude of men has impoverished human life and human relations, we have double reason for cultivating our emotional capacities. Now contemplation of the Heart of Jesus fosters the most positive and sublime emotions, and the noblest passions, by giving us a share in his joys and sufferings, in the exaltation and the woe, the happiness and the distress of his Heart, and by the human heart's growth towards a greater union of life and love with the Heart of Christ.

We need not fear that by cultivating the hidden riches of the emotions by means of devotion to the Sacred Heart, we shall compromise the religious character of the devotion. Any progress made in this direction serves only to open man and his heart to a deeper dedication to God and to an attitude that is essentially religious. The more a man realizes the potentialities of his human nature, the more attraction will he find in God, and the closer will he find himself to his Creator and Father.

The Heart of Jesus is a Heart of the purest love, for love forms the very centre of his Person and the driving force of his life and death. Love is therefore the soul of Christianity and of the Christian life. In the very centre of our faith stands the mighty phrase of St. John that God is love; and we experience for ourselves the blessed truth that he is also wholly love for us. So we must try to realize, not just intellectually but from the depths of our hearts, that we should love him and that we may love him "with our whole heart".

But both the love of God for men and the love of men for God are movingly revealed in the pierced Heart of Christ on the Cross: the wonderful love of the Father and the dedicated love of the Son.

No doubt other mysteries are capable of kindling men's love for God, because they too are revelations of love: the crib of Bethlehem, the Way of the Cross to Golgotha, the miracle of the Blessed Eucharist. But in the Heart of our Lord we meet in its most arresting form the sum and substance of all the revelations of God's love. That is why this sign and this mystery of the Heart has been given with a special urgency to our age, when "love has grown cold". It should challenge us to a warm love for God and men, which will fill our hearts and inspire all our actions. This mystery of the Sacred Heart not only throws down the challenge, but it imparts enthusiasm and strength to those who take it up.

Our Christianity has grown too sober. We would be better for some of the holy intoxication of that Spirit of Pentecost whom we find in the Heart of Jesus: *Laeti bibamus sobriam ebrietatem Spiritus.*

All honour to the Code of Canon Law and the organization of the Church; they fulfil an essential function in the Kingdom of God. But they are never going to set the world on fire. Only love can do that—or hatred. And because hatred toils with such diabolical energy, love is called forth for a last encounter. The well-springs of our human love have run dry; but their divine source flows untiringly from the pierced Heart of Christ on the Cross.

One last benefit of the devotion remains to be indicated, one that includes all the others and gives them their full meaning: a deep personal union of the human heart with the Heart of Christ.

Many a Christian will achieve close and cordial union with our Lord by other ways than this, for true Christian piety is always Christocentric. But the converse is also true; the more closely anyone is joined to Christ, the nearer does he stand to the Sacred Heart, and the more closely will his piety approximate to that of the Sacred Heart devotion.

The devotion to the Sacred Heart is unique in its insistence on the soul's conscious and intimate union with Christ our Lord in grace and faith. Its supreme model is the apostle St. John resting on the breast of our Lord at the Last Supper. The mystics have given us wonderful insights into this intimacy of the heart with their accounts of the exchange of hearts, an experience first recorded by St. Luitgard of St. Trond, and recurring in the life of St. Catherine of Siena, St. Margaret Mary Alacoque and several others. The reality behind these images is an essential part of devotion to the Sacred Heart.

It is in this devotion that Christianity is revealed as a truly personal religion; for at its centre stands a person, who is envisaged not only in his outward aspects but in his Heart, the centre and source of his personality. The act of self-surrender which we make in this devotion is personal in two ways: first, because it involves the innermost core of the human person; and secondly, because every man is unique, and each man's surrender will therefore be stamped by his own inimitable personality. True, the devotion has regular forms of expression, and in its interior development is characterized by certain common features. But within these general norms there are as many types of devotion to the Sacred Heart as there are hearts to pay it their homage.

Where the Spirit of God is, there is freedom. So every man on his journey to God may, indeed must, follow his own spiritual path, under the guidance of the Holy Ghost in the Church.

It is the same Holy Ghost who through St. Margaret Mary and through the mouth of the Church directs us so insistently to the mystery of the Heart of Jesus.

The injunctions of Paray-le-Monial are addressed to all Christians; but every man must fulfil his obligations in his own way.

ENCYCLICAL LETTER
(HAURIETIS AQUAS) OF POPE PIUS XII
ON DEVOTION TO THE SACRED HEART
OF JESUS

The Catholic Truth Society, London, and the Translator, the Rev. Geoffrey Crawfurd B. A., are thanked for their kind permission to reprint this English version, which is based on the Latin text as published in the *Acta Apostolicae Sedis, Vol.* 48, 1956, *num.* 7.

211

"You shall draw waters with joy out of the Saviour's fountains."[1] Words of pregnant imagery by which Isaias the prophet foretold the manifold and bountiful gifts of God which the Christian Dispensation was destined to bring. These words come unbidden to Our mind as the first hundred years run out since Our Predecessor Pius IX of immortal memory yielded gladly to the prayers which reached him from all over the Catholic world and extended the feast of the Most Sacred Heart of Jesus to the universal Church.

It were impossible to enumerate the shower of heavenly blessings which the cult of the Heart of Jesus brings down on the souls of the Christian faithful. It purifies them. It renews them with supernal comfortings. It incites them to the successful quest of all the virtues. We recall the wise saying of the Apostle James: "Every best gift and every perfect gift is from above, coming down from the Father of lights."[2] He who is the Word Incarnate and our Divine Saviour, the one Mediator of grace and truth between our Father in heaven and the human race, has in these latter times bestowed upon the Church, his mystical bride, a gift of inestimable value. This gift has enabled her to undertake gigantic labours, to overcome insuperable difficulties. And in the cult of the Heart of Jesus, flourishing throughout the world like an ever spreading conflagration, we rightly recognize this gift. By this inestimable gift the Church is able to show her Divine Founder a charity more white-hot, and to bring to reali-

---

[1] *Is.* 12, 3.   [2] *Ja.* 1, 17.

zation on a wider scale the invitation of Jesus Christ recorded in St. John's Gospel, where it says: "And on the last great day of the festivity, Jesus stood and cried, saying: If any man thirst, let him come to me; and let him drink who believeth in me. As the Scripture saith: Out of his belly shall flow rivers of living water. Now this he said of the Spirit which they should receive who believed in him."[3] By these words Jesus promised that a fountain of "living water" would take its rise from his bosom; and it was not difficult for those who heard him to compare his words with the utterings of the holy prophets, Isaias, Ezechiel and Zachary, foretelling the Messianic Kingdom; nor to that prophetic rock which Moses struck, and water miraculously gushed forth from it.[4]

Divine charity has its first beginnings in the Holy Spirit who is the personal Love equally of the Father and of the Son in the bosom of the august Trinity. How rightly therefore did St. Paul, echoing almost the words of Jesus Christ, attribute to this Spirit of Love the outpouring of charity into the hearts of believers: "The charity of God is poured out in our hearts by the Holy Spirit who is given to us."[5]

There is according to Holy Scripture the closest connection between divine charity which must burst into flames in the hearts of Christians, and the Holy Spirit whose very *property* it is in God to be Love. And this connection, Venerable Brethren, makes clear to us all the real meaning and nature of that cult which is to be offered to the Heart of Jesus Christ. For on the one hand it is clear that this cult (if we consider its special meaning) is a most excellent act of religion; since it involves on our part a total and unreserved intention of giving and consecrating ourselves to the

---

[3] *John* 7, 37–39. Translator's Note.—In this passage the Holy Father uses the punctuation favoured by St. Irenaeus and St. Cyprian and some other ancient authorities. The translation therefore follows this and not the Douay version.

[4] Cfr. *Is.* 12, 3; *Ez.* 47, 1–12; *Zach.* 13, 1; *Ex.* 17, 1–7; *Num.* 20, 7–13; *I Cor.* 10, 4; *Apoc.* 7, 17; 22, 1.

[5] *Rom.* 5, 5.

Divine Redeemer's love, to which love his wounded Heart is a living pointer and symbol. While on the other hand it is equally, if not more clear that the principal idea of this cult or devotion is that we should ourselves make a return of love to the Divine Love. For it is only by force of charity that the hearts of men can be brought fully and perfectly to accept the sovereignty of Almighty God, when, that is, the affection of our human love so cleaves to the will of God as to become, so to speak, one thing with it; as it is written, "He who is joined to the Lord is one spirit."[6]

The Church has ever held and does hold the cult of the Heart of Jesus in the highest esteem. She seeks by every means to ensure that it shall flourish throughout the world and spread among Christian peoples; and she strives in every way to defend it against false charges of *naturalism* and *sentimentalism*. But, and We grieve to say it, there have been in the past and there are to-day Christians who do not hold this noble devotion in the same esteem and honour. And among these are even some who claim to be inspired by zeal for the Catholic Religion and for their own personal sanctification.

"If thou didst know the gift of God."[7] By these words, Venerable Brethren, conscious of Our duty as the guardian and almoner (chosen by the mysterious counsel of Providence) of that treasure of faith and piety which the Divine Redeemer has entrusted to his Church, We admonish them one and all. They are Our sons. And yet, although the Heart of Jesus is triumphing over error and man's neglect; although this devotion has permeated his mystical Body, still they are led astray by prejudice and some of them go so far as to consider it unsuited, if not actually harmful, to the spiritual needs of the Church and of the human race, so pressing in this our time. Some fail to distinguish between the essential nature of this cult and the various forms in which it

[6] *I Cor.* 6, 17.   [7] *John* 4, 10.

finds expression. These latter the Church encourages and fosters, but does not impose them as of obligation; and so they regard the cult itself of the Heart of Jesus as something non-essential and added, which the individual may adopt, or not, as he pleases. Others regard this same cult as burdensome. They object especially that it is of little or no help to those who are fighting the Christian battle in the Kingdom of God and whose guiding principle it is to toil with all the strength and wealth and time at their disposal to protect, hand on and disseminate Catholic truth; to inculcate the Christian doctrine of social justice and to advance those works and those acts of religion which they deem far more necessary at the present day. Finally there are not wanting those who, so far from welcoming this devotion as of genuine value in the formation of Christian character and the renewal of Christian spirit in the private lives of individuals as well as in the common life of the family, rather dismiss it as a form of piety based on the emotions instead of on man's higher nature, and therefore more suited to women. Indeed they see in it something not quite suited to educated men.

Yet others do not regard this devotion as calculated to revive true piety in the hearts of men to-day. For, they say, it brings out those virtues, such as penance and expiation, which they call *passive* because they do not show any external fruits; whereas true piety to-day must tend towards wholehearted and public action, having as its aim the triumph of Catholic faith and the strenuous safeguarding of Christian behaviour. This latter, as all know, is to-day especially vulnerable to the lying fallacies of men who reject all distinction of true and false in the field of thought and action; who regard all forms of religion as equally valid and some of whom, alas, are tainted by the principles of *anticlericalism* and of *atheistic communism*.

Venerable Brethren, who does not see that opinions of the kind We have described are utterly at variance with the mind of Our Predecessors who from this Chair of Truth have publicly

given their approval to the cult of the Sacred Heart of Jesus?
Did not Our Predecessor, Leo XIII of immortal memory, declare
that this devotion was a most commendable form of religious
piety? Did he not see in it a sure and effective remedy for those
very same ills which, to-day as then, only on a larger scale and
in a more acute degree, afflict and undermine individual men and
human society? How then can anyone dare to brand such a devotion as unprofitable or as unsuited to this age of ours? "This devotion," he wrote, "We recommend to all. For all will profit by it."
And he added these words of advice and encouragement with
reference to the cult of the Heart of Jesus: "Hence we have that
torrent of ills which for so long has beset mankind and which
compel us to turn for help to that One by whose power alone
they may be turned back. And who is that One but Jesus Christ
the Only-begotten of God? 'For there is no other name under
heaven given to men whereby we may be saved.'[8] To Him
therefore must we run for refuge, who is the Way, the Truth and
the Life."[9]

Nor was Our immediate Predecessor, Pius XI of happy memory, less emphatic in affirming the excellence of this devotion
and its value for fostering Christian piety. In his encyclical letter
on the subject he wrote: "This form of piety leads our minds
more quickly than any other to an intimate knowledge of Christ
the Lord and inclines our hearts more effectively to love him
with greater vehemence and to imitate him more earnestly."[10]
This vital truth We too, no less than Our Predecessors, have
perceived and experienced. At the beginning of Our Pontificate
We saw with heartfelt joy, that by God's grace, devotion to the
Sacred Heart of Jesus had increased triumphantly among Christian
peoples; and We rejoiced that blessings innumerable were flowing

[8] Acts 4, 12.
[9] Encl. *Annum Sacrum,* 25th May, 1899: *Acta Leonis,* vol. XIX, 1900, pp. 71,
77–78.
[10] Encl. *Miserentissimus Redemptor,* 8th May, 1928 : A. A. S. XX, 1928, p. 167.

from it upon the whole Church. We saw fit to give expression to Our joy in Our first encyclical letter.[11] And throughout the years of Our Pontificate—years that have been filled not only with sorrow and affliction but also with ineffable consolations—these blessings have not grown less, either in number or in the richness of their beauty. Rather have they increased. For We have seen the successful beginnings of various projects, calculated to rekindle this devotion and at the same time eminently suited to present-day needs. We have in mind associations for the advancement of education, of religion and of good works; the publication of works which set forth the true historical, ascetical and mystical doctrine concerning this whole subject; works of loving reparation; and we must mention especially the ardent gratitude to God of those acknowledgments of favours received which are published by the Confraternity of the Apostleship of Prayer, under whose auspices and direction it has come about that families, colleges, institutions and sometimes whole nations have consecrated themselves to the Most Sacred Heart of Jesus. Our paternal joy at these fruits of devotion to the Heart of Jesus We have expressed on many occasions in Our letters, in allocutions and sometimes even in Our wireless broadcasts.[12]

Wherefore, Venerable Brethren, beholding, as We do, this rich abundance of saving waters (that is of heavenly gifts of divine love) issuing from the Sacred Heart of our Redeemer and, by the breath and impulse of the Spirit of God, penetrating the souls of countless children of the Catholic Church, We cannot but invite you with fatherly affection to join with Us in rendering loud praise and fervent thanks to God, the bestower of all good things. Let Us re-echo the words of the Apostle of the Gentiles: "Now to Him who is able to do all

---

[11] Cfr. Encl. *Summi Pontificatus,* 20th October, 1939 : A. A. S. XXXI, 1939, p. 415.

[12] Cfr. A. A. S. XXXII, 1940, p. 276 ; XXXV, 1943, p. 170 ; XXXVII, 1945, pp. 263–264 ; XL, 1948, p. 501 ; XLI, 1946, p. 331.

things more abundantly than we desire or understand, according to the power that worketh in us; to Him be glory in the Church and in Christ Jesus, unto all generations, world without end, Amen."[13] But after We have rendered due thanks to the eternal Godhead, We desire also to admonish you and all Our beloved children of the Catholic Church by this encyclical letter that you ponder with greater attention those principles, drawn from the Bible and from the teaching of the early Fathers and the Theologians of the Church, on which, as upon a solid foundation, the cult of the Sacred Heart of Jesus is built. For of this We are fully persuaded, that only when, illumined by the light of God's revealed truth, we penetrate through and through the essential and fundamental nature of this devotion, only then, We repeat, shall we be able fully and properly to appreciate its excellence and its inexhaustible abundance of heavenly graces. Furthermore, then only, as we lovingly ponder and contemplate the innumerable blessings to which this cult has given rise, shall we be able worthily to commemorate the first centenary of the extension to the universal Church of the feast of the Most Sacred Heart of Jesus.

Our purpose then is to lead the faithful in Christ to lifegiving pastures, nourished on which they may more easily perceive the intimate nature of this devotion and profit by the abundant blessings it brings. With this purpose in mind We shall first of all expound those pages of the Old and New Testaments in which the infinite charity of God towards mankind is revealed and set before us; which charity indeed we shall never be able sufficiently to explore. Then, as occasion arises, We shall sketch the main outlines of the commentaries (on these pages) left us by the Fathers and Doctors of the Church. Finally it shall be Our care to set forth in clear light the wonderfully close link which exists between on the one hand the worship we must render to

---

[13] *Eph.* 3, 20–21.

the Heart of the Divine Redeemer, and on the other the worship we owe to his love and to that of the august Trinity for all men. For We believe that, if only the fundamental elements of this form of piety are seen in that clear light which comes from Scripture and from Tradition, Christians will be better able to "draw waters in joy from the Saviour's fountains"[14]; that is to say, to realize the altogether special importance of the cult of the Heart of Jesus in the Liturgy of the Church, in her spiritual life and in her external apostolate. And further to reap those spiritual fruits by which each man can return to a more Christian way of life, as the shepherds of Christ's flock desire.

If, however, the faithful are to understand the relevance to this devotion of the texts We shall quote from the Old and New Testaments, then it is altogether necessary that they have a clear grasp of the *motive* or grounds on which the Church renders to the Heart of our Divine Redeemer that supreme cult or worship which belongs to God alone. You, Venerable Brethren, are fully aware that this motive is twofold. In the first place (and this applies equally to all the sacred members of the human Body of Jesus Christ) our worship rests on the acknowledged principle that his Heart, the noblest part of his human nature, is united *hypostatically* to the *Person* of the Word of God; and therefore we render to it the same worship of supreme adoration with which the Church honours the Person of the Incarnate Son of God himself. We are dealing here with a truth which was solemnly defined at the General Council of Ephesus and at the second General Council of Constantinople[15] and which must therefore be held *with Catholic faith*. In the second place—and this applies in an exclusive way to the Divine Redeemer's Heart and provides a motive all its own why the cult of supreme wor-

---

[14] *Is.* 12, 3.
[15] Council of Ephesus, can. 8 ; Cfr. Mansi, *Sacrorum Conciliorum Ampliss. Collectio,* IV, 1083 C. ; II Council of Constantinople, can. 9 ; Cfr. *Ibid.* IX, 382 E.

ship should be paid to it—the Heart of Jesus, more than all the other members of his body, is the natural pointer to, or symbol of, his boundless charity towards humankind. "There is in the Sacred Heart," as Our Predecessor of immortal memory Leo XIII observed, "a symbol, nay an express image, of the infinite charity of Jesus Christ, which moves us to love him in return."[16]

It cannot be denied that nowhere in the Sacred Scriptures is there clear mention of any veneration or love for the physical heart of the Word Incarnate, considered precisely as the symbol of his ardent charity. However, while we freely admit this, it need not cause us any surprise; nor can it lead us in any way to doubt that charity of God towards us which is the primary motive of this cult of the Sacred Heart. For both in the Old Testament and in the New it is preached and inculcated by means of images calculated vehemently to move our hearts. And when these images occur in contexts prophetic of the coming of the Son of God made Man, then may we consider them as a heralding of that noblest of all pointers or signs of God's love, namely the Sacred and Adorable Heart of the Divine Redeemer.

For our purpose We think it hardly necessary to cite many passages from the books of the Old Testament which contain the truths revealed by God in ancient times. Rather do We deem it sufficient to remind you of the Covenant entered into by God and his people and hallowed by the offering of peace-victims. The primary law of this Covenant was published by Moses[17] written on two tablets of stone, and was interpreted by the Prophets. And this was a pact not only forged by the bonds of God's supreme lordship and man's proper obedience, but also strengthened and nourished by the higher motives of love. For the supreme motive for obeying God, offered to the people of Israel, was not that fear of God's punishments which the thunder

---

[16] Cfr. encl. *Annum Sacrum: Acta Leonis,* vol. XIX, 1900, p. 76.
[17] Cfr. *Ex.* 34, 27–28.

that rolled and the lightning that flashed from the peak of Mount Sinai struck into their hearts, but rather the charity they owed to God. As it was written: "Hear, O Israel! The Lord our God is one Lord. Thou shalt love the Lord thy God with thy whole heart, and with thy whole soul, and with thy whole strength. And these words, which I enjoin upon thee to-day, shall be in thy heart."[18]

Small wonder then if Moses and the Prophets—whom the Angelic Doctor rightly calls the "great ones"[19] of the Chosen People—realizing, as they did, that the whole basis of the Law was in this precept of love, described all the relationships which existed between God and his own Nation in terms of images drawn from the mutual love of father and son, and of husband and wife; and not in the forbidding language they might have borrowed from God's supreme Lordship and from the service in fear and trembling that we all owe him. Thus, for example, Moses himself in his famous hymn celebrating the restoration of Israel to liberty from servitude in Egypt, when he wished to signify that this had come about by the power of God, made use of this truly touching simile: "As the eagle enticing her young to fly, and hovering over them, he spread his wings: and hath taken him and carried him on his shoulders."[20] But perhaps of all the holy Prophets none has described so clearly and in such passionate language as Osee the love with which God has at all times pursued his People. This prophet stands out among the other minor prophets both for the sublimity and for the conciseness of his style. In his writings God professes for his Chosen People a love that breathes both justice and a holy anxiety, like that of a compassionate and loving father or of a husband whose wife has been unfaithful. We have here a charity which no

---

[18] *Deut.* 6, 4–6.
[19] *Sum. Theol.* II–II, q. 2, a. 7 : ed. Leon., vol. VIII, 1895, p. 34.
[20] *Deut.* 32, 11.

perfidy on their part, nor crime however great can lessen or destroy. On the contrary it does indeed punish their crimes as they deserve. Yes, but why? To cast them off and send them away utterly? No. It is to purify them, to let them expiate their sins and to embrace them once more in the bonds of a renewed and strengthened love. "Because Israel was a child and I loved him: and I called my son out of Egypt. . . And I was like a foster father to Ephraim, I carried them in my arms: and they knew not that I healed them. I will draw them with the cords of Adam, with the bands of love. . . I will heal their breaches, I will love them freely: for my wrath is turned away from them. I will be as the dew: Israel shall spring as the lily and his root shall shoot forth as that of Libanus."[21]

Similar sentiments are uttered by Isaias the Prophet when he presents the following dialogue, as it were, between God himself and the Chosen People: "And Sion said: the Lord hath forsaken me, and the Lord hath forgotten me. Can a woman forget her infant, so as not to have pity on the son of her womb? And if she should forget, yet will I not forget thee."[22] No less moving are the words by which the author of the Canticle of Canticles describes in the language of conjugal love the bonds of mutual charity by which God and the Nation of his love are knit together: "As the lily among thorns, so is my love among the daughters. . . I to my beloved, and my beloved to me, who feedeth among the lilies. . . Put me as a seal upon thy heart, as a seal upon thy arm: for love is strong as death, jealousy as hard as hell. The lamps thereof are fire and flames."[23]

However, this love of God, forgiving, patient, wondrously tender, which, though roused to anger by the People of Israel, heaping up sin upon sin, nevertheless never casts them off altogether, does indeed seem passionate and carried away; and yet it was but a harbinger of that burning charity which the Redeem-

[21] *Os.* 11, 1 3–4 ; 14, 5–6. [22] *Is.* 49, 14–15. [23] *Cant.* 2, 2 ; 6, 2 ; 8, 6.

er, promised to men, was to pour out upon all from his love-filled Heart, and which was to be both the foundation of the New Covenant and the pattern of our love for him. For indeed only he who is the Only-begotten of the Father and the Word made flesh "full of grace and truth"[24], could come to men groaning under the weight of numberless sins and miseries, and could from his human nature, united *hypostatically* to a Divine Person, open to humankind a "fountain of living water" copiously to irrigate the barren earth and to turn it into a flowering and fruitful paradise. And that this truly wonderful thing would be brought to pass by God's ever merciful and eternal love, Jeremias the Prophet seems in a sense to fortell when he writes: "I have loved thee with an everlasting love: therefore have I drawn thee, taking pity on thee. . . Behold, the days shall come, saith the Lord, and I will make a new Covenant with the house of Israel and with the house of Juda. . . This shall be the Covenant that I will make with the house of Israel after those days, saith the Lord: I will give my law in their bowels and I will write it in their hearts: and I will be their God, and they shall be my People . . .: for I will forgive their iniquity and I will remember their sin no more."[25]

Now the Covenant which Moses made between the People of Israel and God was but a symbol and harbinger of the new Covenant between God and the human race which was foretold by the Prophet Jeremias. And this new Covenant is definitely and clearly set forth only in the Gospels. For it was the achievement of the Word Incarnate, the Mediator of divine grace, to establish this Covenant and to bring it into force. This Covenant must be considered incomparably more excellent and lasting because it was made firm, not with blood of goats and of calves, as was the former one, but by the outpouring of the all-holy Blood of him whom those same dumb animals of the peace-offerings had

[24] *John* 1, 14. [25] *Jer.* 31, 3 31 33–34.

foreshadowed, even "the Lamb of God who taketh away the sin of the world."[26] For the Christian Covenant, much more than the one it replaced, clearly appears as a pact, not based on slavery or fear, but ratified by that friendship which should exist between a father and his children, nourished and strengthened by a more bountiful outpouring of divine grace and truth; as it is written in St John's Gospel: "And of His fulness we all have received; and grace for grace. For the law was given by Moses; grace and truth came by Jesus Christ."[27]

This saying of "the disciple whom Jesus loved, who also leaned on his breast at supper"[28] leads us into the very mystery of the boundless charity of the Incarnate Word, and it seems to Us meet and right, proper and availing to salvation, Venerable Brethren, to pause here for a while in joyous contemplation of this same mystery. Thus, bathed in that light which is reflected from the Gospel and lights up this mystery, we too shall be able to realize that desire of which the Apostle of the Gentiles speaks in his letter to the Ephesians, "that Christ may dwell by faith in your hearts; that being rooted and founded in charity, you may be able to comprehend, with all the saints, what is the breadth and length and height and depth; to know also the charity of Christ, which surpasseth all knowledge; that you may be filled unto all the fulness of God."[29]

The Mystery of our Redemption by God is primarily and of its very nature a mystery of love, that is the righteous love of Christ for his heavenly Father, to whom in loving obedience he offered the Sacrifice of the Cross and rendered satisfaction superabundant and infinite for the sins of the human race. "Christ, by suffering out of charity and obedience, offered to God something greater than was needed to make amends for all the offences

---

[26] Cfr. *John* 1, 29 ; *Heb.* 9, 18–28 ; 10, 1–17.
[27] *John* 1, 16–17.
[28] *John* 21, 20.
[29] *Eph.* 3, 17–19.

of the human race."[30] Moreover it is a mystery of the merciful
love of the august Trinity and of the Divine Redeemer for all
men. Man indeed was incapable by himself of atoning for his
sins.[31] But Christ, by the unsearchable riches of his merits which
he acquired for us by the shedding of his precious Blood, was
able to restore and bring to perfection that ancient Covenant of
friendship twixt God and man which had been shattered first
by Adam's unhappy fall in the earthly paradise and then by the
innumerable sins of the Chosen People. And so the Divine
Redeemer, constituted by God our perfect Mediator, in the
burning intensity of his charity towards us brought about an
absolute harmony between man's trespasses and the obligations
arising therefrom on the one hand and the rights of God on the
other; and thus he was the author of that admirable reconciliation of the justice and mercy of God, which makes the mystery
of our salvation the utterly transcendent thing it is. In this connection the Angelic Doctor utters the following words of wisdom:
"We must say that for man to be set free by the Passion of Christ
was conformable both to his mercy and to his justice. To his
justice, because by his Passion Christ satisfied for the sin of all
mankind; and so man by the justice of Christ was made free. To
his mercy, because, when man of himself was unable to make
satisfaction for the sin of all mankind, God gave him in his Son,
one who should make satisfaction. And this was a proof of more
plentiful mercy than if he had forgiven man's sins outright
and waived all satisfaction. Hence it is written: God, who is
rich in mercy, for his exceeding charity with which he loved us,
even when we were dead in sin, hath quickened us together in
Christ."[32]

But, if we are really to be able, as far as man can in this life,

---

[30] *Sum. Theol.* III, q. 48, a. 2 : ed. Leon., vol. XI, 1903, p. 464.
[31] Cfr. encl. *Miserentissimus Redemptor:* A. A. S. XX, 1928, p. 170.
[32] *Eph.* 2, 4; *Sum. Theol.* III, q. 46, a. 1, ad 3 : ed. Leon., vol. XI, 1903, p. 436.

"to comprehend, with all the saints, what is the breadth and length and height and depth"[33] of the hidden charity of the Incarnate Word towards his Heavenly Father and towards sin-stained man, then we must bear in mind that his love is not *only* a spiritual love, such as befits God (inasmuch as 'God is a Spirit').[34] True the love which God bore our first parents and the Hebrew people was a purely spiritual love. And the language of human love, conjugal and parental, which we find in the Psalms, in the Prophetical writings and in the Canticle of Canticles, is simply a token and symbol of the utterly real yet purely spiritual charity with which God loves the human race. But the love which breathes in the Gospels, in the Epistles and in the pages of the Apocalypse, wherein the love of the Heart of Jesus is depicted, is not merely divine charity, but indicates also human senti-ments of love. This of course is accepted with certainty by every Catholic. For the Word of God did not take to himself a fictitious or phantom body, as certain heretics of the first Christian cen-tury asserted, and were reproved by the Apostle John with words of the greatest severity. "For many seducers," he wrote, "are gone out into the world who confess not that Jesus Christ is come in the flesh. This is a seducer and an antichrist."[35] On the contrary in very truth he joined to himself an individual, integral and perfect human nature, which was conceived by the power of the Holy Ghost in the most pure womb of the Virgin Mary.[36] Nothing therefore was lacking to the human nature which the Word of God united to himself. Neither its spiritual, nor its bodily powers were in any way either lessened or different. It was endowed with mind, will and the other internal and external faculties of knowledge; also with sense desire and all the instincts of our nature. All this the Catholic Church teaches in as much as it has been defined and ratified both by the Roman Pontiffs and by General Councils: "Entire in his own nature, entire in

---

[33] *Eph.* 3, 18. [34] *John* 4, 24. [35] *II John* 7. [36] Cfr. *Lk.* 1, 35.

ours;"[37] "one and the same perfect in Godhead and perfect in manhood;"[38] "a man was wholly God; God was wholly a man."[39]

It is therefore beyond all doubt that Jesus Christ acquired a true body, together with all the emotions proper thereto, amongst which love is pre-eminent. And it is equally beyond all doubt that he possessed a physical heart, a heart just like ours. For without this, the body's noblest member, human life, as far as the emotions are concerned, is impossible. Wherefore without any doubt the Heart of Jesus Christ, *hypostatically* united to the Person of the Divine Word, beat with the pulsations of love and of all the other emotions. At the same time so perfect was the agreement and harmony between these emotions and both his human will, filled as it was with divine charity, and that infinite love itself, which the Father communicates with the Son and with the Holy Spirit, that there was never between these three loves in Jesus Christ any disharmony or disagreement."[40]

The Word of God then took to himself a true and perfect human nature and formed and fashioned for himself a heart of flesh, which, no less than our hearts, could suffer and be pierced. But this truth, unless it be seen and considered in the light that shines forth from the *hypostatic* or personal union, and in that which shines forth from its complement, the Redemption of mankind, is likely to prove a stumbling block and a folly to men, even as Christ crucified was to the Jewish nation and to the Gentiles.[41] For the solemn definitions of Catholic faith, in perfect concord with Sacred Scripture, teach us that the Only-begotten Son of

[37] St. Leo the Great, *Epist. dogm. "Lectis dilectionis tuae" ad Flavianum Const. Patr.*, *13 Jun.*, *a.* 449 ; Cfr. P. L. LIV, 763.

[38] Council of Chalcedon., a. 451 ; Cfr. Mansi, *Op. cit.* VII, 115 B.

[39] St. Gelasius Pope, Tract. III *"Necessarium" de duabus naturis in Christo.* Cfr. A. Thiel, *Epist. Rom. Pont. a S. Hilario usque ad Pelagium* II, p. 532.

[40] Cfr. St. Thomas, *Sum. Theol.* III, q. 15, a. 4 ; q. 18, a. 6 : ed. Leon., vol. XI, 1903, pp. 189 and 237.

[41] Cfr. *I Cor.* 1, 23.

God took to himself a human nature, subject to suffering and death, first and foremost because he wished, hanging on the Cross, to offer a bloody sacrifice which would consummate the work of man's salvation. Is not this what the Apostle of the Gentiles teaches us, when he writes: "For both he that sanctifieth and they who are sanctified are all of one. For which cause he is not ashamed to call them brethren, saying: I will declare thy name to my brethren. . . And again: Behold, I and my children, whom God hath given me. Therefore, because the children are partakers of flesh and blood, he also himself in like manner hath been partaker of the same. . . Wherefore, it behoved him in all things to be made like unto his brethren, that he might become a merciful and faithful high-priest before God, that he might be a propitiation for the sins of the people. For in that wherein he himself hath suffered and been tempted he is able to succour them also that are tempted."[42]

Now the Holy Fathers, those faithful witnesses to the doctrine revealed by God, rightly made this point, upon which the Apostle Paul had already sufficiently insisted; namely that the mystery of God's love is both the beginning and the end as well of the Incarnation as of the Redemption. Again and again we find it clearly stated in their writings that Jesus Christ took a perfect human nature and with it this body of our frailty and decay precisely because he wished to provide for our eternal salvation and to open and display to us his boundless love, human as well as divine.

St. Justin seems to echo the voice of the Apostle of the Gentiles when he writes: "For we adore and love the Word, who was born of the unbegotten and ineffable God; for that on our account he was made man, because he wished by sharing our emotions, to provide for them a healing remedy."[43] St. Basil, outstanding among the three Cappadocian Fathers, declares that the move-

---

[42] *Heb.* 2, 11-14 ; 17–18.   [43] *Apol.* II, 13 : P. G. VI, 465.

ments of Christ's emotional nature were at the same time both real and sinless. "Clearly the Lord took upon himself our natural emotions, because he wished to confirm the truth of the Incarnation, and to confound those who maintained it was but imaginary; but those emotions which soil the purity of our life, he rejected as incompatible with the Holy Godhead."[44] In like manner St. John Chrysostom, that luminary of the Church of Antioch, acknowledges that the emotions of the bodily senses, in which the Divine Redeemer shared, have clearly established that he assumed our human nature whole and entire. "For had he not been of our nature, then he would not have been stricken with grief again and again."[45] Among the Latin Fathers we will mention those whom the Church to-day reveres as the greatest of her Doctors. Thus St. Ambrose attests that the emotions and affections of the senses, which the Incarnate Word of God experienced, arose from the hypostatic union as from their natural source. "And therefore because he took a soul, he took also the soul's passions; for God, as God, could neither have been perturbed nor have died."[46] From these emotions St. Jerome draws his chief proof that Christ really did take a human nature. Our Lord, he argues, to prove the truth of the manhood he had taken to himself, truly gave way to sorrow.[47] It is, however, St. Augustine who in a special way draws our attention to the connection between the emotions of the Incarnate Word and the purpose of man's Redemption. "These emotions of our human weakness, together with the very flesh of our human weakness and death of our human flesh, the Lord Jesus did assume, not indeed through any compulsion in which he was placed, but of his free-will, impelled by pity. For he wished to transform into himself his Body, even the Church whose Head he has deigned to be;

[44] *Epist.* 261, 3 : P. G. XXXII, 972.
[45] *In Ioann.* Homil. 63, 2 : P. G. LIX, 350.
[46] *De fide ad Gratianum*, II, 7, 56 : P. L. XVI, 594.
[47] Cfr. *Super Mt* 26, 37 : P. L. XXVI, 205.

to transform, in other words, his members, that is his saints and faithful ones, so that, if any of them should happen to grieve and sorrow in the midst of human temptations, such a one should not for that reason think himself to be out of his grace, and, like a choir coming in on the opening notes of its leader, so the Body should learn from its own Head that these things are not sins, but merely concomitants of our human weakness."[48] More briefly, perhaps, but no less effectively, the following texts from St. John Damascene illustrate the teaching of the Church: "He wholly assumed me wholly; and Whole was made one with whole, that he might bring salvation to whole. For otherwise what had not been assumed, could not be healed."[49] "All things therefore (of our nature) he assumed, that he might make all holy."[50]

It must be observed, however, that these excerpts from the Sacred Scriptures and from the Fathers, and not a few others like them which We have not quoted, while they bear clear witness that Jesus Christ possessed the emotions and feelings of sense-nature, and had assumed a human nature precisely in order to provide for our eternal salvation, at the same time they do not ever refer these same feelings to his physical heart in such a way as explicitly to point to it as a symbol of his boundless love. But the Heart of our Redeemer is a living heart, endowed no less than ours with the power of feeling, throbbing with the manifold emotions and feelings of his soul, quivering with the burning love of his twofold will. And if the Evangelists and the other Sacred Writers do not actually describe all this, they do nevertheless frequently set in their proper light his divine love and its concomitant emotions of the senses, that is to say desire, joy, sickness of heart, fear and anger, in so far as they are betrayed

---

[48] *Enarr. in Ps.* LXXXVII, 3 : P.L. XXXVII, 1111.
[49] *De Fide Orth.* III, 6 : P.G. XCIV, 1006.
[50] *Ibid.* III, 20 : P.G. XCIV, 1081.

by his facial expression, his words and his gestures. The countenance especially of our adorable Saviour was a token and indeed a mirror most faithful of the emotions which moved his soul in varying manner and, like a succession of waves, reached his Sacred Heart and set it throbbing to their rhythm. For here also is valid that rule of human psychology and its effects formulated from our common experience by the Angelic Doctor, "The disturbance set up by anger reaches even to the external members (of the body); and especially to those members, such as eyes, face and tongue, in which the heart's reflection shines more clearly."[51]

Therefore the Heart of the Word made flesh is rightly looked upon as the principal token and sign of that threefold love wherewith the Divine Redeemer ceaselessly loves both his eternal Father and all mankind. It is the sign of that divine love which he shares with the Father and with the Holy Spirit, but which in him only, that is to say in the Word which was made flesh, is made manifest to us in a frail and corruptible human body, since "in him dwelleth all the fulness of the Godhead corporeally."[52] It is moreover the sign of that white-hot charity which was infused into Christ's human soul, and which enriches his human will. The *acts* of this charity are illumined and guided by Christ's twofold most perfect knowledge, and that is to say his *beatific* knowledge and his *bestowed* or *infused* knowledge.[53] And finally his Heart is a sign—and this in a more direct and natural way—of his emotional affection, since the Body of Jesus Christ, formed by the work of the Holy Spirit in the womb of the Virgin Mary, enjoyed in the fullest degree the power of feeling and perceiving, more perfectly in fact than the bodies of all other men.[54]

Sacred Scripture, then, and the approved sources of Catholic

[51] *Sum. Theol.* I–II, q. 48, a. 4 : ed. Leon., vol. VI, 1891, p. 306.
[52] *Col.* 2, 9.
[53] Cfr. *Sum. Theol.* III, q. 9, aa. 1–3 : ed. Leon., vol. XI, 1903, p. 142.　　[433.
[54] Cfr. *Ibid.* III, q. 33, a. 2, ad 3 ; q. 46, a. 6 : ed. Leon., vol. XI, 1903, pp. 342,

belief teach us that in the all-holy Soul of Jesus Christ there exists a supreme concord and harmony of all parts, and further that Christ openly directed his threefold love to the achievement of his purpose which was our Redemption. We are, therefore, unquestionably justified in contemplating and venerating the Heart of the Divine Redeemer as the striking reflection of his charity, as the witness of our Redemption and as a mystical Jacob's ladder by which we climb up to the embrace of "God our Saviour"[55]. Wherefore his words, his actions, his precepts, his wondrous works, and especially those works which afford clearest evidence of his charity towards us, such as the institution of the Divine Eucharist, his bitter torments and his death, his loving bequest to us of his all-holy Mother, the founding of the Church for our salvation, and the sending of the Holy Spirit upon the Apostles and upon us—all these things, We repeat, we must wonder at as proofs of his threefold love. Likewise we must contemplate lovingly the beats of his Sacred Heart. For by them he would seem to have measured the duration of his earthly pilgrimage up to that supreme moment when, as the Evangelists tell us, "crying out with a loud voice, he said: It is consummated. And bowing his head, he gave up the ghost."[56] Then indeed was the beating of his heart halted, and his emotional love interrupted, until he triumphed over death and rose again from the tomb. But the Divine Redeemer did triumph over death. His Body was reunited to his Soul and attained the state of everlasting glory. And from that moment his Sacred Heart has never ceased, nor will cease, to throb with calm and unshakeable beat, and to betoken his threefold love which binds him, the Son of God, to his Father in heaven and to the worldwide fellowship of men of which he is by fullest right the Mystical Head.

At this point, Venerable Brethren, in order that we may be able to reap rich and saving fruits from these holy considerations,

---

[55] *Tit.* 3, 4.   [56] *Mt.* 27, 50; *John* 19, 30.

we will ponder briefly and contemplate the manifold emotions, divine as well as human, of our Saviour Jesus Christ. By sharing in these emotions during the course of his mortal life, his Heart has made them known to us, and continues now to make them known, and will do so throughout eternity. It is especially from the pages of the Gospel that a light shines forth upon us, illumined and strengthened by which we are able to enter the sanctuary of his Heart, and in company with the Apostle of the Gentiles to wonder at "the abundant riches of his (God's) grace, in his bounty towards us in Christ Jesus."[57]

The Virgin Mary utters that generous word, "be it done", and the Word of God, as the Apostle puts it, coming "into the world, saith: Sacrifice and oblation thou wouldest not; but a body thou hast fitted to me. Holocausts for sin did not please thee. Then said I: Behold I come. In the head of the Book it is written of me that I should do thy will, O God. . . . In the which will we are sanctified by the oblation of the Body of Christ once."[58] Immediately the Heart of Jesus, ever to be adored, has begun to pulsate with love, divine and human. Likewise that Heart stirred with love, a love in perfect concord with the emotions of his human will and with the Divine Love, when in the house at Nazareth he spoke of heavenly things with his sweet Mother and with Joseph, his putative father, in subjection to whom he was toiling at the carpenter's bench. Again he was driven by that same threefold love of which We have spoken, in the daily journeyings entailed by his apostolate; when he worked his countless miracles, healing the sick of every kind and raising the dead to life; in the labours he undertook; when he endured sweat, hunger and thirst; in vigil by night when he communed in prayer most loving with his heavenly Father; in his preaching and when he set forth and explained his parables, especially those whose subject is the *mercy* of God, such as the

[57] *Eph.* 2, 7. [58] *Heb.* 10, 5–7 10.

groat that was lost, the lost sheep and the prodigal son. For in all these words and actions of the Saviour, as Gregory the Great observes, the very Heart of God himself is made manifest. "Learn to know the Heart of God in the words of God, and thou shalt sigh more ardently for things eternal." [59]

But the Heart of Jesus thrilled to a yet more urgent charity when from his lips there fell these words of ardent love. For example, when he beheld the tired and hungry crowds and cried out, "I have compassion upon the multitude." [60] Or when he beheld Jerusalem, the beloved city, blinded by its sins and therefore destined for utter ruin, and uttered these words "Jerusalem, Jerusalem, thou that killest the prophets and stonest them that are sent unto thee, how often would I have gathered together thy children, as the hen doth gather her chickens under her wings, and thou wouldst not?" [61] And did not his Heart throb with love for his Father and with righteous anger when he saw unholy commerce being transacted in the Temple, and upbraided those who violated it in these words, "It is written: My house is a house of prayer; but you have made it a den of thieves." [62]

A special love and fear moved his Heart as he saw the hour of his appalling torments now draw near, and, shrinking by a natural repugnance from the pains and death that threatened him, cried out: "My Father, if it be possible, let this chalice pass from me." [63] Then the traitor greets him with a kiss, and he asks him with unconquerable love and deepest grief: "Friend, whereto art thou come? Dost thou betray the Son of Man with a kiss?" [64] These words seem to be a last appeal of his most merciful Heart to the impious, faithless, obdurate heart of the friend who was about to

[59] *Registr. epist.*, lib. IV, ep. 31 *ad Theodorum medicum*: P. L. LXXVII, 706.
[60] *Mk.* 8, 2.
[61] *Mt.* 23, 37.
[62] *Mt.* 21, 13.
[63] *Mt.* 26, 39.
[64] *Mt.* 26, 50 ; *Lk.* 22, 48.

betray him. The devout women wept for him, because he was about to undergo the unmerited torment of the Cross, and an incredible pity and love moved him and he said to them: "Daughters of Jerusalem, weep not for me; but weep for yourselves and for your children. .. For if in the green wood they do these things, what shall be done in the dry?"[65].

At length the Divine Redeemer, hanging on the Cross, finds that his Heart is seething with many vehement emotions: ardent love, dismay, compassion, burning desire, serene calm. The which emotions are betrayed in his words from the Cross: "Father, forgive them; for they know not what they do."[66] "My God, my God, why hast thou forsaken me?"[67] "Amen I say unto thee, this day thou shalt be with me in paradise."[68] "I thirst."[69] "Father, into thy hands I commend my spirit."[70]

But who can adequately depict the throbbings of the Divine Heart, tokens of his boundless love, at those precious moments when he bestowed his greatest gifts upon mankind? That is to say the gift of himself in the Sacrament of the Eucharist, the gift of his most holy Mother, and the sharing with us of his priestly office.

Even before he ate the Last Supper with his disciples, Christ the Lord, knowing that he was about to institute the Sacrament of his Body and of his Blood by whose outpouring the New Covenant was to be hallowed and ratified, had felt his Heart to be stirred by vehement emotion, which he expressed in these words to his Apostles: "With longing have I longed to eat this Pasch with you, before I suffer."[71] And this emotion was undoubtedly even more vehement when "taking bread, he gave thanks and

[65] *Lk.* 23, 28 31.
[66] *Lk.* 23, 34.
[67] *Mt.* 27, 46.
[68] *Lk.* 23, 43.
[69] *John* 19, 28.
[70] *Lk.* 23, 46.
[71] *Lk.* 22, 15.

brake, and gave to them, saying: This is my Body, which is given for you. Do this for a commemoration of me. In like manner, the chalice also, after he had supped, saying: This is the chalice, the New Testament in my Blood, which shall be shed for you." [72]

Rightly therefore may we reckon among the gifts of the Sacred Heart of Jesus the Divine Eucharist and the Priesthood. And the Eucharist, both as a Sacrament which he gives to men, and as a Sacrifice which he himself continually immolates "from the rising of the sun to the going down thereof." [73]

A further most precious gift of the Sacred Heart is, as we have said, Mary, the dear Mother of God and the loving Mother of all of us. For she who was the Mother of our Redeemer according to the flesh and his associate in raising up the children of Eve once more to the life of divine grace, was rightly hailed as the spiritual Mother of all mankind. Wherefore St. Augustine wrote of her: "Clearly she is the Mother of the members of the Saviour (which is what we are) because she co-operated by charity, so that the faithful, who are the members of that Head, might be born in the Church." [74]

But to the unbloody gift of himself under the appearance of bread and wine our Saviour Jesus Christ willed to add, as the ultimate proof of his intimate and boundless charity, the bloody Sacrifice of the Cross. By this action he has provided an example of that sublime charity which he put before his disciples as the supreme measure of love: "greater love than this no man hath, that a man lay down his life for his friends." [75] Wherefore the love of Jesus Christ the Son of God, through the Sacrifice of Golgotha, sheds light and meaning on the very love of God himself. "In this we know the charity of God, because he hath laid down his life for us; and we ought to lay down our lives for

[72] *Lk.* 22, 19–20.
[73] *Mal.* 1, 11.
[74] *De sancta virginitate* VI : P.L. XL, 399.
[75] *John* 15, 13.

the brethren."[76] And in truth it was his own love, more than the violence of his executioners, that nailed our Divine Redeemer to the Cross. And his voluntary holocaust of himself is his supreme gift to each individual man. As the Apostle pithily expresses it, he "loved me, and delivered himself for me."[77]

The Sacred Heart of Jesus, then, partakes most intimately in the life of the Word made flesh, and therefore, no less than the other members of his human nature, is as it were an instrument which the Godhead has taken up and uses in the work of his grace and his omnipotence.[78] There can therefore be no doubt that this Heart of Jesus is the lawful symbol of that boundless charity which moved our Saviour to shed his Blood and so to enter into mystical marriage with the Church. "Through charity he suffered for the Church, that he might unite her to himself as his bride."[79] And so from the wounded Heart of the Redeemer was born the Church, as the dispenser of the Blood of our Redemption; and from the same Heart flows in copious abundance the grace of the Sacraments, from which the Church's children drink supernal life, as we say in the sacred Liturgy: "From riven Heart is born the Church, espoused to Christ." And, "Who from out his Heart pours grace."[80] Of the meaning of this symbol the early Fathers and writers of the Church were not unaware, and St. Thomas Aquinas seems to echo their words, when he writes: "From the side of Christ there flowed water for washing and blood for redeeming. And so the blood that flowed is associated with the Sacrament of the Eucharist, and the water with the Sacrament of Baptism. Baptism however has its power to make clean from the efficacy of the Blood of Christ."[81] Now what is written here of

---

[76] *I John* 3, 16.
[77] *Gal.* 2, 20.
[78] Cfr. St. Thomas, *Sum. Theol.* III, q. 19, a. 1 : ed. Leon., vol. XI, 1903, p. 329.
[79] *Sum. Theol.*, Suppl., q. 42, a. 1, ad 3 : ed. Leon., vol. XII, 1906, p. 81.
[80] Hymn at Vespers, feast of the Most Sacred Heart of Jesus.
[81] *Sum. Theol.* III, q. 66, a. 3, ad 3 : ed. Leon., vol. XII, 1906, p. 65.

the side of Christ, wounded and laid open by the soldier, is also applicable to his Heart, which the lance's thrust certainly reached, inasmuch as the soldier's purpose in wielding it was to make certain beyond all doubt that Jesus Christ crucified was dead. Hence the wound in the Sacred Heart of the *dead* Christ is for all times a vivid image of that spontaneous charity whereby God gave his Only-begotten Son to redeem men, and whereby Christ has loved us so vehemently that he immolated himself for us a bleeding victim on Calvary's hill. "Christ hath loved us and hath delivered himself for us, an oblation and a sacrifice to God for an odour of sweetness." [82]

Our Saviour has now ascended into heaven, his Body bedecked with the splendours of eternal glory; he has taken his throne at the Father's right hand. But he has not ceased to love his spouse, the Church, with that furnace of love wherewith his Heart still throbs. On his hands, on his feet and in his side he bears the glorious marks of his wounds, showing forth his threefold victory over Satan, sin and death. And in the precious repository of his Heart are stored the fruits of that threefold triumph, even the boundless treasures of his merits which he pours out in flowing abundance on redeemed mankind. This is the consoling truth, proclaimed by the Apostle of the Gentiles, when he says: "ascending on high, he led captivity captive; he gave gifts to men. . . He that descended is the same also that ascended above all the heavens, that he might fill all things." [83]

After his triumphal ascent to the right hand of his Father, the gift of the Holy Spirit, sent upon his disciples, is the first outstanding sign of his munificent charity. For after ten days the Spirit, even the Paraclete given by the heavenly Father, came down upon them, where they were gathered in the Cenacle, according to his promise at the Last Supper: "I will ask the Father, and he shall give you another Paraclete, that he may abide with you for ever." [84]

---

[82] *Eph.* 5, 2.   [83] *Eph.* 4, 8 10.   [84] *John* 14, 16.

And this Paraclete Spirit, since he is the mutual Personal Love, that is of the Father for the Son, and of the Son for the Father, is sent by both Father and Son; and, clothing himself, as it were, in the appearances of tongues of fire, he pours into their hearts an abundance of divine charity and of other heavenly gifts. The torrent of this divine charity rises also in the Heart of our Saviour, "in whom are hid all the treasures of wisdom and knowledge." [85] For this charity is the gift both of the Heart of Jesus and of his Spirit, who is indeed the Spirit of the Father and of the Son. From this Spirit comes the origin of the Church and its marvellous spreading before the face of all those nations and peoples who were sunk in the degradation of idolatry, fraternal hatred, violence and moral corruption. This divine charity is the inestimable gift of the Heart of Christ and of his Spirit. To the Apostles and Martyrs it imparted a fortitude, strengthened by which they strove even unto death, heroically endured, to preach the truth of the Gospel and seal it with their blood. In the Doctors of the Church it instilled a burning zeal to defend and shed light upon Catholic truth. It has nourished the virtues of Confessors and roused them to wonderful works, most profitable to their own and others' eternal and temporal happiness. And lastly it has persuaded the Virgins freely and with joyful hearts to leave behind them the pleasures of body, in order to consecrate themselves entirely to the love of their heavenly Bridegroom. This divine charity flows from the Heart of the Word made flesh, and is poured out by the Holy Spirit in the hearts of all believers. In its honour the Apostle of the Gentiles sang this hymn of victory, which proclaims the triumph of Jesus Christ the Head, and of the members of his Mystical Body, over all those obstacles which in any way hinder the restoration of the Reign of Divine Love among men: "Who . . . shall separate us from the love of Christ? Shall tribulation? Or distress? Or famine? Or nakedness? Or

[85] *Col.* 2, 3.

danger? Or persecution? Or the sword? But in all these things we overcome, because of him that hath loved us. For I am sure that neither death, nor life, nor angels, nor principalities, nor powers, nor things present, nor things to come, nor might, nor height, nor depth, nor any other creature, shall be able to separate us from the love of God which is in Christ Jesus Our Lord."[86]

There is therefore no reason why we should not worship the Sacred Heart of Jesus, both as partaking in, and as being the obvious and expressive symbol of that inexhaustible charity towards men wherewith the Divine Redeemer is still on fire. That Heart indeed is no longer subject to the emotional disturbances of our mortal condition. But still it lives and beats, and is indissolubly united to the Person of the Divine Word, and in him and through him with his divine will. Wherefore, since the Heart of Christ overflows with divine and human love, and is surpassing rich in all the treasures of grace which our Redeemer acquired by his life, his sufferings and his death, it is therefore the perennial fount of that charity which his Spirit pours out upon all the members of his Mystical Body.

The Heart then of our Saviour is in some sense a reflection of the Divine Person of the Word, and likewise of his twofold nature, divine and human; and we may see in it not only a symbol, but also a compendium or summary of the whole mystery of our Redemption. When we worship the most Sacred Heart of Jesus Christ, in it and through it we are worshipping both the uncreated love of the Word of God, and at the same time his human love and his other emotions and virtues. For both these loves impelled our Redeemer to immolate himself for us and for the universal Church, his spouse, as it is written by the Apostle: "Christ loved the Church, and delivered himself up for her; that he might sanctify her, cleansing her by the laver of water in the word of life; that he might present her to himself, a glorious Church, not

[86] *Rom.* 8, 35 37–39.

having spot or wrinkle, or any such thing, but that she should be holy and without blemish."[87]

As Christ loved the Church, so he still loves her most ardently with that threefold love, of which we have spoken, and which moves him, as our advocate,[88] to obtain for us grace and mercy from the Father, "ever living to intercede for us"[89]. The supplications which go from his inexhaustible love to the Father, are never interrupted. As "in the days of his flesh"[90], so now, triumphant in heaven, he pleads no less effectively with his heavenly Father. And to him who "so loved the world, as to give his Only-begotten Son; that whosoever believeth in him may not perish, but may have life everlasting,"[91] he shows his Heart, living, and as it were wounded, and seething with love yet more intense than when, in death, it was wounded by the Roman soldier's lance. "For this reason was (thy Heart) wounded, that through the visible wound we might behold the invisible wound of thy love."[92]

It is therefore beyond doubt that the heavenly Father, "who spared not even his own Son, but delivered him up for us all,"[93] when appealed to with such loving urgency by so powerful an advocate, will, through him, at all times send down upon all men a rich abundance of divine graces.

It was Our desire, Venerable Brethren, by this general outline, to set before you and before the Christian people the intimate nature of the cult of the Sacred Heart of Jesus, and the endless riches that spring therefrom, as they are made clear by the

---

[87] *Eph.* 5, 25–27.

[88] Cfr. *I John* 2, 1.

[89] *Heb.* 7, 25.

[90] *Heb.* 5, 7.

[91] *John* 3, 16.

[92] St. Bonaventure, Opusc. X : *Vitis mystica,* c. III, n. 5 : *Opera Omnia,* Ad Claras Aquas (Quaracchi) 1898, vol. VIII, p. 164 ; Cfr. St. Thomas, *Sum. Theol.* III, q. 54, a. 4 : ed. Leon., vol. XI, 1903, p. 513.

[93] *Rom.* 8, 32.

primary source of doctrine, divine Revelation. And We think that Our observations, guided as they have been by the light of the Gospel, have established that this cult amounts to nothing else than the cult of the divine and human love of the Word made flesh, and of that love too wherewith the Father and the Holy Spirit pursue sinful men. For, as the Angelic Doctor teaches, the charity of the august Trinity is the first source of man's Redemption, inasmuch as that charity flowed copiously into the human will of Jesus Christ and into his adorable Heart, and led him to pour out his Blood that we might be redeemed from the captivity of sin.[94] "I have a baptism wherewith I am to be baptized. And how I am straitened until it be accomplished?"[95]

We are convinced then that the cult or devotion by which we worship the love of God and of Jesus Christ for the human race under the august symbol of the pierced Heart of the crucified Redeemer, was never altogether foreign to the piety of Christians. And this, in spite of the fact that it is only in comparatively recent times that it has been clearly formulated, and has spread so wonderfully in all directions throughout the Church; especially since the Lord himself has disclosed this divine secret by private revelation to certain of his children who were favoured with abundance of supernal gifts and chosen by him to be its apostles and heralds.

For in truth at no time have there been wanting men, especially dedicated to God, who, after the example of the beloved Mother of God, the Apostles and the great Fathers of the Church, have paid to the Sacred Humanity of Christ, and especially to those wounds of his by which his Body was torn when he endured the Cross for our salvation, a tribute or cult of adoration, thanksgiving and love.

Besides, we recall the exclamation of the Apostle Thomas, "My

---

[94] Cfr. *Sum. Theol.* III, q. 48, a. 5 : ed. Leon., vol. XI, 1903, p. 467.
[95] *Lk.* 12, 50.

EARLY HISTORY OF THE DEVOTION

Lord and my God!"[96], words which mark his passage from unbelief to faith. Surely they contain a clear profession of faith, adoration and love, that rises from the wounded human nature of the Lord to the majesty of his Divine Person.

The words of the Prophet Zachary, "they shall look upon him whom they have pierced,"[97] were referred by St. John the Evangelist to Jesus, nailed to the Cross. And whenever these words have fallen upon the ears of Christians of whatever century, men have always been strongly drawn by the contemplation of the pierced Heart of the Saviour to worship his boundless love for mortal men. Still it must be admitted that only little by little and gradually has that same Heart been honoured by the homage of a special devotion, as the mirror of the human and divine love that resides in the Word Incarnate.

But if we wish to touch on the more important stages in the development of this devotion through the centuries, as regards its outward manifestations, then there immediately occur to our minds the names of certain men and women who have won particular renown in this regard. These were the standard-bearers of a form of piety which privately and very gradually, but none the less surely, has gained strength in religious congregations. To cite some examples—in establishing this devotion to the Sacred Heart of Jesus, and in its unceasing propagation, great service was rendered by St. Bonaventure, St. Albert the Great, St. Gertrude, St. Catherine of Siena, Blessed Henry Suso, St. Peter Canisius and St. Francis of Sales. The first liturgical office to be celebrated in honour of the Sacred Heart of Jesus was the work of St. John Eudes, the feast being first solemnly kept on the 20th day of October, 1672, with the approval of many of the French bishops. But without any doubt among those whose labours have established this superlative form of Christian piety the principal place is held by St. Margaret Mary Alacoque. It

[96] *John* 20, 28.   [97] *John* 19, 37 ; Cfr. *Zach.* 12, 10.

was the achievement of this ardent and zealous lover of Christ, assisted by her spiritual director, Bl. Claude de la Colombière, to crystallize the concept of devotion to the Sacred Heart and to enrich that concept with new elements, to the great edification of the Christian faithful, so that it is distinguished from other forms of Christian piety by the special note of loving reparation.[98]

This summary of the period during which the cult of the Sacred Heart of Jesus developed, is sufficient for us to realize that its wonderful growth is due to the fact that it accords perfectly with the very nature of the Christian religion. For this is a religion of love. And therefore we are not to say that this devotion arose as a result of a private revelation from God, nor that it appeared suddenly in the Church. Rather should we say that it was the natural flowering of that living faith and fervent piety by which, in God's grace, men have been affected towards the adorable Redeemer and his glorious wounds; which latter move men's hearts most deeply because they bear witness to his immeasurable love. Wherefore it is clear that the revelations to St. Margaret Mary added nothing new to Catholic doctrine. Their vital importance, however, lies in this: that Christ our Lord, by displaying his Sacred Heart, willed, in a most powerful and unheard of way, to arouse the hearts of men to contemplate and adore the mystery of God's most merciful love for the human race. In these unique revelations Christ again and again clearly indicated his Heart as the symbol by which men might be drawn to a knowledge and appreciation of his love; and at the same time he established it as a sign and pledge of mercy and grace for the Church in the needs of our times.

Furthermore, that this cult is a legitimate development of the very principles of Christian doctrine is established by the fact that the Apostolic See approved the liturgical feast of the Sacred

---

[98] Cfr. encyclical letter *Miserentissimus Redemptor:* A. A. S. XX, 1928, pp. 167–168.

Heart *before* it approved the writings of St. Margaret Mary. For when the Sacred Congregation of Rites, by a decree dated January 25th, 1765, and approved by Our Predecessor Clement XIII on the 6th of February in the same year, gave permission to the bishops of Poland and to the Roman Arch-Sodality of the Sacred Heart to celebrate this feast liturgically, it was not so much taking into account anyone's private revelation from God, as yielding graciously to the prayers of the faithful. And in granting this concession the Apostolic See had in mind the growth of an already established and flourishing devotion, whose purpose it was "symbolically to recall to mind that divine love"[99], by which our Saviour was impelled to offer himself as a victim to expiate the sins of men.

This first approbation took the form of a privilege, hedged by certain restrictions. It was followed nearly a hundred years later by another one of far greater importance and solemnity. We refer to the decree, which We have already recalled, issued by the Sacred Congregation of Rites on the 23rd of August, 1856, by which Our Predecessor, Pius IX of immortal memory, yielding to the prayers of the bishops of France and of almost the whole Catholic world, extended the feast of the Sacred Heart of Jesus to the whole Church and ordered it to be duly observed everywhere.[100] This event deserves a place in the undying memory of the Christian faithful, for as we read in the Liturgy of this feast: "thereafter the cult of the Sacred Heart, as a river that bursts its banks, sweeping all obstacles before it, has spread all over the world."

Venerable Brethren, from what We have so far put before you, it is abundantly clear that the faithful must go right back to Sacred Scripture, to Christian Tradition and to the deep limpid waters of the Sacred Liturgy, if they wish to understand

[99] Cfr. A. Gardellini, *Decreta authentica*, 1857, n. 4579, vol. III, p. 174.

[100] Cfr. *Decr. S. C. Rit.*, apud N. Nilles, *De rationibus festorum Sacratissimi Cordis Iesu et purissimi Cordis Mariae*, 5a ed., Innsbruck 1885, vol. I, p. 167.

the true nature of devotion to the Sacred Heart of Jesus, and, by loving meditation thereon, to receive food for the nourishment and growth of their religious ardour. But if, with illumined and penetrating mind, this devotion is assiduously practised, then it cannot but happen that the faithful soul arrives at that understanding of the charity of Christ, which constitutes the summit of the Christian life, as the Apostle, from his own experience, teaches: "For this cause I bow my knees to the Father of our Lord Jesus Christ . . . that he would grant to you according to the riches of his glory to be strengthened by his Spirit with might unto the inward man; that Christ may dwell by faith in your hearts, being rooted and founded in charity; that you may be able . . . to know also the charity of Christ, which surpasseth knowledge; that you may be filled unto all the fulness of God."[101] Now the clearest reflection of this fulness of God, which embraces all things, is precisely the Heart of Christ Jesus. We refer especially to that fulness of mercy which pertains to the New Testament, in which "the goodness and kindness of God our Saviour appeared."[102] For "God sent not his Son into the world to judge the world; but that the world might be saved by him."[103]

The Church, therefore, in fulfilment of her teaching office, ever since her first official statements regarding the cult of the Sacred Heart of Jesus, has vehemently denied that the primary notions of this cult, namely the acts of love and of reparation by which we honour the infinite love of God for the human race, are infected with the poison of *materialism* or of superstition. On the contrary she has insisted that this devotion is a form of piety by which is brought to perfection that true religion of the spirit, which the Saviour himself foretold when he said to the Samaritan woman: "The hour cometh and now is, when the true adorers shall adore the Father in spirit and in truth. For the

[101] *Eph*. 3, 14 16–19.
[102] *Tit*. 3, 4.
[103] *John* 3, 17.

Father also seeketh such to adore him. God is a spirit; and they that adore him must adore him in spirit and in truth."[104]

It is therefore blasphemous to assert that the contemplation of the physical Heart of Christ is an obstacle to our reaching the innermost love of God, and that the soul is delayed thereby on the road that leads to the height of the virtues. This false mysticism the Church utterly rejects, even as she rejected, through the mouth of Our Predecessor, Innocent XI of happy memory, the vain imaginings of those who uttered the following ineptitudes. "Neither ought they (that is, souls who follow this internal path) to elicit acts of love for the Blessed Virgin, the Saints, or the Humanity of Christ. For since these are objects of our sense-perception, therefore love for them must be a sense-love. No creature, neither the Blessed Virgin, nor the Saints, may reside in our hearts. For God wishes to be the sole occupant and owner thereof."[105] It is clear that those who share this opinion imagine that the representation of the Heart of Christ signifies nothing more interior than his emotional love; and therefore does not offer a new foundation, so to speak, on which to rest that supreme, or *latreutic,* worship which belongs only to that which of its nature is divine. But no one can fail to see that this way of looking at sacred images is altogether false. For it circumscribes within too narrow limits their wide significance. Far different is the opinion and teaching of Catholic theologians, among whom St. Thomas wrote: "Religious worship is not rendered to images for what they are in themselves, as if they had any intrinsic importance; but rather in so far as they are images that lead us on to God made man. The movement of our soul towards an image, precisely as an image, does not stop in the image, but continues towards that thing whose image it is. And therefore from the fact that religious worship is rendered to the representations of

---

[104] *John* 4, 23–24.
[105] Innocent XI, Apostolic Constitution *Coelestis Pastor,* 19th Nov., 1687; *Bullarium Romanum,* Rome 1734, vol. VIII, p. 443.

Christ, the conclusion cannot be drawn either that divine worship admits of differing degrees, or that the virtue of religion is manifold."[106] It follows then that the admittedly relative worship that we render to images is in the last resort offered to the Person of the Word Incarnate, as to its ultimate object. And this, whether it is a question of the relics of the bitter torments which the Saviour endured for our salvation, or whether we are dealing with that representation which surpasses all others in efficacy and meaning, namely the image of the pierced Heart of Christ crucified.

And so from that corporeal thing, which is the Heart of Christ Jesus, and from its natural signification we may and ought, strong in our Christian faith, to ascend not only to the contemplation of that love of his which can be perceived with the senses, but also still higher to consider and adore his sublime *infused* love, and then beyond that, as by a certain delightsome and lofty flight of the soul, to meditate and adore the divine love of the Word Incarnate. For, starting from that faith by which we believe both natures, the human and the divine, to have been united in the Person of Christ, our minds can conceive how incredibly close is the union between the emotional love of the physical Heart of Christ and his twofold spiritual love, the human and the divine. For not only must we say that these loves co-exist in the adorable Person of the Divine Redeemer, but also that they are united one to another by a natural link, inasmuch as the human and the emotional loves are subjected to the divine, and reflect it in an imperfect, or analogical, way. For there is not in the Heart of Jesus, nor do we adore therein, a *formal image,* that is a *perfect*, and completely *adequate* sign of his divine love. Nor do We contend that you should thus conceive of the Sacred Heart. For the essential nature of the divine love cannot possibly be adequately expressed by any created image. Still the Christian,

---

[106] *Sum. Theol.* II–II, q. 81, a. 3, ad 3 : ed. Leon., vol. IX, 1897, p. 180.

when he worships the Heart of Jesus, is adoring, in unison with the Church, a token and as it were a footprint of that divine charity which did not stop short of loving the sin-stained race of men with the Heart of the Word Incarnate.

It is therefore essential that in this vitally important point of Christian doctrine, which calls for so much circumspection, each one should ever retain in mind the fact that the whole validity of the physical Heart of Jesus as a natural symbol of the Person of the Word rests upon the fundamental truth of the hypostatic union. He who denies this truth, resurrects those false beliefs which the Church has rejected on more than one occasion, because they contradict the doctrine that there is one Person in Christ, while the two natures remain distinct and entire.

Once this essential truth is admitted, we realize that the Heart of Jesus is the heart of a Divine Person, that is of the Word Incarnate, and therefore represents and brings before our eyes, so to speak, all the love by which that Person has embraced, and still continues to embrace us. And for this very reason it is impossible to exaggerate the excellence of devotion to the Sacred Heart. If we consider the external practice of the devotion, we must admit that it is a most perfect way of professing the Christian religion. It is indeed no more nor less than the religion of Jesus. For this is entirely centred upon the Mediator, who is both Man and God; and in such a way that we cannot reach the Heart of God, save through the Heart of Christ, even as he himself has said: "I am the Way, and the Truth, and the Life. No man cometh to the Father, but by me."[107] This being so, we can easily understand that devotion to the Sacred Heart of Jesus, of its very nature, involves at one and the same time both worship of the love with which God has loved us through Jesus, and the arousing in us of love both for God and for the rest of men. Or, to put it in different words, the *object* of this devotion is God's

---

[107] *John* 14, 6.

love for us: that we should adore it, give thanks to it, and live by imitation of it; while the *purpose* it has in view is to bring us to absolute perfection in that love which binds us to God and to the rest of men, as with each day that passes we follow out more eagerly the *new* commandment which the Divine Master gave as a sacred heritage to the Apostles, when he said: "A new commandment I give unto you that you love one another, as I have loved you ... This is My commandment that you love one another, as I have loved you."[108] And this commandment truly is *new* and Christ's *very own*. For, as Aquinas says, "it is, in brief, the difference between the New and the Old Testaments; and, as Jeremias says: 'I will make with the house of Israel a new covenant.'[109] And this commandment, although it existed in the Old Testament and was based on fear and on reverential love, still it *belonged* to the New Testament. Whence it is found in the Old Law, not as really belonging to it, but as preparing the way for the New Law."[110]

So far, Venerable Brethren, We have set before you the true nature of this devotion and its outstandingly Christian character. And these considerations are beautiful, surely, and full of comfort. But, mindful of that Apostolic Office, which was first entrusted to Blessed Peter after his threefold profession of love for Christ the Lord, We deem it opportune, before We lay down Our pen, to exhort you once more, and through you all Our beloved children in Christ, that you strive with yet greater zeal to promote this most beautiful form of piety. For We are confident that from it will arise benefits innumerable to-day too, as in former times.

Truly, if the arguments put forward as the foundation for devotion to the pierced Heart of Jesus be duly pondered, it must become clear to all that it is not a question here of any ordinary

[108] *John* 13, 34 ; 15, 12.
[109] *Jer.* 31, 31.
[110] *Comment. in Evang. S. Ioan.,* c. XIII, lect. VII, 3 : ed. Parmae, 1860, vol. X, p. 541.

form of piety, which a man may at his will treat as of little value or set aside as inferior to others. On the contrary we are dealing here with a form of religious homage which is of the greatest assistance in the attainment of Christian perfection. For if *devotion*—according to the accepted theological notion which has come down to us from the Angelic Doctor—"seems to be nothing less than a certain will to give oneself readily to those things which pertain to the service of God,"[111] could there be any service of God more obligatory and needful, and at the same time more excellent and sweeter, than the service which does homage to his love? Could there be anything more pleasing and acceptable to God than that service which is rendered to the Divine Charity, and rendered thereto out of love? For any service which is given *freely,* is in a sense a gift, and love "has the nature of the first gift of all, through which all other free gifts are given."[112] And so we must hold this form of religious piety in the highest esteem, because it helps man to worship and love God more, and to dedicate himself more easily and more promptly to the Divine Charity. Besides, our Redeemer himself has deigned to propose and commend it to his People, while the Supreme Pontiffs, in the official documents which We have quoted, have defended it and have extolled it with the highest praise. For this reason, whosoever belittles this signal gift of Jesus Christ to his Church, is guilty of a rash and harmful action, and one which offends God himself.

This being so, it cannot be doubted that the faithful, when they render their homage to the Sacred Heart of the Redeemer, are fulfilling that gravest of all duties, the duty of serving God. At the same time they are consecrating themselves to their Creator and Redeemer with all that they have, as regards both their intimate affections and the external activities of their life. In this

---

[111] *Sum. Theol.* II–II, q. 82, a. 1 : ed. Leon., vol. IX, 1897, p. 187.
[112] *Ibid.* I, q. 38, a. 2 : ed. Leon., vol. IV, 1888, p. 393.

way they are obeying the divine commandment: "Thou shalt love the Lord thy God with thy whole heart, and with thy whole soul, and with thy whole mind, and with thy whole strength."[113] They have moreover the unshakable conviction that the primary motive of their worship of God is not their own advantage, whether bodily or spiritual, temporal or eternal, but simply God's own goodness. To this they seek to render homage, by loving him in return, adoring him and by offering to him a proper meed of gratitude. Unless this were so, the cult of the Sacred Heart of Jesus would ill accord with the essential spirit of the Christian religion. For man by this kind of devotion would not be honouring first and foremost the Divine Love. And to this extent those who misunderstand this excellent form of piety, or who practise it amiss, lay themselves open to the charge, which is sometimes levelled against them, of excessive self-love or self-interest. Wherefore all must be fully persuaded that in our worship of the august Heart of Jesus the external practices of piety are not the most important thing. Nor should we see the chief reason for this worship in the blessings which Christ our Lord promised in private revelations. For these blessings were promised precisely in order that men might fulfil more fervently the principal duties of the Catholic religion, that is love and expiation, to the more effective enrichment of their own spiritual life.

Therefore We would constrain all Our children in Christ to embrace more eagerly this form of devotion; not only those who are already accustomed to slake their thirst with the saving waters that flow from the Heart of the Redeemer, but also, and more especially, those who look on from a distance, after the manner of curious but hesitant spectators. Let them seriously consider what manner of devotion is here in question. As We have already said, it has now been waxing strong in the Church over a long pe-

[113] Mk. 12, 30 ; Mt. 22, 37.

riod; it is solidly based upon the very words of the Gospels; the teaching of the Fathers and the Sacred Liturgy openly favour it; the Roman Pontiffs themselves have again and again extolled it with unreserved praise. Nor were these latter satisfied to introduce the feast of the august Heart of the Redeemer and to extend it to the universal Church; they must needs as well have the whole human race solemnly dedicated and consecrated to the same Sacred Heart.[114] Let them also consider the happy results which have accrued to the Church in such abundance from this devotion. The return of countless men and women to the Christian religion. The faith of many quickened to new life. The ever closer union of the faithful with the loving Redeemer. And all these blessings have been more abundant and more obvious than ever during these last few decades.

We see around us this wonderful spectacle, burning devotion to the Sacred Heart of Jesus spread far and wide through all the ranks of the Christian faithful; and We are overcome with consolation, gratitude and joy. First We must render due thanks to our Redeemer, inexhaustible treasure-house of goodness that he is. Then We feel Ourselves constrained to offer Our fatherly congratulations to all those, whether of the clergy or of the laity, who have actively helped to spread this devotion.

Devotion to the Sacred Heart of Jesus has engendered everywhere salutary fruits of Christian living. Still, Venerable Brethren, no one can fail to see that the Church Militant on earth, and still more Civil Society, has not yet attained that full and complete perfection which responds to the ardent desire of Jesus Christ, mystical Spouse of the Church and Redeemer of the human race. Not a few of the Church's children make hideous the reflection they bear of their Mother's beauty, by their all too numerous

---

[114] Cfr. Leo XIII, Encyclical *Annum Sacrum: Acta Leonis,* vol. XIX, 1900, p. 71 f. ; *Decree of the Sacred Congregation of Rites,* 28th June, 1899, in *Decr. Auth.* III, n. 3712 ; Pius XI, Encyclical *Miserentissimus Redemptor: A. A. S.* XX, 1928, p. 177 f. ; *Dec. S. C. Rit.,* 29th January, 1929 : A. A. S. XXI, 1929, p. 77.

sins and imperfections. Not all the faithful are distinguished by that holiness of life to which God is calling them. Not all sinners have returned to their Father's house (which they should never have left), there to be clothed anew in the "first robe"[115] and to receive on their finger the ring which betokens their fidelity to the Bridegroom of their souls. Not all the heathen have yet been incorporated into the Mystical Body of Christ. Nor is that all. Bitter indeed is Our grief at the languishing faith of good people, in whose hearts, misled by vain longing for earthly goods, the ardour of divine charity grows cold and is gradually being extinguished. But much more cruelly is Our heart wrung by the strivings of those impious men who, as if inspired by the infernal enemy, are beside themselves with open and implacable hatred for God, for the Church, and especially for him who takes the Divine Redeemer's place on earth and represents his charity for men. The Doctor of Milan (St. Ambrose) was referring to this in his oft-quoted words: "He is questioned, about whom the questioner doubts. But the Lord does not doubt when he questions him (Peter), not to learn, but because he wishes to teach him whom, on his own elevation into heaven, *he was leaving behind for us as the vicar of his love.*"[116]

In truth hatred of God and of those who lawfully represent God is the greatest sin that man, made in God's image and likeness and destined to enjoy perfect friendship with God for all eternity in heaven, can commit. For by hatred of God man is separated in the most complete possible way from the Supreme Good, and is driven to repel utterly from himself and from those near to him whatever comes from God, whatever joins man to God, whatever leads to the possession of God, that is to say truth, virtue, peace and justice.[117]

---

[115] *Lk.* 15, 22.

[116] *Expos. in Evang. sec. Lucam,* l. X, n. 175 : P. L. XV, 1942.

[117] Cfr. St. Thomas, *Sum. Theol.* II–II, q. 34, a. 2 : ed. Leon., vol. VIII, 1895, p. 274.

Alas, one can see that the number of those whose boast it is that they are God's enemies is increasing in some places. The lying slogans of *materialism* too are spreading in practice as well as in theory, while the unrestrained indulgence of sensual desire is everywhere extolled. What wonder then, if in the hearts of many charity grows cold? Charity, which is the highest law of the Christian religion, the unshakable foundation of true and perfect justice, and the principal fount of peace and of chaste delight. Did not our Saviour warn us: "because iniquity hath abounded, the charity of many shall grow cold."[118]

To-day, more than at any other time, we behold individual men and women, families, nations, the whole world attacked and undermined by innumerable evils. Where, Venerable Brethren, are we to seek a remedy for them? Consider this holy cult of the Heart of Jesus. Could we find a more excellent form of devotion, or one which accords more perfectly with the essential spirit of the Catholic faith, or is more apt to succour the Church and the human race in the needs of the present day? What form of religious observance is more exalted, sweeter, more health-giving than this? For are we not dealing here with a cult, which is totally directed towards the very charity of God himself as its object?[119] And lastly, devotion to the Sacred Heart of Jesus increases and fosters the charity of Christ in our hearts at a rate that grows each day. And what, more powerfully than the charity of Christ, can move the faithful to put into application in the activities of their daily lives the law of the Gospel? And, if that law be set aside, true peace among men can in no wise be achieved, as indeed we are clearly warned by the words of the Holy Spirit: "and the work of justice shall be peace."[120]

Wherefore, following the example of Our immediate Predecessor, We wish to address once more to all Our children in

[118] *Mt.* 24, 12.
[119] Cfr. Encl. *Miserentissimus Redemptor:* A. A. S. XX, 1928, p. 166.
[120] *Is.* 32, 17.

Christ those words of warning which at the close of the last century Leo XIII of immortal memory spoke to all Christians, and indeed to all men of good will who cared for their own survival and for that of human society: "Behold, to-day another sign appears before our eyes, auspicious and divine, even the Sacred Heart of Jesus, . . . enveloped in flames, shining in resplendent glory. In it must all our hopes be placed. From it must men seek and await their salvation."[121]

It is also Our dearest wish that all those who glory in the name of Christian, and who labour to establish the Reign of Christ in the world, should regard the practice of devotion to the Heart of Jesus as a standard and source of unity, salvation and peace. At the same time no one must think that this devotion entails any belittlement of the other forms of religious piety whereby the Christian people, under the Church's guidance, honour the Divine Redeemer. Far from it. Without any doubt a burning devotion to the Heart of Jesus will cherish and advance our reverence for the Holy Cross especially, and our love for the august Sacrament of the Altar. For We dare assert—and this is wonderfully borne out by the revelations vouchsafed by Jesus Christ to St. Gertrude and to St. Margaret Mary—that only those have a proper understanding of Jesus Christ crucified, who have penetrated the mystic secrets of his Heart. Nor is it easy to fathom the might of that love, constrained by which Christ has given himself to us as the food of our souls, unless we go out of our way to foster the cult of the Eucharistic Heart of Jesus; the which cult, if We may borrow the words of Our Predecessor of happy memory, Leo XIII, recalls that "act of supreme love by which our Redeemer, pouring out all the riches of his Heart in his desire to be with us all days even to the end of the world, instituted the adorable Sacrament of the Eucharist."[122] "For not the least

---

[121] Encl. *Annum Sacrum: Acta Leonis,* vol. XIX, 1900, p. 79 ; Encl. *Miserentissimus Redemptor:* A. A. S. XX, 1928, p. 167.

[122] *Litt. Apost. quibus Archisodalitas a Corde Eucharistico Jesu ad S. Ioachim de Urbe*

gift of his heart is the Eucharist, which he bestowed upon us out of the immense charity of his Heart."[123]

Finally, in Our urgent desire to set a strong bulwark against the wicked designs of those who hate God and his Church and at the same time to lead the family and the state back to the love of God and of neighbour, We do not hesitate to affirm that the cult of the Sacred Heart of Jesus is a most effective school of divine charity. That divine charity, We repeat, which is the foundation on which the Kingdom of God must be built up in the souls of men, in the family circle and in the lives of nations; even as that same Predecessor of Ours of pious memory wisely reminds us: "The Reign of Jesus Christ takes its power and its quality from divine charity. To love holily and with *right order* is its foundation and its perfection. The which Reign must bring forth these fruits: that we should fulfil our duties without blame; that we should in no wise wrong our neighbour; that we should esteem earthly things of less worth than heavenly; that we should put the love of God before all things."[124]

But if from their devotion to the august Heart of Jesus riches more abundant are to be poured out upon the family of Christians, and indeed upon the entire human race, then the faithful must see to it that to this devotion of theirs is linked indissolubly devotion also to the Immaculate Heart of the Mother of God. For in the eternal Will of God the Blessed Virgin Mary has been joined indissolubly to Christ in the accomplishment of the work of man's Redemption, in such a way that our salvation has proceeded from the charity of Jesus Christ and his bitter sufferings, together with the love and sorrows of his Mother most intimately associated thereto. This being so, it is altogether fitting

---

erigitur, 17th Febr., 1903 : *Acta Leonis,* vol. XXII, 1903, p. 307 f. ; cfr. encl. *Mirae caritatis,* 22nd May, 1902 : *Acta Leonis,* vol. XXII, 1903, p. 116.

[123] St. Albert the Great, *De Eucharistia,* dist. VI, tr. 1, c. 1 : *Opera Omnia,* ed. Borgnet, vol. XXXVIII, Paris, 1890, p. 358.

[124] Encyclical *Tametsi: Acta Leonis,* vol. XX, 1900, p. 303.

that the Christian people, who have received the divine life of grace from Christ through Mary, should, after paying their rightful homage to the Sacred Heart of Jesus, also render to the loving Heart of their heavenly Mother the corresponding debt of filial loyalty, love, gratitude and reparation. Entirely in keeping with the above-mentioned disposition of God's most sweet and wise Providence is the memorable form of consecration by which We Ourselves solemnly dedicated Holy Church and the whole world to the sinless Heart of the Blessed Virgin Mary.[125]

In the course of this year, as We have already mentioned, we shall celebrate with joy the first centenary of the extension of the feast of the Most Sacred Heart of Jesus to the universal Church by Our Predecessor of happy memory Pius IX. And We earnestly desire, Venerable Brethren, that the Christian people everywhere shall solemnly observe this centenary by the offering of public acts of adoration, thanksgiving and reparation to the Divine Heart of Jesus. And, while the faithful everywhere will be united in the bonds of charity and of common prayers, We are confident that this feast of Christian joy and Christian piety will be celebrated with special religious fervour by that nation from which, in God's Providence, came the Virgin-Saint who was the fosterer and the tireless herald of this devotion.

Meanwhile, refreshed by sweet hope, We already foresee the abundant spiritual fruits which We are confident will accrue to the Church from the cult of the Sacred Heart of Jesus, provided it be correctly understood and practised, as We have explained it. And We earnestly entreat Almighty God that he would graciously bring to fulfilment this Our ardent desire by the mighty help of his grace. By God's inspiration may this great mercy befall us, that from the celebration appointed for this year the loving devotion of the faithful towards the Sacred Heart of Jesus may grow day by day. May his sweet Empire and Kingdom spread

[125] Cfr. A. A. S. XXXIV, 1942, p. 345 f.

ever more widely throughout the whole world and open its gates to all men; "the Kingdom of truth and life; the Kingdom of holiness and grace; the Kingdom of justice, of love and of peace."[126]

As a pledge of these favours, with overflowing heart We bestow Our Apostolic Benediction upon each one of you, Venerable Brethren, together with the clergy and faithful committed to your charge, and in particular upon those who, by their devoted labours, foster and promote devotion to the Most Sacred Heart of Jesus.

Given at Rome, at St. Peter's, on the 15th day of the month of May, in the year 1956, the eighteenth of Our Pontificate.

PIUS PP XII.

[126] From the Roman Missal, *Preface of Christ the King*.

BIBLIOGRAPHY

The last complete bibliography of English books on the devotion to the Sacred Heart was that compiled by N. NILLES S.J., in *De rationibus festorum SS. Cordis Iesu et purissimi Cordis Mariae* (Innsbruck 1885). The following list gives the more important works published in English since 1885.

Papal

LEO XIII	Encyclical letter *Annum Sacrum*, 1899. (C.T.S.)
PIUS XI	Encyclical letter *Miserentissimus Redemptor*, 1928. (America Press)
	Encyclical letter *Caritate Christi Compulsi*, 1932. (C.T.S.)
PIUS XII	Encyclical letter *Haurietis Aquas,* 1956. (C.T.S.)

Doctrinal

J. BAINVEL S.J.	*Devotion to the Sacred Heart.* London, Burns Oates & Washbourne, 1924.
J. GALOT	*The Heart of Christ.* Maryland, Newman Press, 1953.
H. NOLDIN S.J.	*The Devotion to the Sacred Heart of Jesus.* New York, Benziger, 1905.
C. PESCH S.J.	*Our Best Friend.* Milwaukee, Bruce, 1953.
L. VERHEYLEZOON S.J.	*Devotion to the Sacred Heart.* London, Sands, 1955.
A. WATKIN O.S.B.	*The Heart of the World.* London, Burns Oates, 1954.

BIBLIOGRAPHY

Historical

Ancient Devotions to the Sacred Heart by Carthusian Monks of the 14th to 17th Centuries. London, Burns Oates, 1953.

St. Margaret Mary   *Autobiography*. Kent, Visitation Library, 1952.

K. Richstaetter S.J.   *Medieval Devotions to the Sacred Heart*. London, Burns Oates, 1925.
Illustrious Friends of the Sacred Heart of Jesus. London, Sands, 1930.

Devotional and Apostolic

F. Charmot   *The Sacred Heart and Modern Life*. New York, Kenedy, 152.

E. F. Garesche S.J.   *The Sacred Heart and the Catholic Home*. Milwaukee, Bruce, 1927.

F. Konz   *Sacred Heart of Christ*. New York, Benziger, 1936.

J. McDonnell S.J.   *The Litany of the Sacred Heart*. London, Washbourne, 1912.
The Promises of the Sacred Heart. Dublin, Irish Messenger Office, 1925.

A. McGratty S.J.   *The Sacred Heart: Yesterday and Today*. New York, Benziger, 1951.

R. Plus S.J.   *Reparation*. London, Burns Oates & Washbourne, 1931.

A. Vermeersch S.J.   *Practical Devotion to the Sacred Heart*. London, Washbourne, 1918.

INDEX

St. Paulinus of Nola, 51
Pelagianism, 205
Pergmayr, 101
St. Peter Canisius, 38, 40, 50 n., 74,
  80, 91–2, 98–9, 101–2, 164, 243
St. Peter's, Rome, 98, 102
Peterson, Eric, 21
Pictures of Sacred Heart, 2, 3, 46,
  88, 89, 106–7, 116, 120, 133–4,
  247–8
Pistoia, Pseudo-Council, 16
Pius IX, 1, 129, 212, 245, 258
Pius X, 110, 168
Pius XI, 1, 12, 37, 129, 137, 144, 151,
  167, 216
Pius XII, 30, 59 n., 204, 211–59
Pleroma, 183, 246
Poland, 128, 245
St. Polycarp, 43
de Ponte, Luis, 102
Porto, 129
Portuguese Mysticism, 98
Prayer to Sacred Heart, 3–4, 66, 74,
  75, 88, 105–6, 137, 150–1, 153,
  165, 167–9, 203–5
Preachers of St. George, 71
Premonstratensians, 66
St. Priscilla Catacomb, 48
Private Revelations, 67, 85–7, 114–9,
  127, 135, 139–44, 154–5, 242,
  244–5, 252
Promises of Sacred Heart, 4, 10–11,
  116–7, 119, 154–5, 252
Protestantism, 15–16

Q

Quas primas, 167
Quodvultdeus, 55

R

Raymond of Capua, 85, 87
Reformation, 87, 91, 96
Regensburg, 71, 80
Reparation, 12, 88, 117–9, 121,
  129–30, 140, 142, 147–50, 152,
  158–60, 161–3, 166, 167, 168, 170,
  179, 187, 244, 246, 258

Richard of St. Victor, 64
Richstaetter, 37, 63, 103
Rigoleuc, 102
Roermond, 90
Rome, 124, 125, 126–8
Rufinus, 49
Rupert of Deutz, 65
Ruysbroek, 88, 90, 93, 95

S

Sacraments, 42, 55, 60, 79, 163–4,
  168, 180, 200, 237
Saint-Jure, 102
de Sales, see St. Francis
Sanctus, Deacon, 44
Saumaise, Mother, 118, 123
Septuagint version, 23
Society of Jesus, 92, 97–103, 122–6
Solomon, Temple of, 176
Spain, 63, 98, 128
von Spee, Friedrich, 99
Spiritual Exercises of St. Ignatius, 92,
  98, 140, 175
Steinfeld, 66
Suarez, Francis, 102
Summi Regis Cor Aveto, 66, 97
Surin, 102
Surius, Laurence, 92
Suso, see Bl. Henry
Swiss monasteries, 66 n., 84
Swenshed, 64
Symbolism of the Heart, 78–9,
  133–4, 146–7, 198, 207, 220,
  230–1, 240, 242, 244, 245, 247–9
Syrian Popes, 63

T

Tabernacle, 176–7
Tabernacles, Feast of, 31–3, 186–7,
  196, 201
Tauler, 80, 88, 92
Temple, 176, 185, 186
Terreau, 111
Tertullian, 47, 53–4
Theology of the Sacred Heart, 5–7,
  127–9, 131–55, 193–202, 212–59
  passim